The "Spiritual Presence" in the Theology of Paul Tillich

THE "SPIRITUAL PRESENCE" IN THE THEOLOGY OF PAUL TILLICH

Tillich's Use of St. Paul

by
John Charles Cooper

Mercer University Press
Macon, Georgia
—1997—

BT
119
.C67
1997

©1997
Mercer University Press
6316 Peake Road
Macon, Georgia 31210
All rights reserved

Library of Congress Cataloging-in-Publication Data

Cooper, John Charles.
The "Spiritual presence" in the theology of Paul Tillich:
Tillich's use of St. Paul / John Charles Cooper.
p. cm.
Includes bibliographical references and index.
ISBN 0-86554-535-9 (alk. paper)
1. Tillich, Paul, 1886-1965—Contributions in doctrine of spiritual
presence. 2. Holy Spirit—History of doctrines—20th century. 3. Presence
of God—History of doctrines—20th century. 4. Bible. N.T. Epistles of
Paul—Theology. 5. Paul, the apostle, Saint—Influence. I. Title.
BT119.G67   1997
97-30334
231′.3′092—dc21
CIP

Table of Contents

Foreword

This book originated as a doctoral dissertation at the *Divinity School*, the University of Chicago, while I was a student of Paul Tillich (1963-66). Since Tillich would not be "doctor father" for a study of himself, Langdon Gilkey, who had recently joined the faculty in Christian Theology, agreed to serve as dissertation advisor. Joseph Sittler and Norman Perrin (in New Testament) rounded out the dissertation committee. Many others contributed to both input and oversight of what may be a multidisciplinary study: Robert Grant (Greek, New Testament), Joseph Haroutunian (Christian Theology, Philosophy—especially Pragmatism), Bernard Loomer (Christian Theology and Philosophy, especially Whitehead, Pierce, James, Plato, Augustine, Anselm), Bernard Meland (Theology) and Arthur Vööbus of the Maywood Lutheran Seminary faculty (Greek, Hebrew, Syriac, Coptic, Latin and the textual witnesses to the N.T.). For the many works of sermons, philosophy, social and political criticism and the three volumes of the systematic theology by Tillich, I must credit the man himself for the insights contained herein, or, perhaps stated better, for *confirming* the insights that came to the author during several years of concentrated study that actually began ten years before Tillich graciously accepted me as his student in 1963. My thanks to all of these learned gentlemen and my gratitude to my family who suffered through those years with me. Any errors of fact or interpretation are mine alone.

Sola Deo Gloria.

Preface

The historic creeds of the Ancient Catholic Christian Church, especially the Niceo-Constantinopolitan (325 AD—386 AD) and the so-called Athanasian Creed (*Quicunque vult*) define the relationships of the three persons (*larva*, "masks") of the Holy Trinity to the Divine essence and to each other. These Counciliar definitions are ecumenical (Universal) and final for Christians *until* another truly ecumenical Council is called. While I by no means desire to challenge the decisions of the great Universal Councils, indeed, I have sworn loyalty to them in my ordination vows, I believe it is not generally recognized that, like most legislative efforts, the Councils' decisions did not deal with all the contemporary (i.e., Fourth Century, AD) problems, nor did it harmonize the teachings of the great Church Fathers of East, West, and North Africa (including Egypt) and the many and varied comments and observations about the Triune Persons in the Textus Receptus of the New Testament. Indeed, the fact that the Ecumenical Symbols have stood for so long is due to the early separation of the church Catholic into Eastern and Western branches by the Pope's excommunication of the Eastern patriarch in the late Eighth Century, AD. There simply has *not* been a truly *Catholic* or Universal Church since that time, although the Latin Church took pains to "balance" The Trinity by adding the *fileoque* clause, so that the Spirit is said to "proceed" (i.e., *process* or *emanate*, as in Plotinus) "from the Father *and the Son*". The Eastern Church has never accepted this. Indeed, very little of the Nicene and Athanasian language was accepted by those Near Eastern and African churches known as "monophysite" ("one nature" in Christ) or "Coptic", referring to the Christianity of the ancient Ethiopian and Egyptian Churches.

To sum up: The Ecumenical Symbols or creeds *are* fully authoritative for us (dispite the rejection of them by cultists and sectarians like Jehovah's Witnesses, Latter Day Saints, and the World-wide Church of God), yet those Symbols did not settle all the legitimate issues raised on Scriptural bases. All that is required to open these Trinitarian issues again is the convening of a genuinely ecumenical Council (which is *a very big "all"*). This is the position of the "Counciliarists" during the Middle Ages, and the stance of the Lutheran Reformers in the Sixteenth

Century, AD (See *The Augsburg Confession* and its *Apology*). It is the real underlying principle behind the multi-partied and bilateral talks and arguments between interfaith partners (such as the Lutherans and Episcopalians) today: The belief in *ecumenical convergence*.

All of these issues make Tillich's approach to the Divine presence even more exciting to me now than it was 30 years ago. Fundamentally, Tillich is a Lutheran, Pauline based theologian, underneath the questioning of Existential Philosophy. The "answers" Tillich gives to these questions are not drawn from Existentialism but from the Bible, and more, from a Bible interpreted by St. Paul. So it is not surprising that Paul's famous observation: *"The Lord is the Spirit"* is the basis of Tillich's pneumatology.

INTRODUCTION

The problem proposed for study here is not a simple one to explain. Essentially it is a proposal to extricate one strand of the multi-sided conversation which Tillich carries on with the history of philosophy and theology in his *Systematic Theology*. Specifically, I propose to delineate the dialogue Tillich is carrying on with the first Christian theologian, St. Paul, on the subject of the Spiritual Presence. In order to illustrate this dialogue, I propose to establish first what St. Paul has to say regarding the Spiritual Presence. I will then give particular attention to what Tillich calls Paul's "Spirit-Christology" and the spiritual participation of persons "in Christ." I will then continue by making a careful study of the Pauline passages with a view to reaching an historical understanding of them in their significance for Paul and their meaning for his theology. This will be done with the guidance of the best available scholarship in the New Testament field.

The basic thrust of this thesis is that St. Paul's teachings concerning the Holy Spirit and the Spirit of Christ are determinative for the formulation of Tillich's doctrine of the Spiritual Presence, as he develops that doctrine in Part IV of his *Systematic Theology*, "Life and the Spirit."

Chapter two will investigate Tillich's doctrine of the Spirit, unfolding the doctrine of the Spiritual Presence and placing it in its proper place within Tillich's system. I will study all of Tillich's published works, in order to specify the importance of the doctrine of the Spirit in Tillich's thought. The three volumes of the *Systematic Theology* will be analyzed, but major attention will be given to Volume 3, Parts IV and V. I will proceed by giving a brief description of Tillich's systematic thought, covering its apologetic intention, its demonstration of the method of correlation, and Tillich's revivification of theological symbols. I shall discuss Tillich's conception of the media of the Spiritual Presence, the manifestation of the Spirit in the spirit, and the manifestation of the Spiritual Presence in historical mankind. I will conclude my study of Tillich on the Spirit by investigating the adequacy of Tillich's doctrine for the conveying of the Biblical conception of the presence of the Spirit.

Chapter three will be devoted to the hermeneutic of Paul Tillich. After the materials relating to St. Paul and the Spirit and Tillich's development of the doctrine of the Spirit have been investigated, I shall attempt to establish the hermeneutical principles that underlie Tillich's use of Saint Paul in his description of the doctrine of the Spiritual Presence. In order to adequately deal with this topic, I will offer an introduction to the modern theological discussion concerning hermeneutic, including a description of several prominent theological movements. I shall then turn to a study of Tillich's approach to myth, symbol, and the technique of the deliteralization of religious symbols. In order to establish Tillich's hermeneutic, I shall analyze Tillich's treatment of the myth of Creation-Fall and his interpretation of Christology. I will conclude this study by identifying the hermeneutical considerations in Tillich's theological method, and attempt to specify the operational concept in Tillich's hermeneutical approach. I shall offer several hermeneutical principles that are found In Tillich's theology which I believe are based on Tillich's primary operational concept in the interpretation of religious symbols.

The study will be completed by an assessment of Saint Paul's significance for Tillich's doctrine of the Spiritual Presence. Chapter four will introduce the various evidences of St. Paul's importance for Tillich's theological thought concerning the Spirit. A number of rather definite Pauline influences on Tillich's doctrine of the Spirit will be identified, with particular emphasis given to the Pauline conception of the Spirit as the Spiritual Presence of the Risen Christ (II Corinthians 3:17). I shall demonstrate at some length that this is a very important theological influence on Tillich's development of the doctrine of the Spiritual Presence. I shall also draw together the Pauline teachings concerning the Spirit studied in chapter one, and point out the fact that St. Paul himself ontologized the doctrine of Christ and that this hitherto disregarded aspect of St. Paul's thought is quite influential on Tillich's doctrine of the Spirit. This book concludes with a general discussion of how Tillich used his hermeneutical principles to deal with the Pauline doctrine of the Spirit, and a brief evaluation of the importance of Tillich's interpretation of St. Paul for modern theology.

1

THE PAULINE TEACHING CONCERNING THE SPIRITUAL PRESENCE

Introduction

What does Saint Paul say about the Holy Spirit and the *Spiritual Presence of Christ*? I am especially concerned to investigate those passages in Saint Paul's Epistles that deal with what has been called "Spirit-Christology." I concentrate on the epistles that have been generally accepted as genuine: Romans, 1 and 2 Corinthians, Galatians, Philippians, 1 Thessalonians and Philemon. I shall also refer to the "deutero-Pauline" Epistles, Colossians and Ephesians, for reference to the Christology developed in them. An assumption of this study is that these two Epistles reflect the teachings of disciples of Saint Paul, if they are not actually from Saint Paul himself.

My first task is to survey the usage of the term, *pneuma*, and the phrases, "in Christ"; "in the Spirit" and "The body of Christ" in order to make a judgment about Saint Paul's conception of the Spirit and the relationship of the Spirit to Christ.

The methodological approach of this chapter will be to analyze and interpret the incidences of *pneuma* in Paul, and to investigate the unique Pauline phrase, "in Christ." I will then proceed to discuss the theological concept basic to Paul's thought, union with Christ. On this basis I will develop the Christ-mysticism taught by Saint Paul, assisted by the insights of older scholars such as Albert Schweitzer and Adolf Deissmann, as well as by the extensive literature on the subject. In order to establish the validity of the assertion that Paul was a Christ-mystic, I will survey and analyze the passages in his Epistles that speak of "union with Christ" or the presence of Christ in believers. In my investigation of the "in Christ" passages, there are references to several tables in the appendix that illustrate the significant features of the phrases "in Christ," "in the Spirit," "in the Lord," and "the body of Christ." I conclude the chapter with an analysis of the Pauline textual data and draw conclusions about Paul's beliefs concerning the Spirit and the presence of Christ in the believer.

Introduction to Saint Paul's Conception of *Pneuma*

The conception of *pneuma* (or the Spirit) is a major element in Paul's theology. On occasion, Paul uses the term *pneuma* in the same two senses that occur in the common speech of the English and German languages. I shall distinguish these two uses by referring to them as A and B.

A is the usage in Paul—and in English and German—of *pneuma* or spirit to refer to human personality ("the human spirit").

B is in reference to God in which the term Spirit denotes the quality which distinguishes God from all else that is not God ("God is Spirit," as the Fourth Gospel proclaims).

An example of Paul's usage A of *Pneuma* is Philemon, vs. 25: "The grace of our Lord Jesus Christ be with your spirit." Another example is 1 Thessalonians 5:23: "... and may your spirit and soul and body be kept sound."

This usage is analogous to the Old Testament use of the Hebrew word *nephesh* for soul, life, or self, and is also analogous to *ruah* or spirit. Actually, usage A is a minor element in Paul's treatment of the term *Pneuma*. Generally, Paul uses *psyche* (vitality or life) to refer to "the human spirit." Predominantly, Paul uses *pneuma* for the Divine Spirit (e.g., 1 Thessalonians 1:5-6; 4:8), which he carefully distinguished from man's spirit as in Romans 8:16. An example of Paul's differentiation of *Pneuma A* from *Pneuma B* is 1 Corinthians 2:10ff. where Paul declares that as only one's own spirit knows what is within him, so the depths of God are available only to the Divine Spirit.

Nevertheless, Paul can and does use *pneuma* to refer to humans in 1 Corinthians 7:34 where "body and spirit" are used to designate the totality of a person. This is the case in 1 Thessalonians 5:23 as I showed above. This ambiguous usage of *pneuma* is illustrative of the unsystematic thinking of Paul and it requires us to note carefully the context in which *pneuma* occurs in the Pauline writings. Used in the sense of *Pneuma A, pneuma* can mean the person and can even take the place of the personal pronoun, e.g., 1 Corinthians 16:8: "They refreshed my spirit,...." which is equal to "They refreshed me." The conclusions of several of the Epistles, "with your spirit," as in Galatians 6:18;

Philippians 4:23; and Philemon 25 are all instances of the use of *Pneuma A* as a personal pronoun.

Since Paul uses *Pneuma* in two senses, it may be possible to discern something of the meaning of *Pneuma* in the second sense, referring to the Divine, from his usage of *Pneuma* in the first sense, referring to man.

Paul uses *Pneuma* to refer to persons simply to denote the self, or some higher principle within him. Thus in Romans 1:9 the phrase, "God ...whom I serve with my spirit," is equal to "with my whole being or self." Indeed, in 1 Corinthians 2:11, the statement that "man's spirit knows what is within him" (paraphrased), uses *Pneuma* in the sense of human consciousness or "mind," a concept usually denoted in Paul — and in Greek literature generally — by the term *nous*.[1]

As noted above, Paul uses *Pneuma* in the second sense to refer to the Divine unsystematically. Rudolf Bultmann[2] has written that this may be due to the background overtones of *Pneuma* in Greek thought, by which Bultmann means *Pneuma*'s animistic and dynamistic connotations. Additionally, I find inconsistency in Paul's reference to the Divine Spirit because of a broad variation in Paul's terminology which I shall note later in this chapter. Some of Paul's variant terms are "the Holy Spirit," "the Spirit of God," and "the Spirit of Christ."

So far as the Spirit concept is concerned, Paul's basic idea in referring to the Divine is clear. *Pneuma* does not mean spirit in the Platonic, idealistic sense, i.e., it does not mean "mind" in contrast to body (regarded as the vehicle of sensuous life), or in contrast to nature. "Mind" in this sense, the active subject in mental or spiritual life, is called in Greek *nous* or *psyche* or *logos*.[3] Rather *Pneuma B* (in the second sense) is the divine power that stands in absolute contrast to all that is human. Arndt and Gingrich's *Greek-English Lexicon of the New Testament and Early Christian Literature* (Bauer)[4] defines *Pneuma* as "that which differentiated God from all that is not God, as the divine power that produces all divine existence, as the divine element in which all divine life is carried on, as the bearer of every application of the divine will." This term can occur as "the Spirit of God," the "Spirit of Christ," the "Spirit of the Lord," and as "The Holy Spirit." All of these usages are

---

[1]Cf.. Rudolf Bultman, *Theology of the New Testament*, I, trans. Kendrick Grobel (New York: Chas. Scribners' Sons, 1951), 203-207.

[2]Ibid., p. 155.

[3]Ibid., p. 153.

[4]Wm. F. Arndt and F. W. Gingrich translated and adapted the 1952 edition of Walter Bauer's German work in 1957. *Greek-English Lexicon of the New Testament and Early Christian Literature* (Chicago: University of Chicago Press, 1959), p. 682, Heading No. 5.

found in Paul.[5] Thus we may define *Pneuma B* as a term denoting the living quality of God, His power, His dynamic, creative aspect.

From the fact that Paul uses *Pneuma* in a dual sense, we may gather that for Paul there is an analogy between the spirit of humans and the Spirit of God. Arndt and Gingrich, however, have defined the spirit as the differentiating element of God from all that is not God. This seems to be a contradiction. Perhaps the way out of this seeming contradiction is to reconsider the above definition, for the Spirit is traditionally understood as the presence of the Divine in the world of humanity. In this sense the Spirit is the element in which the Divine Will is applied in the world and it is thus the symbol under which we may understand the living quality of God. We believe that there is reason to understand *Pneuma B* as a symbol which is related to *Pneuma A*. It is necessary to see such a relationship in order to affect a reasonable theological understanding of *Pneuma A*, on the one hand, and to adequately deal with the occurrences of *Pneuma* in the dual senses we find in Saint Paul. The spirit is the dimension of creativity in humanity, and therefore it seems a fitting symbol for the dimension of creativity in God. Man is aware of the spiritual aspect of his own nature and in this sense he is able to grasp after the nature of God under the symbol of Spirit. The differentiating quality of the Spirit of God from the spirit of humanity for Paul lies in the dimension of power. Man's spirit is dependent upon the Spirit of the Divine.

Man's spirit alone is ineffectual and powerless. God's Spirit is self-sufficient and all-powerful. Thus *Pneuma B* serves a term both of contrast and of analogy. The experience of *Pneuma B* is at once a point of contact between humanity and God and the reason why humanity needs contact with the Divine.

The Spirit (*Pneuma B*) is also connected with the revealing activity of God, that is, with the occurrences of prophecy. It is in the dimension of the Spirit—in the encounter of one's spirit with the Divine's Spirit—that man becomes aware of God and of God's demand upon his life. It is in the event of being grasped by the Spirit that man becomes aware of his sinfulness and the need of grace. This is the usage that we will see is most common in Saint Paul, for whom "life in the Spirit meant life in the new creation, the new creative order."[6] For Paul, however, the presence of the Divine Spirit was clearly connected with the appearance

---

[5]E.g., God—1 Cor. 2:11b, 14; 3:16; 6:11; Christ - Rom. 8:9c; Phil. 1:19; 2 Cor. 3:17b; Gal. 4:16; Holy Spirit—1 Cor. 6:19; 2 Cor. 13:13. Arndt and Gingrich, *BAGD*, 680-658.

[6]Eduard Schweitzer, "Spirit of God," in *Bible Key Words*, III (London: A. & C. Black, 1960), 57.

of Jesus Christ; consequently, the chief interest was contained in the question: "How is the proclamation of the Spirit connected with that of the crucified, risen and coming Lord?"[7] We shall see that Paul answered this question by identifying the Lord (Christ) with the Spirit (2 Corinthians 3:17). For Paul, the Spirit is the risen, glorified (ascended) Lord, and turning to Christ in faith is union with the Spirit or Christ. Thus, Paul can declare that by the Resurrection, Christ has become "the Spirit that makes alive" (1 Corinthians 15:45).

As mentioned above, Bultmann[8] points out that *Pneuma* in Paul's usage B (to refer to God) has two different "overtones" or backgrounds. The first "overtone" is the *animistic*, which conceives of the Spirit as an independent, personal power that can fall upon a man and take possession of him, enabling him or compelling him to demonstrate a personal manifestation of power (e.g., Romans 8:16; 1 Corinthians 2:10-16; 14:14). This animistic "overtone" is classically illustrated in the Old Testament passage, 1 Samuel 19:23-24, where the Spirit of God is said to have come upon Saul so that he prophesied, and fell into such a frenzy that he stripped off his clothes and lay naked on ground a day and a night. This usage is not the same as the animistic usage found in Paul, and yet it is related to it. In fact, the animistic usage is only infrequently found in Paul's letters as he preferred the second or *dynamistic* conception of the Spirit. In the dynamistic conception, *Pneuma* appears as an impersonal force which fills a man like a fluid. This conception is operative wherever "infusion" or "pouring into" or "giving" or "supplying" is mentioned (e.g., Romans 5:5; 2 Corinthians 1:22-5:5; I Thessalonians 4:8; Galatians 3:5; Philippians 1:19). In this conception, Spirit and Power are synonymous, and since "power" and glory" can be synonymous (Romans 6:4; cf.. 1 Corinthians 6:14), so "spirit" is related to "glory" (1 Corinthians 15:44). "Spirit" so conceived (usage B., dynamistic) is also synonymous with grace, considered as a spiritual power (1 Corinthians 15:10; 2 Corinthians 12:9).

Bultmann also points out that there is an inconsistency in Paul's conception of the manner in which Christians possess the Spirit.[9] On the one hand, Paul speaks as if all Christians possess the Spirit, having received it in Baptism (2 Corinthians 3:6; 1 Corinthians 15:45; Romans 8:2), but on the other hand, there are people who are to be regarded as bearers of the Spirit in a special sense (1 Corinthians 2:13-3:3; esp. 1 Corinthians 12:31, and the whole discussion of the various gifts of the Spirit in 1 Corinthians 12).

---

[7]Ibid., p. 55.
[8]Bultmann, *Theology of the New Testament*, pp. 155–57.
[9]Ibid., pp. 158–60.

Precisely because there is this inconsistency in Paul's conception of the Christian's Spirit-possession, it becomes necessary to investigate that aspect of Paul's religious life which revolves around his experiences or visions of the risen Lord. Paul's assessment of the Lord's appearance to him on the road to Damascus and the continuing visions which he experienced during his lifetime has been termed Paul's "Christ-mysticism." This "Christ-mysticism" forms the center of Paul's religion and consequently of his theology.

Paul's Spiritual Experiences

Adolf Deissmann declared that in Paul's case access to Christ was through the Christophany at Damascus and that stemming from this event Paul felt himself to grow closer and closer to the risen Lord until he could declare that Christ was "in him" and he was "in Christ." This is what is meant by Christ-mysticism.[10] In this discussion of Paul's Christ-mysticism, Deissmann's classic study is the starting point. The term "mystic" is used in the sense which Deissmann gives it, i.e., in the sense of the old German word *mystik*.[11] *Mystik* refers to "every religious tendency that discovers the way to God directly through inner experience without the mediation of reasoning."[12] This means that Paul's mysticism involves an immediate contact with God without the aid of sacraments or rituals or elaborate personal preparation. God speaks to Paul in the "visions" that he has of the Lord, and it is God who fills him when he feels the Spirit at work within him.

Union with Christ: The Center of Paul's Theology
A Brief Survey of the Scholarly
Study of the Problem

Every student of Saint Paul's Epistles has noted that Paul gives heavy emphasis to the topic of union with Christ. James S. Stewart in his popular study of Paul's experiences, *A Man in Christ*,[13] declares "the heart of Paul's religion is union with Christ."[14] William Barclay in his book, *The Mind of Saint Paul*,[15] has observed: "Every man who speaks

---

[10]Adolf Deissmann, *Paul: A Study in Social and Religious History*, trans. W. E. Wilson (New York: Harper & Brothers, 1957 [orig. 1912]) pp. 146-147.

[11]Ibid., p. 149.

[12]Ibid.

[13]James S. Stewart, *A Man in Christ* (New York: Harper & Brothers, n.d.).

[14]Ibid., p. 147.

[15]William Barclay, *The Mind of Saint Paul* (New York: Harper & Brothers, 1958).

or writes a great deal has favorite expressions, and Paul's is 'In Christ'."[16] The position of Deissmann has already been noted, and the positive assessment of Albert Schweitzer concerning Paul's mysticism underlies most modern interpretations of Paul.[17] Indeed, Paul uses the phrase "in Christ" in every Epistle generally accepted by scholars as genuine. According to the study made by this writer, the phrase is used seventeen times in Romans; seventeen times in 1 Corinthians; eleven times in 2 Corinthians;[18] fifteen times in Galatians; six times in 1 Thessalonians; fifteen times in Philippians and four times in the twenty-five verses of Philemon. Paul's use of the related phrase "in the Lord," clearly referring to Christ, is also notable.[19] Deissmann informs us that the phrase "in Christ" or its cognate, "in the Lord", occurs 164 times in the Epistles traditionally attributed to Paul.[20] Although many scholars have spoken of the close connection of the Spirit and the Risen Christ in Saint Paul's theology, among them, W. Bousset, A. Harnack, H. J. Holtzmann, Paul Feine, E. F. Scott, and Dean Inge,[21] it was Adolf Deissmann who developed the close connection between Christ and the Spirit in Paul's thought. This interpretation of the connection of Christ and the Spirit has exercised a remarkable fascination on Bible scholars for many years as can be seen from the works of F. W. Farrar [22]in the nineteenth century, to the increasing interest it has elicited in our century.[23] Among the interpreters who have dealt with the identification of the Spirit with the risen Christ are J. A. Allons,[24] F. J.

---

[16]*Ibid.*, p. 121.

[17]Albert Schweitzer, *The Mysticism of Paul the Apostle* (London: A. & C. Black, 1953).

[18]It is noted that 2 Corinthians is really a collection of two or more letters of Paul that have been loosely joined together in the transmission of the Pauline corpus.

[19]Deissmann, *Paul: A Study in Social and Religious History*, p. 140.

[20]Ibid.

[21]R. Birch Hoyle, *The Holy Spirit in Saint Paul*, (Garden City, N.Y.: Doubleday, Doran & Co., 1929), p. 19.

[22]F. W. Farrar, *The Life and Work of Saint Paul* (New York: E. P. Dutton & Co., 1880).

[23]See the list of articles in the bibliography. See also *New Testament Tools and Studies*, Vol. I: *Index to Periodical Literature on the Apostle Paul*, ed. Bruce M. Metzger (Grand Rapids: Eerdmans Press, 1951). See also *Ephermerides Theological Lovanienses*, Anius XL (Belgium: The Catholic University of Louvain, June, 1964), facililus 2.

[24]J. A. Allen, "The 'In Christ' Formula in Ephesians," *New Testament Studies*, 1958, and "The 'In Christ' Formula in the Pastoral Epistles," *New Testament Studies*, 1963.

Badcock,[25] W. Bartling,[26] Gerard Boll,[27] J. W. Buckham,[28] Prosper Grech,[29] D. R. Griffiths,[30] R. B. Hoyle,[31] R. M. Hughes,[32] D. W. Martin,[33] D. H. Ralston,[34] J. A. T. Robinson,[35] and M. J. Shrayer.[36] While not all of the scholars mentioned here have concluded that the Spirit is identical with the Risen Christ in Paul's theological thought, many of them have, and all of then remark on the indefiniteness of any distinction drawn between the presence of the Spirit with the believer and the presence of the Risen Christ. Deissmann, in his study of Paul, did not hesitate to speak of "the Spirit-Christ," meaning the living presence of the Risen, Glorified Savior.[37] This writer takes the close connection of Christ and the Spirit in Pauline theology, which is demonstrated by the alternation of the phrases "in Christ" and "in the Spirit," as the center of Paul's theology.

Albert Schweitzer in his book, *The Mysticism of Paul the Apostle,*[38] clearly demonstrates that mystical union with Christ and its correlate, union through Christ's Spirit with all other Christians in the body of Christ, are recurrent themes throughout Paul's letters. This is the point where we must begin if we would understand Saint Paul, for union with Christ is Paul's key thought.

---

[25]F. J. Badcock, "'The Spirit' and Spirit in the New Testament," *Expository Times*, XLV, No. 5 (February, 1934), 2, 8-22.

[26]W. Bartling, "The New Creation in Christ: A Study of the Pauline Formula," *Concordia Theological Monthly*, XXI (1950), 401-418.

[27]Gerald Boll, "Studies in Texts; II Cor. 3:17-18," *Theology*, VI (1923), 166-169.

[28]J. W. Buckham, "Are Christ and the Spirit Identical in Paul's Teaching?" *Exposition*, 8th Series, XXII (1921), 1154-1160.

[29]Prosper Grech, "II Cor. 3:17 and the Pauline Doctrine of Conversion to the Holy Spirit," *Catholic Biblical Quarterly*, XVII (1955), 420-437.

[30]D. R. Griffiths, "'The Lord is the Spirit' (II Cor. 3:17-18)," *Pastoral Theology*, LV (1943-1944), 81-83.

[31]R. B. Hoyle, "Paul's Doctrine of the Spirit," *Biblical Research*, XIII (1928), 45-62. "Spirit in Saint Paul's Experience and Writings," *Biblical Research*, II (1926), 491-507.

[32]H. M. Hughes, "II Cor. 3:17," *Expository Times*, XLV (1933-1934), 233-236.

[33]D. W. Martin, "'Spirit' in the 2nd Chapter of I Cor.," *Catholic Biblical Quarterly*, V (1943), 381-395.

[34]D. H. Ralston, "The Union of Christ with the Believer and the Inference Therefrom," *Union Seminary Quarterly Review*, XXI (1909-1910), 285-292.

[35]J. A. T. Robinson, "The Most Primitive Christology of All?" *Journal of Theological Studies*, New Series, VII (1956), 177-189.

[36]M. J. Shrayer, "The Lord Is the Spirit," *Religion in Life*, XX (1951), 21-35.

[37]Deissmann, *Paul: A Study in Social and Religious History*, p. 143.

[38]A. Schweitzer, *The Mysticism of Paul.*

Illustrations of the Use of "In Christ" in Paul

The chief expression of Paul's key idea we find in his confession: "If anyone is in Christ, he is a new creation" (11 Corinthians 5:17). This central idea receives expression in many and varied ways, some of which are:

"Redemption in Christ" — Romans 3:24
"Baptism in Christ" — Romans 6:3
"Alive to God in Christ" — Romans 6:11
"Eternal Life in Christ" — Romans 6:23
"Love of God in Christ" — Romans 8:39
"One Body in Christ" — Romans 12:5
"Sanctified in Christ" — 1 Corinthians 1:2
"The Day of Christ" — 1 Corinthians 1:8
"Wise in Christ" — 1 Corinthians 4:10
"Participation in the Blood of Christ" — 1 Corinthians 10:16
"Participation in the Body of Christ" — 1 Corinthians 10:16
"Asleep (death) in Christ" — 1 Corinthians 15:8
"Glory of God in Christ" — 2 Corinthians 4:6
"God was in Christ" — 2 Corinthians 5:19
"A Man in Christ" — 2 Corinthians 12:2
"Freedom in Christ" — Galatians 2:4
"Faith in Christ" — Galatians 2:16
"Justified in Christ" — Galatians 2:17
"Hope in Christ" — 1 Thessalonians 1:3
"Will of God in Christ" — 1 Thessalonians 5:18
"Encouragement in Christ" — Philippians 2:1[39]
"Mind in Christ" — Philippians 2:5
"Call of God in Christ" — Philippians 3:14
"Good in Christ" — Philemon v. 6
"Prisoner in Christ" — Philemon v. 23[40]

Saint Paul apparently thought of the whole church as being "in Christ" and each of the individual churches as also being "in Christ." This can be seen in the opening verse of 1 Thessalonians where the church in Thessalonica is said to be "in God and in the Lord Jesus Christ" (1:1). Again the churches—in the plural—of Judea are said to be "in Christ" (Galatians 1:22). In Paul's thought, churches may be located

---

[39]Which is equated with "participation in the Spirit."
[40]See the complete table on the instances of the phrase "In Christ" in Paul's writings at the end of this work.

in widely separated parts of the world but they are all "in Christ." The life of the church is life "in Christ."

"In Christ" and "In the Lord"

Individual members of the church are declared to be "in Christ" by Paul also. The Epistle to the Philippians is addressed to the saints in Christ Jesus who are at Philippi (1:1). Greetings are sent to every saint in Christ Jesus (Philippians 4:21). The members of the Church at Philippi are brethren in the Lord (Philippians 1:14). When Epaphroditus is sent back to Philippi after his serious illness in Rome, he is to be received in the Lord (Philippians 2:29). Those who are set in authority in the church are over the others in the Lord (1 Thessalonians 5:12).

The fact that all individual Christians are in Christ is the source of that unity which should characterize all members of the Church. All Christians are the children of God by faith in Christ Jesus (Galatians 3:26); and because of that, circumcision and uncircumcision are irrelevant (Galatians 5:6). In Christ there is neither Jew nor Greek, male nor female, bond nor free (Galatians 3:28). All Christians are "one body in Christ" (Romans 12:5). Two women in Philippi who have quarreled are urged to be reconciled "in Christ" (Philippians 4:2).

For Paul, life was lived "in Christ." His ways are "in Christ" (1 Corinthians 4:17). He has begotten the Corinthians "in Christ," and they are his work "in the Lord" (1 Corinthians 4:15; 9:1). He speaks "in Christ" (2 Corinthians 2:7 – 12:19). He sends his love to the Corinthians "in Christ" (1 Corinthians 16:24). In speaking of himself and of his own spiritual experience, he says that he knows "a man in Christ" (2 Corinthians 12:2). In prison his bonds are "in Christ" (Philippians 1:12).

Sometimes "in Christ" simply means Christian. In Romans 16, "in Christ" occurs no fewer than nine times in fifteen verses. Phoebe is to be received "in the Lord" (vs. 2). Priscilla and Aquila are Paul's helpers "in Christ Jesus" (vs. 3); they are his helpers in his Christian work. Andronicus and Junias were "in Christ" before Paul (vs. 7); they were Christians before Paul was. Ampliatus is Paul's beloved "in the Lord" (v. 8); he is the fellow-Christian whom Paul loved. Urbanus is a helper "in Christ", i.e., a helper in Christian work (vs. 9). Apelles is approved "in Christ" (vs. 10); he is a well-proved Christian. The household of Narcissus are "in the Lord" (vs. 11); they are Christians. Tryphaena and Tryphosa labor "in the Lord" (vs. 12); they are engaged in Christian work. Persis labored in the Lord and Rufus was eminent "in the Lord" (vs. 13). It can be seen that in nearly all these cases the phrase, "in Christ," or its equivalent, could be translated "Christian."

For Paul, all spiritual qualities are "in Christ." We have consolation "in Christ" (Philippians 2:1). We are bold "in Christ" (Philemon 8). We have liberty "in Christ" (Galatians 2:4). We have truth "in Christ" (Romans 9:1). The promises of God are guaranteed "in Christ" (2 Corinthians 1:20). We are sanctified "in Christ" (2 Corinthians 5:17). We are called "in the Lord" (1 Corinthians 7:22). The high calling of God is "in Christ" (Philippians 3:14). We are babes in Christ (1 Corinthians 3:1). God has established us "in Christ" (2 Corinthians 1:21).

It can be seen that for Paul the whole process of the Christian life is "in Christ." The call to it is "in Christ" — we begin by being babes "in Christ"; we are established "in Christ"; the gifts of nurture and of strength are "in Christ." For Paul the Christian life is begun, continued and ended "in Christ." Deissmann is correct in saying that Paul's chief achievement was uniting Christian piety with the person of Jesus Christ.[41] Paul did it precisely through his Christ-piety (or mysticism).

On the other hand, special powers and gifts come to us in Christ. In times of persecution, it is "in the Lord" that Christians stand fast (1 Thessalonians 3:8; Philippians 4:1). It is "in Christ" that we find joy in times of sorrow (Philippians 1:26; 3:1; 4:7; 10). It is "in Christ" that His servants are faithful. Thus Timothy is faithful "in the Lord" (1 Corinthians 4:17). Every good thing that we experience is "in Christ." Paul speaks of every good thing which is in the Christian, "in Christ" (Philemon 6).

Deissmann has suggested that "in Christ" can be interpreted by using the analogy of the way in which we live in the air. Just as everyone lives in the air and cannot live without the air, so the Christian lives in Christ. And just as the air is inside all living things, in a person's lungs and in the body, so Christ is in the person. Just as all men live in the air so the Christian lives in Christ. Just as the air within them gives all persons life, so Christ within them gives the Christian newness of life. To be "in Christ" is to live a life in which Christ is the atmosphere which one breathes.[42]

This is a helpful analogy, and yet it has in it a nebulousness which is not in the Pauline conception. Deissmann is much closer to the truth about Paul's conception when he defines what he means (and what this study means) by calling Paul a *Mystik*: A *Mystik* is one who discovers the way to God directly through inner experience without the mediation of reason or sacrament or ceremony. "The constitutive element in mysticism is immediacy of contact with the Deity."[43] In

---

[41]Deissmann, *Paul: A Study in Social and Religious History*, pp. 207ff.
[42]Ibid., p. 140.
[43]Ibid., p. 149.

Deissmann's analysis, it is the Christophany or appearance of Christ to Paul on the Damascus Road that is at the root of Paul's understanding of "being in Christ." At the moment Paul experienced this appearance of Christ, the Risen Christ took possession of him, transforming him from a persecutor to a believer and calling him to be an Apostle (Galatians 1:16ff). Thus Deissmann can say: "All that can be called Christ-mysticism is the *reaction* [my italics] to this initial experience."[44] This is the key—and Deissmann's great contribution to the understanding of Paul. Paul is a *reacting mystic*, his Christ-union (and communion) arises from his response to the Divine Initiative. Paul does not create his own ecstatic breakthrough to a new understanding of himself or to an oceanic feeling of being at home in the universe (*"acting mysticism,"* which is often achieved through a technique like Zen or Yoga), but rather responds to a present energy that "grasps him" and takes possession of him—in the same manner that the Divine Spirit "grasped" the Old Testament prophets and moved them to prophecy (e.g., Jeremiah 11:1-5). Hence it was an "invasion" of Divine Spirit that Paul experienced, the Spirit that is the Spirit of Christ took "possession" of him. It is interesting to note that this conception of Paul's theological expression as an essentially mystical one goes back (in modern scholarship) to Otto Pfleiderer, in his work, *Das Urchristentum*, written in 1887.[45]

It is legitimate to refer to Paul's experiences as mystical because feelings such as Paul describes are expressions of that feeling of man's creaturehood, of man's littleness in the face of that which is above all creatures.[46] Paul's mystical expressions are full of his sense of his own weakness and of the majestic power of the Divine.

Mysticism thus primarily consists of self-introspection. Because of its subjective nature, mysticism has been often condemned by theologians, and yet there is nothing of self-deception or a desire for self-salvation in the Pauline form of mysticism; it is but the reaction of a human spirit to the Divine Spirit which has encountered it. Here the emphasis must be placed upon the element of encounter. Paul believes that the Spirit has come to him from beyond himself and that his inward communion is a response to the Divine which has "grasped" him. Paul cannot be correctly understood as teaching an ultimate identity of the human spirit and the Divine Spirit. God, for Paul, is not the "within." The

---

[44]Ibid., pp. 130-131.

[45]Discussed in Albert Schweitzer, *Paul and His Interpreters*, trans. W. Montgomery (London: A. & C. Black, 1948), p. 31.

[46]Rudolf Otto, *The Idea of the Holy*, trans. J. W. Harvey (2nd ed.; London: Oxford University Press, 1957), pp. 20-21.

Divine transcends the human spirit, as it transcends the world and is the ultimate Ground of both without being identical with either. For Paul, the Spirit is the source of the power which strengthens him and enables him to work, preach and pray (Romans 8:9-27). There is no evidence in Paul's writings that would lead us to consider his Christ-mysticism as the reflection of a Vedanta-like philosophy of identity. Whenever Paul is declared to be a mystic in this study, the term mystic is to be understood in the sense of reacting mysticism that responds to the invasion of the Divine Spirit that comes to man from beyond himself (Galatians 1:11-16).

A Textual Analysis of Paul's Mystical Phrases:
"In Christ," "In the Lord," and "In the Spirit"[47]

In order to arrive at a precise understanding of the meaning of the Pauline mystical phrases I turn now to a detailed textual analysis of the phrases, "In Christ," "In the Lord," and "In the Spirit." In this analysis I limit myself to instances of these phrases found in Romans, 1 and 2 Corinthians, Galatians, Philippians, 1 Thessalonians and Philemon. I shall review the scholarly consensus of the meaning and usage of *en*, as that information is found in the *Theologisches Worterbuch*,[48] and other standard reference works. I shall limit this study to occurrences of *en* that have the sense of the *Theologisches Worterbuch zum Neuen Testament*, types 2, 3, and 4 ("in the spirit, " "in Christ," and "in the Faithful").

---

[47]In this study only materials from Romans, 1 and 2 Corinthians, Philippians, 1 Thessalonians and Philemon will be used. Most scholars agree that these epistles are undoubtedly by Paul. Thus by excluding the rest of the Pauline Corpus, I will try to eliminate the risk of "later theological developments" entering into this study. I do not mean to pass judgment on the question of authorship of these other epistles in doing this. Obviously some sort of control of the material is needed, and this seems to be a useful one.

[48]G. V. Kittel, *Theologisches Worterbuch zum Neuen Testament* (Stuttgart: W. Kohlhammer, 1935). (Hereafter cited as *T.W.N.T.*) Article on en, pp. 534-539. Esp. See p. 536, No. 2: "*En* in verbindung mit *pneuma*." I shall also use information from Arndt and Gingrich, *BAGD.*, pp. 257-261; and W. F. Moulton and A. S. Geden, *A Concordance to the Greek Testament* (New York: Charles Scribner's Sons, 1897); J. H. Moulton and George Milligan, *The Vocabularies of the Greek Testament* (2nd ed.; London: Houghton & Stoughton, 1915); F. Glass and A. Debrunner, *A Greek Grammar of the New Testament and Other Early Christian Literature*, trans. Robert W. Funk (Chicago: University of Chicago Press, 1961); *The Analytical Greek Lexicon* (London, n.d.); Alfred Schmoller, *Handkonkordanz sum griechisen Neuen Testament* (Stuttgart: Privilegierte Württ. Bibelanstalt, 1949).

The General Meaning of *En*

The Greek preposition, *en,* is used with the dative case. Arndt and Gingrich speak of *en'*s usage as "so many-sided and often so easily confused, that a strictly systematic treatment is impossible."[49] It can mean: in (within); at; near; before; in the presence of; among; with; or equipped, depending on the context. But for our purposes, most importantly, it can mean the denotation of a state of being. In the Greek language, the dative case is the case of the indirect object and of locative and instrumental relationships. With the perfect passive system, the perfect middle and perfect passive verbs plus the pluperfect, the dative may be used without a preposition to express personal agency. This construction is found chiefly with verbs which are impersonal, i.e., which have a thing and not a person as their subject. The construction which includes the proclitic *en* plus the dative, however, can express a very close connection such as indicating the state of being filled with something or gripped by something. Examples of this are Romans 8:10, "But if Christ is in you, although your bodies are dead because of sin, your spirits are alive because of righteousness." Other examples are: 2 Corinthians 13:5 and in non-Pauline instances, Luke 16:23 and 1 John 3:14. In Luke 16:23 we find the expression ". . . and in Hades, being in torment, . . ." where the state of being in torment is expressed by the proclitic *en.* In 1 John 3:14 there is the statement "He who does not love remains *in* death." Here the state of being spiritually dead is expressed by the proclitic *en* thus demonstrating that *en* plus the dative case may express a state of being. In the Pauline usage, therefore we are justified in understanding *en* as designating a state of being.[50]

Kittel's *Worterbuch* gives us three major categories of usage of *en* that bear on our problem. Those are numbers 2, 3.. and 4.[51] Usage number 2 refers to *en* in connection with *Pneuma* or Spirit.

The *Worterbuch* says that the place of the Spirit in man is localized by the use of *en.*[52] For an example look to: "The Spirit of God in man," in Numbers 27:18 and Ezekiel 36:27. In Paul, an example would be Romans 3:5: "The love of God is shed abroad in our hearts through the Holy Spirit."

---

[49] Arndt and Gingrich, *BAGD,* p. 257.

[50] All information from *ibid., passim.* See also Rom. 6:11, 23; 8:39; and Gal. 2:4; 3:14; 28.

[51] See *T.W.N.T.,* pp. 534-539.

[52] Ibid., p. 536.

Secondly, en is used to speak of man's being in the Spirit (Matthew 22:43; Revelation 21:10). Very often this relationship is spoken of by Paul, i.e., the relation of the individual to Christ. Romans 6:9 illustrates this: "But you are not in the flesh, you are in the Spirit, if the Spirit of God really dwells in you."

Usage number 3 refers to *en* in the phrases "in Christ," "in Christ Jesus" and "in the Lord." In the *Worterbuch*, such "formulas" as these were not used before Paul, and they are seldom used outside the Pauline Corpus. Paul, then, is the originator, perhaps even the creator, of such usage.[53] However, Paul's use of *en* in this general way is not all on one level, there are differences of meaning within this general framework that become apparent upon closer examination.[54]

As, we have previously noted, *en* used in such expressions as "in Christ," is used by Paul to designate Christ's connection with the Christian congregation or church. In the section "Illustrations of the Use of 'In Christ' in Paul," note that the church as a whole and individual churches in particular are spoken of as being "in Christ" (1 and 2 Thessalonians 1:1). In Romans 8:l, we read "There is therefore now no condemnation for those who are *in* Christ Jesus." This is the same idea as expressed in Philippians 1:1, where Paul greets "the saints in Christ Jesus who are at Philippi." Romans 16:11, "Greet those *in* the Lord who belong to the family of Narcissus" and Romans 16:7, ". . . they are *in* Christ before me," are other examples of this use of *en* which we will designate "*en*, use a."

En may also be used to designate an activity or position as characteristically "Christian." Romans 14:14 illustrates this, as Paul says, "I know and am persuaded *in* the Lord Jesus that nothing is unclean in itself." This use was noted in the previous section where Romans 16 was cited as containing the phrase "in Christ," nine times, each occurrence of which use denoted the person as being a Christian. Other examples of this Pauline usage are Romans 15:17, "in Christ Jesus, then, I have reason to be proud of my work for God." Romans 16:2, 12, 22 and Galatians 5:10 ("I have confidence in the Lord") are other examples of this use of *en* which we will designate "*en*, use b."

A third use of *en* in the Pauline Epistles is in expressions that describe value-judgments in the moral sphere. It was noted in the illustrations given above that in Paul's view all spiritual qualities are enjoyed by the Christian in Christ. Galatians 2:4, which speaks of the Christian's "liberty in Christ," illustrates this use. Other examples are

---

[53]"Paulus ist ihr eightentlicher trager, vielleicht ihr Schopfer." Ibid., p. 537.

[54]In the following I have omitted all reference to usages outside the seven epistles under discussion. For a full treatment see *T.W.N.T.*, pp. 534ff., itself.

Romans 16:8, "beloved *in* the Lord"; Romans 16:10, "approved *in* Christ"; and Romans 16:13, "eminent *in* the Lord." 1 Corinthians contains several examples of this usage, which may be illustrated by 1 Corinthians 4:10, "We are fools for Christ's sake, but you are wise *in* Christ." 1 Corinthians 9:1-2 is an appropriate example, "Are you not my workmanship *in* the Lord....? You are the seal of my apostleship *in* the Lord." We shall designate this usage as "*en,* use c."

Paul also uses the Greek proclitic *en* to present the objective foundation of our salvation and of the Kingdom of God. This was illustrated in the foregoing section by calling attention to the fact that for Paul our call into the church is "in Christ" and we are established "in Christ." Romans and the Corinthian correspondence contain many examples of this usage, such as Romans 3:24, "... the free gift of God is eternal life *in* Christ Jesus our Lord." 1 Corinthians 1:2 speaks of " . . . the church of God which is at Corinth, ... those sanctified *in* Christ Jesus." 2 Corinthians 5:19 declares, "... God was in Christ reconciling the world to himself."[55] Galatians 2:4 uses *en* to speak of "... our freedom which we have *in* Christ Jesus."[56] These usages demonstrate that *en* is used by Paul very frequently to designate the objective foundations of the Christian's salvation. This usage we will designate as "*en,* use d."

Paul exhibits one final usage of *en* in several of his letters, to express the idea of unity. Romans 12:5 expresses this comprehensive use of *en* very clearly, "So we, though many, are one body *in* Christ, and individually members one of another." Galatians 3:28 declares, " ... you are one *in* Christ Jesus." First Thessalonians 2:14 is a final illustration. This usage will be designated "*en,* use e."

Evaluation

From the above survey of the five possible meanings of *en* in Paul's writings, several important facts stand out. The first is that Paul does lean heavily upon phrases beginning with *en* to express his theological insights. Secondly, we can gather from the many illustrations cited that *en* can and does mean "in the presence of"; "with" or "equipped." Such overtones of meaning are readily discernible in many of our

---

[55]2 Corinthians 5:19 may also be translated as "*in* Christ God was reconciling . . ."

[56]All these usages and many others can be found in table 1 in the appendix, "A Typological Breakdown of the 'In Christ' passages in Paul." There are three "Typological Breakdown" tables containing information about the phrases "in Christ," "in the Spirit," and "in the Lord" at the end of this book.

illustrations. But most important for our purpose is the insight that *en* can denote a *state-of being*. As was pointed out in the discussion of the general meaning of *en* when Paul says "Christ is *in* you," he is expressing a state of being. The phrase, "in Christ," then is logically equivalent to saying that "you are in a state in which Christ participates in your very life." On the other hand when Paul declared that Christ is "in him" as he does in Galatians 2:20, and that he henceforth lives "in Christ," he is explicitly using *en* to denote a state of being in which Christ not only participates in his own life, but also says that, in some way, Paul participates in the life of the Risen Christ. The basis of Paul's idea of "participation in Christ" is particularly brought out by use a. of *en* where *en* designates the connection of the individual Christian or of the church with Christ. Use d. of *en* which expresses the foundation of our salvation is also enlightening for our understanding of Paul's belief that the Christian can and does participate in the Risen Christ. Expressions that show use d. declare that the Christian's redemption is "in Christ," that his eternal life is "in Christ" and that he is sanctified "in Christ." But perhaps most significant of all is the passage in Galatians 3:28 which illustrates what we have called use e. This passage states: "There is neither Jew nor Greek, ... slave nor free, ... male nor female, for you are all one in Christ Jesus." Thus usage of *en* expresses Paul's conception of the unity of the Christian with his Lord and the unity of Christians with each other in the church. Paul apparently is attempting to put in words his personal experience of being grasped by the Spiritual, Risen Christ. In order to express what he probably felt was beyond human comprehension, Paul made use of the proclitic en, *in phrases that suggest that Christ is a dimension of life*—a dimension into which men are drawn by an encounter with the Divine Spirit, either in a vision experience such as his own Christophany on the Damascus Road or through a confrontation with the Christian kerygma through the witness of the church.

We must attempt to understand what Paul was trying to communicate here before we can understand the meaning of the "in Christ" passages. In Galatians 2:20 there is the significant passage "I am crucified with Christ; nevertheless I live, yet not I, but Christ liveth in me." What does this mean? Does it mean that Paul's personal center is dead and that in the place of his "self" Christ now lives? Or does it mean that Paul's unredeemed, i.e., untouched by the encounter with the Divine he experienced in his Christophany, self—his "old" self, Romans 6:6—was now spiritually dead and that a new self was born? On the basis of Paul's writings we must conclude that it is Paul's unredeemed or "old" self that has died, and not that Paul's personal center has been replaced by the Risen Christ. As he concluded his description of baptism in Romans 6, "So you also must consider yourselves dead to sin and alive to God in Christ Jesus" (vs. 11). Thus Paul founds his entire line of thought upon the Damascus Road experience. In a moment of time, Paul, the enemy of Christ, became Paul, the slave of Christ. Paul found it impossible to describe it except in the graphic terms of Romans 6. It seemed to him that one man (the "old" man) had died, and another man (the "new" man) was born. And who was responsible for this change? None other than the Risen Christ. From that moment Paul felt that between him and Christ there was so real, so close, so indissoluble a union that it could not be expressed in any other way than to say that he lived in Christ, and Christ lived in him.

It was not a case of complete identification with Christ. Paul did not lose his personality, but rather it had changed. Paul still lived, but he lived in a new dimension and for new purposes. Paul could still worship and long for a closer union with Christ, as we see expressed in Philippians 1:22-23 and 3:8, but something had happened to him which brought Christ into the life of Paul and joined Paul's life to the life of Christ in such a way that we could say he was forever in Christ.[57] Thus Paul's religion was a participation in a living Spirit that he, again, in a graphic way expressed in a radically objective sense. Thus Paul could declare "I live, yet not I, but Christ lives in me" (Galatians 2:20), and "He that is joined to the Lord is one spirit" (1 Corinthians 16:17).

The Theologisches Worterbuch zum Neuen Testament records a usage of *en* that expresses the participation of Christ in the faithful or in the believer. This usage of *en* is found in Paul although it is not as prominent as the "in Christ" instances. An example of this usage (which the *Worterbuch* designates usage four) is Romans 8:9b-11:

> Anyone who does not have the Spirit of Christ does not belong to him. But if Christ is in you, although your bodies are dead because of sin, your spirits are alive because of righteousness. If the Spirit of him who raised Jesus from the dead dwells in you, he who raised Christ Jesus from the dead will give life to your mortal bodies also through his Spirit which dwells in you.

---

[57]Deissmann, *Paul: A Study in Social and Religious History*, pp. 217–19. According to Deissmann, Paul thought of being "with Christ" as a higher stage of Christ-communion than that experienced "in Christ" here on earth. Q.v. 1 Thessa. 4:17; 5:10; Phil. 1:23; 2 Cor. 13:4 and Rom. 8:32.

This passage is especially noteworthy because within its few sentences we find all the elements of this study associated together. The ideas of "Christ in you," of the "Spirit in you," and a close connection of the work of the Spirit to the accomplished work of Christ, all occur here. This illustrates the possibility of using *en* to denote the participation of Christ (and the Spirit) in the inner life of the believer. This passage becomes increasingly important, however, when we note that the phrase "the Spirit of Christ" occurs here and the phrase "Christ is in you" appears as a synonym or parallel to both "the Spirit of Christ" (vs. 9b) and to the phrase "the Spirit of him who raised Jesus from the dead" (vs. 11). Thus Christ and the Spirit are apparently identified by Paul as being one and the same experience of the Divine which Christians enjoy in their inner life. Galatians 2:20 carries this thought even further: "I have been crucified with Christ; it is no longer I who live, but Christ who lives in me; and the life I now live in the flesh I live by faith in the Son of God, who loved me and gave himself for me." Here Christ is said to dwell in the believer—at his very personal center—*and the Spirit is not mentioned.*

Here we must compare 1 Corinthians 15:22, 45-49 and Romans 5:12-21 with what we have already surveyed.

> For as in Adam all die, so also in Christ shall all be made alive.... Thus it is written, "The first man Adam became a living being.," *the last Adam became a life-giving spirit....* The first man was from the earth, a man of dust; the second man is from heaven. As was the man of dust, so are those who are of the dust; and as is the man of heaven, so are those who are of heaven. Just as we have borne the image of the man of dust, we shall (or let us)[58] also bear the image of the man of heaven. (1 Cor 15)

> Therefore as sin came into the world through one man and death through sin, and so death spread to all man because all men sinned.... For if many died through one man's trespass, much more have the grace of God and the free gift in the grace of that one man Jesus Christ abounded for many .... Then as one man's trespass led to condemnation for all men, so one

---

[58]The hortatory "let us" is found in p. 46 and the Western Text, Codex D (Cantabrigiensus) as well as other significant MS traditions and Irenaeus and Clement. Information from E. Nestle, *Novum Testamentum Graece* (Stuttgart: Wurttembergische Bibelanstalt, 1956).

man's act of righteousness leads to acquittal and life for all men
... so by one man's obedience many will be made righteous ...
(Rom 15)

These two passages take us to the midst of Paul's Adam-Christ
speculation. Because of the scholarly research of people like W. D.
Davies and Fritz Neugebauer[59] we now know this Adam-Christ strand
of Paul's thought was based on pre-Christian Jewish Apocalyptic
speculation about "the primitive man" and the body of Adam. The
"first Adam" and the "last Adam" are to be understood as original or
primal men, *in illo tempore*, as Eliade would say.[60] The first and last
Adam are pioneers who in themselves set in order a whole creation
either in the order "life to death" (Adam) or "death to life" (Christ).
These pioneers bind all their descendants under the order they
established. This kind of speculation is akin to the cosmologies of the
ancient Semitic peoples as well as to the Apocalyptic mysticism within
Judaism that helped produce the sufferings of the Bar-Kochba Rebellion
in the second century, A.D. Deissmann, who sees the "In Christ"
formula and its parallels as being indicative of a Christ mysticism in
Paul, is thus borne out by Davies' studies of the influence of Rabbinic
Judaism on Paul. Paul's oft-used phrase, "In Christ," arose from the
ancient mystical conception of the primal man, Adam, and his universal
personality. From such speculation on "the mystical Body of Adam" the
ancient thinkers were able to draw those ideas that express the
conception of original (or universal) sin, as well as of the possibility of
universal salvation which is at least open to all, if not effective in all.
There is evidence that this type of speculation has influenced Paul in his
phrase, "in the flesh" which occurs in Romans 7:18; 8:3; 2 Corinthians
10:3 and Galatians 2:20. This phrase, "in the flesh," which Paul uses as
a term for a state of being estranged from God, is used at least 32 times
in the Pauline epistles, discounting entirely the occurrences of flesh as a
synonym for the physical body. The passage that expresses this Pauline
conception most clearly is Galatians 5:16-17: "But I say, walk by the
Spirit, and do not gratify the desires of the flesh. For the desires of the
flesh are against the Spirit, and the desires of the Spirit are against the

---

[59]W. D. Davies, *Paul and Rabbinic Judaism* (London: S.P.C.K., 1962). Also, Fritz
Neugebauer, *In Christus: En Christoi* (Gottingen: Vandenhoeck & Ruprecht,
1961); and Basil Stegmann, "Christ, the Man from Heaven—A Study of I Cor.
15:45-47 in the Light of the Anthropology of Philo Judaeus" (unpublished S.T.D.
thesis, Catholic University, Washington, D.C., 1927); also, C. K. Barrett, *From
First Adam to Last* (London: A. & C. Black, 1962).

[60]Mircea Eliade, *Cosmos and History* (New York: Harper Torchbooks, 1959), pp.
14f and 59.

flesh; for these are opposed to each other, to prevent you from doing what you would." The phrase, "in the flesh," usually has as its counterweight the phrase "in the Spirit" in Paul's usage (Romans 8:8ff).

Paul creatively draws the ancient speculation on the primal man, represented in his thoughts by the phrase, "in the flesh," and the mysticism of his spiritual theology together in the statement: "Those who are in the flesh cannot please God. But you are not in the flesh, you are in the Spirit, if the Spirit of God really dwells in you. Anyone who does not have the Spirit of Christ does not belong to him. But if Christ is in you, although your bodies are dead because of sin, your spirits are alive because of righteousness" (Romans 8:9-10). In this declaration Paul coordinates the Adam-Christ speculation with his own Christ-mysticism based on his Christophany and developed through his experiences of participation in the life of the Risen Christ. To be "in the flesh" is to be in Adam, to be "an old man," to be untouched by the renewing qualities of an encounter with the second Adam who restored to man a right relationship with God that was lost to the natural man by the primal "disobedience of the first man" *in illo tempore*.

The passages concerning the relationship of Christ to Adam give us the insight that just as Adam, the originator of the "fleshly" man, lives on in natural men, even so Christ the pioneer of the new aeon lives on in the believer. Paul can speak of this indwelling of Christ in the believer as being almost a physical process, like pregnancy. In Galatians 4:19, Paul says, "My little children, with whom I am again in travail until Christ be formed in you." The Christian who is so "indwelt" will not, thereby be wafted to paradise, but must continue to "do and suffer" here on earth. In a real sense Paul says the sufferings of the indwelt Christian are then Christ's sufferings, and are necessary because the church, Christ's Body, is not yet fully subject to Christ in this present aeon of sin and death. 2 Corinthians 1:5 illustrates this: "For as we share abundantly in Christ's sufferings, so through Christ we share abundantly in comfort too." Paul is even more explicit in 2 Corinthians 4:8-10 where he compares the sufferings of the Christian to a manifestation of Jesus' death. He declares, "We are afflicted in every way, but not crushed . . . always carrying in the body the death of Jesus, so that the life of Jesus may also be manifested in our bodies.[61]

---

[61]"For while we live we are always being given up to death for Jesus' sake, so that the life of Jesus may be manifested in our mortal flesh" (2 Cor. 4:11). Does this mean that "Paul must decrease that Christ-in-him can increase?" Also, cf.. "Col." 1:24: "Now I rejoice in my sufferings for your sake, and in my flesh I complete what is lacking in Christ's afflictions for the sake of his body, that is, the church, ..."

Perhaps Paul's last word on this subject is his confession in Philippians 1:21, "For me to live is Christ, and to die is gain."

Paul's Theological Position

The detailed study we have made of Paul's theological language has now brought us to the point where we can speak of the theology which lies behind the words and phrases of the Pauline epistles. For this writer the disputed epistle, Colossians, expresses Paul's theological position quite clearly.[62] J. B. Phillips has given us an excellent translation of this epistle, especially of the passage in which we see Paul's theological program concisely expressed:

> For I am a minister of the church by Divine commission, a commission granted to me for your benefit and for a special purpose: that I might fully declare God's word—that sacred mystery which up till now has been hidden in every age and every generation, but which is now as clear as daylight to those who love God. They are those to whom God has planned to give a vision of the full wonder and splendor of His secret plan for the sons of men. And this secret is simply this: Christ in you!
>
> Yes, Christ in you bringing with Him the hope of all the glorious things to come.
>
> So naturally, we proclaim Christ! We warn everyone we meet, and we teach everyone we can all that we know about Him, so that, if possible, we may bring every man to his full maturity in Christ.[63]

As we have noted several times before, Paul's theology grows out of his experience with "the Kerygmatic Christ"—the Risen, Spirit-Christ of faith. The roots of Paul's Spirit-Christ mysticism lie in his Damascus Road experience and in his assessment of the meaning of Christ's Resurrection which is controlled by his own visionary experience, recorded for us in 1 Corinthians 15:8. Paul's mysticism rests on his evaluation of what was accomplished by the death of Christ, which he

---

[62]I accept Colossians as "Pauline" in the general sense that it was written by a disciple of Paul if not by Saint Paul himself.

[63]J. B. Phillips, *Letters to Young Churches* (New York: Macmillan Co., 1948), Colossians 1:25-28, p. 126.

never considered in isolation, but always in connection with the Resurrection. All of those experiences and reflections flow together into his primal doctrine: that we have entered *a new reality*, become *new creatures* by participation in the death and resurrection of Christ *now* when we come to faith. This new reality is experienced in the indwelling of Christ's Spirit in us, and by immersion in the external nexus of love-and-faith-relationships created by Christ's indwelling in believers, who are thus members of the Body of Christ, the Spirit-built congregation or Church.

The declaration, "If anyone is in Christ, he is a new creation," is the compressed proclamation of the meaning of Christ's death and resurrection and of Paul's own experience with the Spirit-Christ[64] on the Damascus Road. At the center of Paul's understanding of Christ, growing out of his contemplation of the Christ-Spirit who is his ever-present contemporary — freed from the limitations of space and time, flesh and blood[65] — is the figure of the Living One, who Paul confesses was pre-existent (Philippians 2:5ff.), took on flesh (Romans 1:3, 9:5; also 8:3c.), suffered and died (1 Corinthians 15:3), and is now alive (and omnipresent) again (1 Corinthians 15:4-58). Paul's understanding of the meaning of Christ is thus from Spirit to flesh to Spirit, for "He who is the crucified" (Galatians 3:1; 1 Corinthians 1:23; 2:2 — note the present tense) is now alive and will remain alive, near the believer, forever. Thus the "Real Presence" of Christ, so often invoked in terms of sacramentalism, is a fact for Paul in that this presence is an ever-present participation that follows upon Baptism, the means of entry into the Body of Christ (Romans 6:1-11; 8:9-11). Once one is "joined to the mystical Body," it may be said of him that

> ...you are not in the flesh, you are in the Spirit, if the Spirit of God really dwells in you. Anyone who does not have the Spirit of Christ does not belong to him. But if Christ is in you, although your bodies are dead because of sin, your spirits are alive because of righteousness. (Romans 8:9-10).

Therefore, the Christian can be said to

---

[64]I understand the Pauline experience of participation in the life of the Spirit-Christ to be the equivalent of "the Kerygmatic Christ" or "the Christ of Faith."

[65]"From now on, therefore, we regard no one from a human point of view; even though we once regarded Christ from a human point of view." RSV, 2 Cor. 5:16—The Greek is *kata sarka christon*, i.e., to regard Christ according to the flesh. This statement is followed by the confession that if anyone is in Christ, he is a new creation.

have this treasure in earthen vessels, to show that the transcendent power belongs to God and not to us .... Always carrying in the body the death of Jesus, so that the life of Jesus may also be manifested in our bodies. For while we live we are always being given up to death for Jesus' sake, so that the life of Jesus may be manifested in our mortal flesh ... [2 Corinthians 4:7, RSV].

These two passages are an attempted explanation of the meaning of Christ in terms of the operative power and presence of the Spirit-Christ. As they are based on personal experience, obviously these passages possess a psychological power that is missing from the metaphors or symbol-constructs Paul uses in more homiletic passages, such as Romans 1:16-17. They attempt to illuminate personal experience to directly relate to those "confessions" of Paul's inner life, i.e., of his Christ-mysticism, such as that in Galatians 2:15-21, where Paul links together the metaphor of justification and his experiences of Christ-communion:

For I through the law died to the law, that I might live to God. I have been crucified with Christ; it is no longer I who live, but Christ who lives in me; and the life I now live in the flesh I live by faith in the Son of God, who loved as and gave himself for me. I do not nullify the grace of God; for if justification (righteousness) were through the law, then Christ died to no purpose (Galatians 2:19-21, RSV).

The disruption between "the historical Jesus" (who lived in Palestine about B.C. 4–29 A.D.) and the Kerygmatic Christ—the Christ of Faith—who is the Spirit (2 Corinthians 3:17-18, also 3:4ff.), is quite marked in Paul. The point of cleavage is not just his disclaimer that he no longer regards Jesus "after the flesh" or "according to a human point of view" (i.e., as an historic, material personality), which is explicit in 2 Corinthians 5:16b; rather the cleavage of Historical Jesus and Spirit-Christ grows out of *Paul's emphasis upon Christ's death.* Jesus of Nazareth was crucified, died and was buried (1 Corinthians 15:3-4), and Paul preached (1 Corinthians 15:1) that Christ was raised from the dead(Romans 6), and was "raised by the glory of the Father" to newness of life, and "will never die again" (Romans 6:4, 9), thus:

The death he died he died to sin, once for all, but the life he lives he lives to God. So you also must consider yourselves dead to sin and alive to God in Christ Jesus. [Romans 6:10-11].

Indeed, the historical Jesus thus fades out of the picture for Paul, *having been the necessary precondition for the Christ-Spirit, but having now fulfilled his function — by His death.* In a real sense, Jesus of Nazareth could have said, "It is finished"; (John 19:30) and "Into thy (God's) hands, I commit my Spirit.' (Luke 23:46).

No matter where we take our start, at Jesus' conception — by the Divine Spirit (Luke 1:35) — or at his Baptism (Luke 3:21-22), when the Spirit fell upon Him, or at the moment of Jesus' passage from flesh through death to life as a Spirit (Luke 23:46), Paul, and much of the New Testament, teaches a Spirit-Christology. In this same Epistle Paul says:

> The gospel concerning his Son, who was descended from David according to the flesh — and designated Son of God in power according to[66] the Spirit of Holiness by His Resurrection from the dead, Jesus Christ Our Lord [Romans 1:3-4].

Thus the Resurrection, too, in Paul's theology, is accomplished by the Divine Spirit. By saying, "who *is* the crucified," rather than using the aorist, "who *was* crucified," Paul confesses that the Christian has fellowship with the very one who died for our sins (1 Corinthians 10:16), but who is now free from every limitation, ambiguity, finite quality and threat of existence, so as to be able to be "our Lord." Paul can write of this Spiritual-Christ:

> The cup of blessing which we bless, is it not a participation in the blood of Christ? The bread which we break, is it not a participation[67] in the body of Christ? Because there is one bread, we who are many are one body, for we all partake of the one bread [1 Corinthians 10: 16-17].

The bread is none other than a symbol for the Body of Christ — the sphere of his Spirit. For Paul, the death on the cross of Jesus of Nazareth and the Resurrection of the Glorified (or Spirit) Christ are not two separate events, but one unity. Crucifixion-Resurrection thus forms the center-point of all the centrifugal forces (of which Paul was one) which were now spreading the proclamation of the New Reality (in which God

---

[66]*Kata*, that "by".

[67]*Koinonia*: Participation, sharing in something. Phile. 6: "That your participation in the faith may be made known by your deeds." See 2 Cor. 13:13: "Participation in the Holy Spirit." Arndt and Gingrich, *BAGD*, p. 440

accepts man, justifying the sinner, adopting the fatherless, reconciling the estranged, redeeming the sin-enslaved) across the Eastern Mediterranean area. These central events are inseparable from one another for Paul. The Crucifixion, considered alone, seems but the tragic end of a good, but possibly incautious man; while the Resurrection alone, without attachment to the life of a genuinely historical figure seems but the recounting of a fragment of the myth of the dying and rising god, so well known to Paul's area and time. Only in unity with one another does either event make its full impact. Only in reference to one another did they "make sense" even to Paul. We may remember that Saul-Paul persecuted the infant Christian congregation after Jesus died on the cross— and after he was said to be risen by those earliest Christians. Saul-Paul became a believer only when the Risen Spirit-Christ appeared to him (1 Corinthians 15:8), thus confronting him with the (to him, at least) reality of the Living Christ. Paul could offer no evidence concerning Christ's Resurrection as an "event," except the evidence of his own experience. Yet, however it came about— and Paul believed that God brought it about— Christ was alive! Thus, because he believed in the reality of the Spirit-Christ's present life, Paul accepted the Resurrection, since Jesus' death was a matter of record, at least in the tradition he received. Indeed, as he points out in 1 Corinthians 12:23ff., the cross is a stumbling block and foolishness only to those who have not experienced the power of Christ's Resurrection (i.e., participation in his Spirit). On the other hand, the Resurrection is mere wishful thinking (and the Christian's experiences perhaps delusions) if one does not accept the confession: "Christ died." Paul thus believed in the reality of Christ's death and His new dimension of life—as Spirit—which was his experience,[68] of "the power of His Resurrection."

> ... that I may gain Christ and be found in him, not having a righteousness of my own, based on law, but that which is through faith in Christ, the righteousness from God that depends on faith; that I may know him and the power of his resurrection, and may share his sufferings, becoming like him in his death, that if possible I may attain the resurrection from the dead [Philippians 3:8b-11].

This Resurrection is a matter of faith, not demonstration; it is part of the Kerygma, that is, of the proclamation of the Church which is

---

[68]And that of all the witnesses listed in 1 Cor. 15:5-8, none of whom saw Christ's body rise up, but to whom Christ appeared alive after his death.

interpretative. We must assume from 1 Corinthians 15, the earliest record, that the early Christians experienced the presence of Christ as a Spirit, as Paul records: "He appeared to Cephas... He appeared to James" in 1 Corinthians 15:5,7. On the other hand, the Kerygma is the distillation of the apostles' reflections upon their experiences with Jesus called the Christ. Paul and the early disciples presented this living experience of participation in mystic communication with the Spirit of Christ as an objective event. The wisdom of this Kerygmatic procedure lies in its inseparable connection of Christ's death and His new mode of life (Spirit, "Risen," "Glorified"), so that the experience of communion with the Spirit was always understood (and even received) in connection with the name of and the tradition about the "historical Jesus." In fact, there could be, for Paul, no cult (church) or piety that was participant in the New Reality that appeared in Jesus Christ apart from a living Christ. The Paulinist who produced Colossians particularly stresses that the Christian's life in hid with Christ in God and that Christ is our life (Colossians 3:3-4). Otherwise, Christianity would have developed into a minor sect of Judaism, bound to the law, in which the freedom and joy of Jesus (theonomy) would have shortly degenerated into a new legalism (heteronomy, as in the Ebionite sect) or else it would have cut loose all its moorings in the acts of God in history and become a Palestinian strain of gnosticism, as in Valentinianism. The significance of Paul, and of the struggle reflected in Galatians 2, is that under this rigorous thinker, who was also a "reacting mystic,"[69] the church was guided away from both of these blind alleys and was enabled to develop in fidelity to its own Spirit.

---

[69]In Deissmann's phrase (*Paul*, p. 152), Paul is both a reacting and a communion mystic. He writes of Paul's communion in terms similar to Wilhelm Herrmann's in *The Communion of the Christian with God*, trans. J. S. Stanyon (London: Williams and Norgate, 1895). Deissmann, *Paul*, pp. 147, 157, elaborately explains what he means by mysticism and why he applies the term to Paul's religion. Paul is a re-acting mystic or follower of catabatic mysticism in Deissmann's terminology. In this form of communion with the Divine, God approaches man first rather than man seeking to approach God first as in anabatic or acting mysticism. Paul's mysticism is a mysticism of grace or of the Divine gift, says Deissmann. This form of re-acting mysticism is the response of the religious personality to an encounter with God, such as Paul's Damascus Road experience. Paul's mysticism is aimed at communion with God rather than union with God in that it aims at the sanctification of the personality through the presence of God rather than at a transformation of the person into the deity. Thus Deissmann concludes that Paul's mysticism affirms human personality rather than denying it.

Therefore Paul teaches that he, too, and all Christian believers, have also died (Romans 6) and have already passed from death to new life—after the manner of Christ's experience and under the control of Christ's own Spirit. Hence, Paul can use his own experience as a guide in preaching the Gospel, and can even call upon believers to imitate him, as he imitates Christ (1 Corinthians 4:15-17; 11:1; and Philippians 3:17). The Cross, Christ's death, and his Resurrection, then, mystically understood, are not only "once for all" events, but a living reality that is continually going on for the believer. This is the case because through the power of God, death was not able to annihilate Christ's Spirit, and through this "resurrection" Christ (as Spirit) was liberated from his self-accepted (Philippians 2:5ff.) limitations in the fleshly mode and has become Spirit once more.[70] For this reason Paul could say "...if Christ has not been raised, than our preaching is in vain and our faith is in vain. We are even found to be misrepresenting God ... If for this life only we have hoped in Christ, we are of all men most to be pitied (1 Corinthians 15:14-19). "But in fact Christ has been raised from the dead ..." Paul concludes, basing his conclusion not only on the Kerygma proclaimed to him, but also on that personal participation in the Spirit of Christ of which he said:

And we all, with unveiled face, reflecting the glory of the Lord, are being changed into his likeness from one degree of glory to another; for this comes from the Lord who is the Spirit [2 Corinthians 3:17-18].

The Idea of the Corporeity (or Common Life) of the Christian Life: The Body of Christ:
The Connection of the "Body of Christ" Passages to the "In-Christ" and "In-the-Spirit" Passages

In the preceding sections, I have pointed out that, for Paul, having a relationship with the Divine is understood as being filled by the Spirit and "being in Christ." I have designated Paul's religion "Christ-mysticism" and noted that the Pauline theology may be understood as a development of this continuing communion with Christ which began for Paul with the Damascus Road Christophany. Albert Schweitzer has been cited as an authority for this interpretation along with Adolf Deissmann, who might be termed the father of the modern emphasis on the mystical element in Paul's theology. Schweitzer has noted in his

---

[70]See 1 Cor. 15:4, 50, 51, 54, also 1 Cor. 3:21 and 2 Cor. 13:4; Phil. 2:9. Cf.. Ephesians 2:17-18: "And he came and preached peace . . . for through him we both have assess in one Spirit to the Father." And 4:4-7: "There is one body and one Spirit . . ."

classic study, *The Mysticism of Paul the Apostle*, that Paul's teaching concerning Christ's mysticism was appropriate for the time immediately following the death and Resurrection of Jesus Christ.[71] Deissmann has observed the same appropriateness of Paul's teaching in his own great works declaring that the Pauline Spirit-Christ is not a fantasy of Paul's religious imagination, but on the contrary, the Spirit-Christ is grounded in the concrete reality of the cross. The Spiritual Christ is the Christian believer's present experience of the Crucified One who could not be overcome by rejection and death. Paul's mystical communion with the Spirit-Christ, therefore, transforms all that had been entrusted to him as tradition or teaching about Jesus into a present reality.[72]

If I were to introduce a modern set of terms into this discussion, I might borrow the unusually penetrating terminology of Joseph Sittler and Jaroslav Pelikan.[73] These terms are the "ecology of the Christian life" used by Sittler in his book, *The Ecology of Faith*,[74] and the "shape" of the Christian's communion with his Lord taken from Pelikan's *The Shape of Death*.[75] Both Pelikan and Sittler use their terms in different senses in these works, but I will borrow them and point them in another direction as they possess the power of expressing what I mean by the Pauline Christ-communion, particularly on its external or inter-personal side, the corporeity or common life of Christians in the church.

An evaluation of Paul's usage of the "In-Christ" passages reveals the fact that the imagery inherent in Paul's usage is that of spatiality or of *Lebensraum*. For Saint Paul, being in Christ meant that the Divine Spirit was the environment, the milieu[76], the living space in which the believer lived and moved and had his being. This environmental or spatial image underlies both the external reference in Paul's "In-Christ" passages where he declares "I am in Christ," and the internal "In-Christ" passages where Paul declares "Christ is in me."

In my survey of the various usages that have been identified in the Pauline "In-Christ" passages, I noted that there was one type (denoted Usage 3, type a) which designates the relationship of Christ to the Christian congregation. To use only one example, the letter to the Romans, note that the proclitic *en* is used six times to emphasize the relationship of Christ and the congregation, twice more to emphasize

---

[71]A. Schweitzer, *The Mysticism of Paul the Apostle*, pp. 109ff.

[72]Deissmann, *Paul*, p. 143.

[73]I have borrowed the term "ecology" used in a theological sense from Joseph Sittler and the term "shape" used in a theological sense from Jaroslav Pelikan.

[74]Joseph Sittler, *The Ecology of Faith* (Philadelphia: Muhlenberg Press, 1961).

[75]Jaroslav Pelikan, *The Shape of Death* (New York: Abingdon Press, 1961).

[76]Pierre Teilhard de Chardin, *The Divine Milieu* (New York: Harper Torchbooks, 1965).

Christian unity and once to denote Christ's presence in the believer. There are only seventeen instances of the phrase "in Christ" in Romans; thus ten out of seventeen times "In Christ" has the meaning of the unity of the Christian with his Lord. What is especially noteworthy is that of these ten instances of "in Christ" donating the unity of the Christian with Christ, nine of them refer to that mystical Christ-communication as being experienced in the church, in the unity of believers. Paul's other letters reveal a similar pattern. 1 Corinthians gives six out of seventeen instances of the "In-Christ" passages to Usage 3, type a, while 2 Corinthians gives at least four instances of the same type and Galatians contains four more instances of this type of usage. Indeed, we may say that the emphasis is on a correlation of the inner communion with Christ, with an external communion with other Christians. This emphasis on unity with other Christians is found in all the Epistles under study, being absent only in 2 Corinthians. Thus, Paul's conception of Christ-mysticism holds that an inner mystical union takes place precisely in and through the community.

The related phrase "In the Lord" has a similar profile. Usage 3, type a, referring to Christ's connection with the congregation, is found in I and 2 Corinthians as well as in Philippians and Philemon. The brief note of Paul to Philemon contains four instances of "In Christ" and two instances of "in the Lord" in its twenty-five verses. This fact alone reveals the importance of Christ-communion for Paul's thought. It also underscores the mystical cast of his theology and the importance of the spatial image for his religious vocabulary.

The fact that the "In-Christ" passages are used, in a two-fold sense, to point to an external communion as well as an internal communion, means that Paul's mysticism is not an individualistic affair. "I in Christ" expresses the state of being in unity with Christ's body, the Christian Church, and "Christ in me" means to be empowered to meet the demands of the Christian life from within by a sharing of one's personal life with the universal and ubiquitous Christ-Jesus who was now freed from the limitations of the categories that bind men by his Resurrection. Such an inner and outer mystical relationship of union with Christ is for this writer the root of all Paul's theological thought. It is also the explanation for the development by Paul of his unique ecclesiology, his view of the church as being the *soma tou christou*, the body of Christ. Albert Schweitzer clearly expressed this same insight saying "The common denominator behind the ideas of 'in Christ' and 'with Christ' and 'Christ in us' is the corporeity of the common life of the body of Christ."[77] Schweitzer explains Paul's Christ-mysticism on the basis of the

---

[77]A. Schweitzer, *The Mysticism of Paul the Apostle*, p. 122.

early Christian belief in the Messianic Kingdom. He interprets the Pauline Epistles as revealing that Paul believed that he and all other Christians shared with the Risen Christ a new life which is none other than the Resurrection mode of existence.[78] In this new relation of solidarity, Christ and the Christian share a common life open to and receptive of influences flowing from the powers of the Resurrection. Therefore, the "Elect are in reality no longer natural men, but, like Christ Himself, are already supernatural beings, only that in them this is not yet manifest.[79]

To turn from the older analyses of Schweitzer and Deissmann to a more modern one, we may say that the ecology of the Christian life for Paul, the environment in which one grows into the fullness of Christ-likeness, is the community of believers. A new shape is given to the life of men who have been grasped by the Spirit; they are shaped into a living community that acknowledges the Lordship of Christ and which shares in his spiritual power. A new creation, indeed, has come about in the interpersonal life of those touched by the Christian message. A new milieu has come into being, the sphere of the spirit., and a new shape is given to life—a shape that points toward the future and the eschatological consummation. Schweitzer has remarked at length on this eschatological bent of Paul's mysticism and of its implications for his doctrine of the Body of Christ, that is, of the Church.

The Pauline Mysticism is therefore nothing else than the doctrine of the making manifest, in consequence of the death and resurrection of Jesus, of the pre-existent church (the community of God). The enigmatic concept, which dominates the mysticism of the "body of Christ" to which all believers belong, and in which they are already dead and risen again, is thus derived from the pre-existent church ....[80]

From his analysis of the close connection between Paul's mysticism and Paul's doctrine of the church with the eschatological hope of the early Christians, Schweitzer concludes that Paul's teaching is an "eschatological mysticism." Schweitzer holds that this future hope of the coming Kingdom of God which Jesus had preached, raised to a high degree of intensity by the passage of time and by Paul's and other Christians' continuing experiences with the Spirit, produced the Pauline mysticism as well as the other aspects of his theology.[81]

In order to complete my assessment of the Pauline doctrine of communion with Christ, which passed into his doctrine of the church by

---

[78]Ibid., p.109.
[79]Ibid., p. 110.
[80]Ibid., p. 116. (See Romans 6.)
[81]A. Schweitzer, *The Mysticism of Paul the Apostle*, pp. 241-242.

an inner necessity, I will examine the passages in Paul's epistles which refer to "the body of Christ." The same control over the Pauline material that was used in the study of the "In-Christ" and "In-the-Spirit" passages will be exercised here. I will limit myself to those Epistles generally accepted as Pauline, which in this case means that I will examine only Romans and 1 Corinthians. I will omit reference to the very rich development of the concept of the body of Christ in the disputed Epistles, Ephesians and Colossians.

The Body of Christ Passages in Paul[82]

In Romans 12:5, Paul declares, that "the many are one body in Christ ..." "*Hoi pollio hen soma esmen en Christo.*" Here the term now under discussion, *soma*, occurs in close connection with "in Christ." Paul's point is that it is "in Christ" that men ("the many") become "one body." The unity of believer with believer in the Christian congregation is accomplished "in Christ," for "in Christ" the believer enters a new environment, indeed, a new reality. "In Christ" man's spiritual life enjoys a new ecology and his physical life takes on a new *shape*. In Romans 9:4, Paul explains (to the Corinthians) that they have "died to the law through the body of Christ," i.e., they have changed one spiritual environment for another by their participation in the life of the Risen Christ. Undoubtedly the term *soma* in Romans 7:4 refers to the sacrifice of Christ, to the bodily death of Christ on the cross. However, the intention of the passage is to stress the Christian believer's spiritual participation in Christ's sacrifice and aims to show the believer that they now belong to"him who has been raised from the dead." Thus spiritual participation in Christ is indicated in this passage.

Arndt and Gingrich tell us that *soma* is used in at least five different ways in the New Testament. It may have its obvious use to refer to the body of a man or animal; in the plural it can mean slaves; it can refer to the stalk or stem of a plant (1 Corinthians 15:35); and it may mean reality in contrast to a shadow (Colossians 2:17). None of these uses, except perhaps the reference of *soma* to Christ's physical body as it was involved in the sacrifice of the cross, is of interest in this investigation. It is the fifth usage of *soma* that is under study here. This last usage occurs in Romans 12:5; 1 Corinthians 10:17; 12:13 and 27, as well as Ephesians 1:23 and Colossians 1:18, where it signifies the Christian community, the church as an organic unity.[83]

---

[82]See Table 4, "The 'Body of Christ' Passages in Romans and 1 Corinthians" in the appendix.

[83]Arndt and Gingrich, *BAGD*, pp. 806-807.

In Romans 12:4-5, *soma* is used as a metaphor in verse 4, where Paul says "as in one body we have many members." In verse 5, however, Paul draws a simile, or comparison, and declares that "We (i.e., Christians) though many are one body in Christ." This use of the term *soma* by Paul is apparently closely related to his usage of the phrases "in Christ" and "in the Spirit" to express the Christian's new situation in the world, that of being in a mystical participation with Christ's Spirit and in a nexus of inter-relations with one another that is characterized by Christ's Spiritual Presence among them. It might be said that the *soma* in this sense refers to the spiritual environment (in its external manifestation) of the Christian.

First Corinthians 10:16-17 occurs in the context of Paul's teaching concerning the Lord's Supper, but it obviously refers to Paul's belief that those who commune at the Christian Eucharist participate in the spiritual effect of the sacrifice of Christ. Paul does go on to draw a moral from this spiritual experience at the Communion in verse 17 where he uses the phrase "one body" to designate the unity of Christians in the church.

First Corinthians 11:24ff, is the Pauline tradition concerning the institution of the Lord's Supper, and the term *soma* here refers to the sacrifice of Christ. The same meaning of *soma* is intended in 1 Corinthians 11:27 and 29, where the term refers to the Communion elements and to the sacrifice of Christ by analogy.

Paul's fullest discourse on "the body" occurs in 1 Corinthians 12:12-27. Actually Paul's discussion carries through as far as verse 31 and if we examine this larger context we find that he uses the term *soma* nineteen times in these twenty verses. Paul describes the Christian congregation as an organic unity in which each Christian believer may be compared to a *mele* or member. Each member Paul declares to be equipped to fulfill various needful religious services by the indwelling of the Holy Spirit. The use of *soma* throughout this passage is, of course, metaphorical.

Verse 13 is of chief interest to us, for in this declaration Paul unites the activity of the Spirit with the concept of the church as a unity of believers with one another and with Christ. Paul says: "For by one Spirit we were all baptized into *one body*—Jews or Greeks, slaves or free—all were made to drink of *one Spirit*." This passage strengthens the insight that the phrase "the body of Christ" is an expression of Paul's Christ-mysticism in the same sense as his phrase "in Christ." Here the "one body" mentioned in verse 13 is coordinated with "Christ" in verse 12:

(12) For just as the body is one and has many members, and all
the members of the body, though many, are one body, so it is
with Christ. (13) For by one Spirit we were all baptized into one
body— ... and all were made to drink of one Spirit.

This passage demonstrates Paul's equation of the church (the body)
and the spiritually present Christ. Therefore we will be close to Paul's
intention if we understand the phrase "in Christ" to refer to the
environment of the Christian, his organic relatedness to other believers
and to the Lord in the church.

The English scholar, George Johnston,[84] who was convinced that
Paul had borrowed the term *soma* from Stoic philosophy, found himself
forced to say about this passage, "Such a conception is on the verge of
passing beyond the stage of metaphor, if it has not yet done so. Christ
and the Church are practically identified."[85] We would say that Paul
does make such an identification on the basis of his Christ-mysticism,
for he had experienced Communion with Christ in the church and
therefore equated the organic unity of believer and Lord he found there
with his own experience of being "in Christ" that dated from the
Damascus Road event. Such a mystical background, once presupposed,
explains the point that Paul attempts to make in this lengthy passage.
Paul's point is that the church is an organic unity in which each
believer is included in the same fashion as a physical organ is included
in the totality of the physical body. In this situation the Spiritual gift
possessed by each individual member is needed for the organic growth
or up-building (*oikodome*) of the body, the church. Unless the mystical
participation background is presupposed, any speech about an organic
unity of one member (believer) with the total membership is
groundless. Only such spiritual participation (based on Christ-
mysticism) gives meaning to verse 26: "If one member suffers, all suffer
together; if one member is honored, all rejoice together." The fact that
Paul does pass beyond metaphor into the language of religious
mysticism is further borne out by verse 27: "Now you are the body of
Christ and individually members of it." This verse specifically points
out that "you," the Corinthian church members, *are* the body of Christ.
The totality of believers, with the nexus of inter-relationships that
prevail among them, are seen by the man who mystically participated
in fellowship with the Risen-Spirit-Christ as forming a *Gestalt*, an
organic unity larger than the sum-total of the number of church

---

[84]George Johnston, *The Doctrine of the Church in the New Testament*
(Cambridge: The Cambridge Press, 1943).
[85]Ibid., p. 90.

members and greater than the totality of their spiritual talents. Among the various members of the body there are evidences of the indwelling of the Spiritual Christ, who makes himself known by the new powers of the believers and especially by the presence of love among them (1 Corinthians 13).

A Constructive Analysis of Paul's "Christ-Mysticism" and Conception of "The Spirit"
An Analysis of the Pauline Textual Data

Now that we have examined the Pauline textual material and the literature on it, let us turn to the following analysis of Paul's theology and some conclusions about the meaning of his language in regard to his conception of Christ and the Spirit. It should be noted that this is not an attempt to develop a full-blown Pauline Christology and/or Pneumatology, but only to point out the relationship between the Christ and the Spirit in the passages discussed above.

In this section the various Pauline passages studied previously are grouped into general classes that illustrate Paul's usage and intention. First I will summarize my findings concerning Paul's use of the term *pneuma* or spirit. Then I will investigate his usage of the "in Christ" and "in the Spirit" passages, and finally try to relate these to Paul's use of the "body of Christ" passages.

In the first section of this chapter I pointed out that Paul uses *pneuma* in two ways, the first way (use a) to refer to the spirit of man, and the second way (use b) to refer to the Divine Spirit. Paul's general meaning in using the term *pneuma* in sense *a* was to refer to the self or the principle of personality within humans. As such *pneuma a* refers to the dimension of man's total being that expresses his feelings, drives and will. *Pneuma a* is the dimension in which man becomes self-conscious, self-aware and is able to transcend himself in acts of faith and human creativity. Paul uses *pneuma* in the second sense, to refer to the Divine, in a less definite way because he has a number of phrases that he uses apparently unsystematically to refer to the Divine. Examples of this varied terminology are "the Holy Spirit," "the Spirit," "the Spirit of Jesus," and even the unique phrase, "the Lord is the Spirit," which occurs in 2 Corinthians 3:17. Due to this variation of terminology, it is not always clear just what aspect of the Divine is intended to be designated by Paul. However, the two passages, Romans 1:9 and 1 Corinthians 2:11, tend to lead to the opinion that there is at least an analogy between *pneuma a* and *pneuma b* in Paul's thinking. These passages refer to the human spirit in the sense of the selfhood of man and imply that "only a man's spirit knows what is within him," and that this same internal structure is true of the Divine life, also. Paul declared that "the Spirit searches everything, even the depths of God," and that "no one comprehends the thoughts of God except the Spirit of God." Therefore we may conclude from this that as the spirit is the dimension of self-awareness, of volition and of creativity in man, even so the Spirit is the dimension of self-awareness, of volition and of creativity in God. I noted in the above discussion that the difference between the spirit of man and the Spirit of God lies in the aspect of power, as man's spirit is dependent upon the Divine, while the Divine Spirit is self-sufficient.

When we turn to the "in Christ," "in the Spirit," and" in the Lord" passages we immediately note the close connection in Paul's thought of the Spirit and Christ. Indeed the passage from 1 Corinthians 2 quoted above is itself a demonstration of this. Just as Paul tells us that the Spirit interprets spiritual truths to those who possess the Spirit in 2 Corinthians 2:13, even so in verse 16 Paul declares that the Christians who know these spiritual truths "have the mind of Christ." We noted especially in our discussion of Paul's "in Christ" passages that these phrases and their cognates appear to be related to Paul's visionary experiences of the Risen Christ. Thus Paul tends to use the phrase "in Christ" synonymously with the phrase "in the Spirit." The unique passage in 2 Corinthians 3:17 which identifies "the Lord" with "the Spirit" serves to emphasize this synonymous use. While there is a disagreement among scholars as to the meaning of the term "the Lord" in this passage, the reference to Christ in verse 15 and its obvious synonym "the Lord" in verse 16 tends to bear out the contention that "the Lord" in verse 17 means Christ. 2 Corinthians 3:17 goes on to speak of "the Spirit of the Lord," and verse 18 speaks of "the Lord who is the Spirit."

In our analysis of the "in Christ" passages and its cognates, we observed that Paul apparently has a spatial analogy in mind when he speaks of "being in Christ." Not only is one "in Christ" when he is in "the body of Christ" but he is "in Christ" simply by being a Christian. As we noted above, "in Christ" often bears the simple meaning of "Christian." However, there is a deeper sense to "in Christ" than this surface meaning. Paul's phrases beginning with the Greek proclitic *en* seem to have the meaning of having "a state of being." We illustrated this possible meaning of phrases beginning with *en* by reference to the phrase "in torment" in Luke 16:23 and "in death" in 1 John 3:14, as well as by referring to Romans 8:10 "if Christ is in you," where Paul concludes that if one does have Christ in him then his spirit is alive."

Paul sometimes uses the phrase "in Christ" or "in the Lord" to refer to the presence of the church in an actual spatial location such as "the church in Phillipi." However, the more cogent usage is Paul's usage of *en* to refer to the environment of the Christian's life which is lived in communion with the Risen Christ Jesus. This environment is expressed in an ecological sense, both externally and internally. By this we mean that one can be said to be "in Christ" (which we have designated in Table 1 as usage 3, types a, c, and d) and also one may be able to say that "Christ is in him" (which Table I designates as usage 4).[86] The analogous usage of the phrase "in the Spirit" we designated as usage a which speaks of the Spirit as localized in man, and as usage b which designates the state of man's being in the Spirit.[87] Because Paul uses the phrases "in Christ" and "in the Spirit" alternately, apparently referring to the same spiritual experience, and uses them to speak of both the internal and external communion, we may conclude that to be "in Christ" and to be "in the Spirit" represent the same experience for Saint Paul.

The Pauline usage of the phrase "the body of Christ" which was investigated above, was seen to be related to Paul's phrases "in Christ" and "in the Spirit." "The body of Christ'" is an obviously spatially oriented metaphor that speaks of the Christian's spiritual participation in the Spirit-Christ under the analogy of an organic unity in which the Spirit-Christ is the framework to which each Christian belongs as a structural part. Thus the "body of Christ" is an environmental or ecological metaphor that makes even plainer the Pauline conception of participation in the Risen Lord than does the more elliptical "in Christ" and "in the Spirit" passages. 1 Corinthians 12:12-13 dramatically expresses Paul's equation of "the body" and "the Spirit" and "the Christ." In this passage Paul speaks of Christ, the body and the "one Spirit" all in one sense. Thus it is justifiable to conclude that the Pauline expression "the body of Christ" belongs to Paul's Christ-mysticism and expresses his conception of the nature of the Christian life.

Constructive Analysis

Our investigation of Paul's "mystical passages" reveals that his theology is neither consistent nor systematic. However, there is an underlying metaphor discernible in Paul's thought, that of the spatial,

---

[86]See Table 1, "The 'In Christ' Passages" in the appendix.
[87]SeeTable 2, "The 'In the Spirit' Passages" in the appendix.

environmental, ecological image of being "in" some spiritual reality which Paul alternatively refers to as "Christ," "Spirit," "Lord," and as "the body of Christ." Paul's theology is an existential theology as it is bi-polar, having at one pole the message of Christ which he felt constrained to preach, and at the other pole the "situation" in which his readers lived, feared and worked. Thus Paul's theology arises on the basis of the felt needs of the Christian people under his care who asked for advice and counsel on the problems they faced in their personal and congregational experiences. One might say that Paul's theology, therefore, is given in the form of a dialogue between the needs of the Christian community (of which he himself was a member) and the historic traditions about Jesus Christ, along with Paul's own personal "mystical" experiences with the Risen Spirit-Christ.

We may document the unsystematic nature of Paul's theology by pointing out the various ways in which Paul used the terms "Christ" and "Spirit." In the following paragraphs we will give examples (a) of Paul's use of "Christ" and "Spirit" in an interchangeable way; (b) of Paul's use of these terms in a separate and distinct way; and (c) we will document the variety of terms Paul uses to refer to "the Spirit."

(A) *Paul's use of "Christ" and "Spirit" interchangeably.* The chief passage in Paul's Epistles that apparently identifies Christ with the Spirit, due to its interchangeable use of the two terms, is 2 Corinthians 3:17. In this passage, and in the context surrounding it, we have the phrases "the Lord is the Spirit" and (in 3:18) "the Lord who is the Spirit." The context of these passages makes it apparent that "Lord" and "Spirit" are synonyms for Christ, as verse 3:14 speaks of Christ and there to no apparent change of subject before verses 3:17-18.

Other passages in Epistles that use "Christ" and "Spirit" interchangeably are Romans 8:2 and 8:9-10: "For the law of the Spirit of life in Christ Jesus" (8:2); "... anyone who does not have the Spirit of Christ does not belong to him" (8:9-10). But if Christ is in you ...

These passages are among the clearest in their identification of Christ as Spirit. Romans 8:2 speaks of "the Spirit of life" which is apparently localized "in Christ Jesus." Romans 8:9-10 very precisely refers to the "Spirit of Christ" and implies that the possession of the Spirit of Christ is a necessary condition for one's being a Christian. Paul declares that a person who does not possess (or participate in) the Spirit of Christ is not a Christian and goes on to state that if "Christ is in you" then one is freed from the spiritual death of sin and is now a participant in the new spiritual life that is characterized by the righteousness of Christ.

Philippians 2:1, in a beautiful series of parallel phrases that are reminiscent of the parallelism of the Psalms, makes the apparent identification of the state of being "in Christ" and the state of being "in the Spirit:" "So if there in any encouragement in Christ, any incentive of love, any participation in the Spirit ..."

This passage uses the phrases "in Christ" and "in the Spirit" synonymously and goes on to identify this state as one of participation. This apparently underscores our identification of the Pauline basic metaphor of participation in a spatial or organic environment which he designates as "Christ" or "Spirit" or "body." It is interesting to note that this state of spiritual participation can be identified as the state of having *agape* or Christian love by Saint Paul.

(B) *Paul's use of "Christ" and the "Spirit" separately.* In these passages we must note that Paul is very indefinite about the referent of the term "Spirit," as his terminology varies from passage to passage. We will note that there are two chief terminological differences here: (1) passages which speak of the "Spirit from God" or "Spirit of God;" and (2) passages which speak of "the Holy Spirit." Three examples of Paul's use of the terms "Spirit from God" are:

Now we have received not the spirit of the world but the spirit which is from God. (1 Cor 2:10-16)

Do you not know that you are God's temple and that God's Spirit dwells in you? (1 Cor 3:16 [Also 1 Corinthians 6:19])

No one speaking by the Spirit of God ever says "Jesus be cursed." (1 Cor 12:3 [Also Romans 8:9])

In these passages we are impressed by the lack of distinctness in 1 Corinthians 2:12, where we have the reference to the "Spirit ... from God," which is an antithesis to the "Spirit of the World." In this reference, "the Spirit from God" could be simply a general way of speaking of the Spiritual-Christ or it could refer to the Old Testament usage of "the Spirit" as a synonym for God himself. It could also refer to a third possibility, a concept something like the later Christian doctrine of the Holy Spirit. First Corinthians 3:16 is an obvious allusion to the indwelling of the Divine Spirit in the believer. Here Paul utilizes the metaphor of spatiality by referring to the Christian's body as "God's temple." First Corinthians 6:19 makes this even more obvious by speaking of "your body ... a temple of the Holy Spirit within you, which you have from God ... " First Corinthians 12:3 refers to the "Spirit of God," which is put in parallelism with the phrase "the Holy Spirit," in the second half of the same verse. What is of interest here is that Paul is maintaining that no one who has the Spirit of God or the Holy Spirit can curse Jesus, and that only one who has this Spirit can say "Jesus is Lord." First Corinthians 12:4-5 also is of interest for it parallels Spirit and Lord, "Now there are varieties of gifts, but the same Spirit; and there are varieties of services, but the same Lord ..."

This passage very definitely speaks of Spirit and Lord as the same spiritual entity. And verse 6 goes on to say "... but it is the same God, ..." which seems to equate Spirit, Lord, and God. The remainder of the lengthy passage goes on to speak of the Spirit until verse 18 where God is mentioned as the arranger of the organs in the body. God is also mentioned in verses 24 and 28, and the Corinthian Christians are identified as "the body of Christ" in verse 27.

(C) *Paul's use of the "Holy Spirit" as a term without reference to God or Christ.* First Thessalonians 1:5-6 speaks of Paul's spiritual credentials saying "... for our Gospel came to you not only in word, but also in power and in the Holy Spirit ..." Here the Holy Spirit is referred to twice without any kind of correlation to Christ or God. However, "... hope in our Lord Jesus Christ" is mentioned in verse 3, and in verse 4 the brethren are said to be " ... beloved by God ..." This kind of reference would lead one to conclude that Paul has some specific idea of the Holy Spirit in mind, which can not be reduced to language about Christ.

Romans 9:1 states "I am speaking the truth in Christ, I am not lying; my conscience bears me witness in the Holy Spirit ..." This passage might be taken as an example of the parallelism of "in Christ" and "in the Spirit" treated in Section a above, because this sentence actually throws the two phrases in synonymous parallelism. If it is an instance of Paul's interchangeable use of "Spirit" and "Christ," then we would be justified in saying that Paul equated "the Holy Spirit" with the Risen Christ. However, there is apparently an intention to speak of an *external* reference in the first phrase "the truth of Christ," and of an *internal* reference in the second phrase, which refers to Paul's conscience bearing his witness "in the Holy Spirit." Whatever Paul's intention, the Holy Spirit here seems to be thought of as somehow distinct from Christ. However, we can see the Pauline spatial metaphor of the organic body of Christ underlying this passage, as verse 3 speaks of "being cut off from Christ."

Romans 14:17-18 again mentions the Holy Spirit as a distinct entity but uses the term in close connection with the term "Christ:"

For the kingdom of God does not mean food and drink but righteousness and peace and joy in the Holy Spirit; he who thus serves Christ is acceptable to God and approved by men.

Here "acceptance by God" and "the kingdom of God" are equated with the spiritual gifts the Christian experiences when he is "in the Holy Spirit." And the "kingdom," "God," and "Spirit" are put in close connection with "serving Christ." This passage also might be taken as an equation of the state of "being in the Spirit" with the state of "serving Christ." However, "the Holy Spirit" is more correctly taken as a reference to a special spiritual entity due to the syntax of the sentence.

First Corinthians 12:11 has been treated above, but deserves mention here also as it, along with a number of passages before and after it, refer to "the Spirit" without close reference to Christ or to God. However, we note above that the entire passage seems to be controlled by an equation of God, Christ and the Spirit. The variety of expression Paul reveals in his Epistles tends to bear out our previous comment that Paul is not wholly consistent in his language about Christ and the Spirit. This analysis might be summed up in three propositions:

(1) In some passages "the Spirit" is equivalent to the Risen Christ.

(2) In other passages "the Spirit" is apparently equivalent to expressions that denote the extension of God's personality or activity into human life.

(3) In a few passages "the Spirit" apparently is used by Paul to denote a distinct "hypothesis" of the Godhead or a specific spiritual entity.

After looking objectively at the raw material of Paul's writings in this way, we might well conclude from Paul's imprecision that he did not have any clear conception of an hypostasis of the Spirit. *We believe this to be the case.* Looked at from our own assessment of our experiences, there is little that can be said that would distinguish between the indwelling of the Holy Spirit and the indwelling of the Risen Christ. However, it remains true that Paul does occasionally try to make such a distinction.

On the basis of these passages we must conclude that Paul enjoyed a rich mystical life with the Risen Christ. Paul speaks of Christ as present with him now, not just as a "memory" from the past, even if that memory is of the "vision" he had on the Damascus Road. This mystical experience can be best described as participation—which Paul might well have understood by anamnesis or "remembrance," but which would have meant a living presence for Paul, as in the words of institution at the Lord's Supper (1 Cor 11:23-30). Actually, Paul thought of this participation in an ecological, environmental sense, basing his language upon the spatial metaphor of the body of Christ. Some examples of the rich spiritual life of Paul that we have designated "Christ-mysticism," following Deissmann and Schweitzer, are: The passage in Romans 6:11 where Paul speaks of being "dead to sin and alive to God in Christ Jesus" and the passage in Romans 6:23 where Paul refers to the Christian's possession of "eternal life in Christ Jesus our Lord." In Romans 15:17 Paul feels himself able to say "In Christ Jesus, then I have reason to be proud of my work for God." In 1 Corinthians 10:16 Paul speaks of the Christian Eucharist as "a participation in the blood of Christ" and as "a participation in the body of Christ." In 1 Corinthians 15:19 Paul says "We who are in Christ" have hope for the future. 1 Corinthians 15:31 speaks of Paul's "pride in you which I have in Christ Jesus our Lord." 2 Corinthians 12:2 is Paul's famous reference to "a man in Christ." 1 Corinthians 13:3 speaks of Paul's "proof that Christ is speaking in me." 2 Corinthians 13:5 shows Paul asking the Corinthians if they do not "realize that Jesus Christ is in you?"

On any assessment of Paul's Christ-mysticism the passage in Galatians 2:20 must be considered the crowning passage:

"I have been crucified with Christ; it is no longer I who live, but Christ who lives in me; and the life I now live in the flesh I live in by faith in the Son of God, who loved me and gave himself for me."

A conclusion is that for Paul, if one is a Christian he leads such a life of *unio mystica*, of an inner communion with Christ which is correlated with an external communion with the body of Christ, the Church, and with its individual members. This union is present from the beginning of the Christian life and becomes clearer as one becomes more aware of it and realizes its possibilities in one's relationship with others.

The Pauline textual data investigated in this chapter bear out the contention that Paul was a Christ-mystic and that his conception of his mystical relationship with Christ is at the root of Paul's theological thought. As we have mentioned above, Paul's conception of union with Christ had its inception at his Christophany on the Damascus Road. This sense of having been grasped or seized by the Spirit of Christ increased as Paul matured in the Christian life. In time he came to see it as having an external, environmental sense in that he felt that he was "in Christ." Paul felt that he was a participant in some spiritually grounded organic unity that bound together all Christian believers in the body of Christ. On the other hand, Paul came to believe that his mystic unity has an internal sense as well as an external one. In some way "Christ was in Paul." Paul could speak of the "Christ in me," always referring to this mystical participation in the Risen Lord as the indwelling of Christ in his own soul. This indwelling, Spiritual-Christ was understood by Paul to empower him to meet the demands of the

Christian life. Paul felt that he was sharing his most personal, inmost spiritual life with the ubiquitous Spirit of the Risen Lord. Paul's Spiritual-Christ was the universal Lord and was available at all times and in all places as the source of strength that strengthened him for the trials he had to undergo and the task he had to do. The Spiritual-Christ was the manifestation of the Divine for Paul, a manifestation that was universally present because he was freed from the limitations of the categories that bind one to the structures of life and the world by the power of his resurrection (Romans 1:4).

In conclusion, Paul's emphasis upon his inner and outer union with the Risen Spiritual-Christ prevented him from developing his Pneumatology any further than he did. As we have seen above, Paul's terminology varies from place to place when he discusses his experience with the Spirit. It is not easy to say just what he is attempting to communicate when he refers to "the Spirit," "the Holy Spirit," and the "Spirit of Christ." And yet a pattern of meaning can be discerned in Paul's varied references to the Divine as Spirit.

The Pattern of Meaning Discernible in Paul's References to "The Spirit"

For Saint Paul the decisive element of the Christian religion was the manifestation of the Divine in the world of men in the Incarnation of the Christ-Messiah in Jesus. This was not only a manifestation of divine power, but a series of actions by the Divine-human Christ. Christ had broken down the barriers of estrangement that separated sinful men from God (when they believed in his atoning death) and had shown that God was a gracious and loving Father who freely gave men that righteousness the Law demanded but could not give. But this "Justification" or "reconciliation" or "adoption" or "redemption" (or whatever metaphor for this act of acceptance by God, one might use) must be made operative in and be applied to human lives in every generation. Paul was preaching and writing in the decades after the Crucifixion and Resurrection, and hence faced the same problem of understanding how the external fact of atonement is to be made internal in the Christian's life that we face in the twentieth century. To make this connection Paul had recourse to the traditional Jewish theological language about "the Holy Spirit" or "the Spirit of the Lord." Here was the living connection of the act of Christ on the cross and the act of God in the Resurrection-event, with the act of faith in the Christian-removed-from-those-decisive-acts in time and space. Therefore, Paul certainly does have a doctrine of the Spirit and it lies at the very foundation of his theological reflection.

As to how Paul conceived of the Holy Spirit, we must conclude, on the basis of the evidence examined above, that Paul was not clear in his own mind to the precise "status" of the Spirit in relationship to the Godhead. He does give evidence that he at times thought of the Spirit as the extension of the personality of God (the Father) into the world. At other times, Paul thought of the Spirit as a more or less "separate" divine presence, and in the majority of times he thought of the Spirit as *the way in which the Risen Christ is mediated to the believer*. It is in reference to this thought of the Spirit as the "bringer" of the real presence of the Spirit-Christ that Paul is most imprecise. He does identify the Spirit and Christ in several places, as in 2 Corinthians 3:4-5, 17, 18. It is certain that it is this kind of participation in the continuing life of the universal (and ubiquitous) Spirit of Christ that is the basis of Paul's own religious life, as can be seen from the passages in Galatians 2:20 and Philippians 1:21. However, as tempting as it is to say that Paul simply conceived of the Holy Spirit as the Risen, Spiritual-Christ, we cannot do this because the evidence herein studied shows that Paul avoided making this strict identification in all cases *except when he was discussing his own spiritual life*. In such cases he usually confined his statements to Christ, speaking of "Christ in me"; "I in Christ"; as, for example, "I know a man in Christ" (2 Corinthians 12:2-3), and, "It is no longer I who live but Christ who lives in me" (Galatians 2:20). Only rarely, as in 2 Corinthians 3:4-5, 17-18, does Paul identify this Spiritual-Christ with the Holy Spirit in a strict manner.

Thus, we must conclude that in Paul's theological thought, *the Holy Spirit is an imprecise term* that is used to refer to what Trinitarians would call each one of the three "Persons" of the Trinity. The chief emphasis in Paul's thought about the Spirit falls, however, on the Spirit as the mediator of the presence of the Risen Christ to the believer. As such, the Holy Spirit was experienced by Paul as a manifestation of the Divine power, but the content of that manifestation was the Spirit-Christ, he who had died for the sin of the world and was alive again, reigning in the believer's heart by the power of the Almighty God. To put this in Tillich's theological terms, a manifestation of the spiritual presence grasps the believer by the power of the new reality revealed in Jesus the Christ.

The kind of imprecision in thought that we have attributed to Paul is not due to a lack of interest or competence on his part as much as it is due to the fact that the development of a fuller Christology seems inevitably to prevent the growth of a separate Pneumatology. Cyril C. Richardson has remarked on this phenomena of theological development in his discussions at Union Seminary on the Tri-unity of God.

The plain fact is that the more primitive structures of thought in which the trinitarian formulas originally made sense became inapplicable when a more developed Christology appeared on the scene. Thus the binitarian formulas superseded the trinitarian ones in the New Testament. Colossians 1:15-20 and John 1:1-17, by employing the Logos Doctrine, have no place for the Spirit, for the Logos is everything that the Spirit is. In earlier formulas as Romans 1:3-5 and Acts 2:31-2; 10:36-41, it is different. There the three names refer to the God of the Jewish tradition, to the man who is exalted to a unique place in the heavenly sphere, and to the Spirit as the medium of all God's activity. Thus Jesus is born of the Spirit, endowed with the Spirit at baptism or raised from the dead by the Spirit. But when Jesus is understood as the incarnation of the Logos, such references to the Spirit no longer apply. The indwelling Christ and the indwelling Spirit, for instance, become indistinguishable, for Logos is exactly what Spirit is, God in action, God expressing Himself, whether the one metaphor is taken from speaking or the other from the desert wind.[88]

Richardson speaks of a confusion which arises when one tries to separate sharply the second and third persons of the Trinity after the development of a high Christology. This confusion arises because the meanings of the names, Christ and Spirit, are seen to overlap when they are investigated closely. The Spirit becomes a theological embarrassment, an embarrassment which is at least partially caused by the fact that all the Spirit's functions are logically subsumed under the Logos doctrine.

Richardson has also observed that there is a development within the New Testament from more primitive structures of thought in which trinitarian formulas were used in a straightforward manner (e.g., Romans 1:3-5 and Acts 2:31-32; 10:36-41), to a later development in which binitarian formulas superseded the earlier ones (Colossians 1:15-20 and John 1:1-17). This kind of observation undergirds our theory that Paul was prevented from developing a full Pneumatology by his rich development of Christ-mysticism. We might say, as Richardson does, that for Paul, as for the early Christian theologians, "Any attempt to distinguish Son and Spirit could not but be artificial in the last resort.[89]

---

[88]Cyril C. Richardson, "Discussion: The Tri-Unity of God," *Union Seminary Quarterly Review*, XXI, No. 2 (January, 1966), pp. 216-218.

[89]Ibid., p. 217.

A Final Evaluation of Paul's "Christ-mysticism"

The most simple statement of Paul's position is: being in the Spirit is synonymous with being in Christ and *vice versa*. As Albert Schweitzer notes, Paul teaches Christ-mysticism in a way appropriate to the time immediately following the death and resurrection of Jesus Christ.[90] Deissman echoes this by saying:

> The Spirit-Christ of Paul is no feeble, indistinct image ..., on the contrary, He has his hold on concrete reality at the cross. He is, and remains, the crucified. That is to say, mystical communion with the Spirit-Christ transforms all that we call the "historical" Christ, all that found its climax on Golgatha, all that had been entrusted to the apostle as tradition about Jesus, into a present reality.[91]

Schweitzer, developing his insight that Jesus' message was primarily eschatological, which was to influence the future of New Testament theology, explains Paul's Christ-mysticism on the basis of the early Christian belief in the Messianic Kingdom. Schweitzer sees Paul as believing that he and other Christians share with the Risen Christ the resurrection mode of existence,[92] and in this relation of solidarity, Christ and the Christian thus share a common life, open to and receptive of the influence of the powers of the resurrection. Thus the "Elect are in reality no longer natural men, but, like Christ Himself, are already supernatural beings, only that in them this is not yet manifest."[93] Schweitzer thus says that Paul thinks of this union with Christ (the Head of the now present and soon to come Messianic Kingdom) in a "quasi-physical" way.[94] In this study we refer to such a conception of union with Christ as being a spatial, ecological or environmental union, and thus we do not wish to use the term "quasi-physical." However, the term might be useful in understanding some of Paul's statements about the relationship of the Christian to Christ, which he occasionally compares to the marriage union. This material will be examined later in this chapter. Deissmann speaks of Paul's mysticism as being

---

[90]A. Schweitzer, *The Mysticism of Paul the Apostle*, pp. 109ff.

[91]Deissmann, *Paul*, p. 143.

[92]A. Schweitzer, *The Mysticism of Paul the Apostle*, p. 109.

[93]Ibid., p. 110.

[94]Ibid.

... nothing else than the doctrine of the making manifest, in consequence of the death and resurrection of Jesus, of the pre-existent church (the community of God). The enigmatic contempt, which dominates that mysticism, of the "body of Christ" to which all believers belong, and in which they are already dead and risen again, is thus derived from the pre-existent church . . .[95] [T]he corporeity, which is common to Christ and the Elect, is called the Body of Christ by reference to the most exalted personality which shares in it, and because its special character was first consummated and made manifest in Christ; the general is expressed through the individual.[96]

Schweizer is able to conclude from this analysis that because the concept of the body of Christ and the concomitant Christ-mysticism have their roots in Jesus' own (Jewish) eschatology, it is impossible to find their sources in Hellenistic religion.[97]

Deissmann generally agrees that the Pauline Christ-mysticism[98] is conceived of in an ecological, environmental way, i.e., as being in a spiritual body, such as Paul mentions in 1 Corinthians 15:45ff., especially in vss. 47ff.[99] Paul believed that he and other believers in Christ were "participant in" a "spiritual body" of which Christ was the head, in which they had, as their vital power, the Spirit of God, which is also the power which lives in Jesus Christ and which flows through Him to all those joined to Him in faith (Romans 3:9-10). Thus, Christ, the Spiritual Christ, is Himself in them ("Christ in me") and the believer is "in Christ" ("I in Christ"). Deissmann traces Paul's sense of union with Christ to Paul's Christophany when he was grasped by the Risen Christ-Spirit (the Christ of Faith, the Christ of the Kerygma) who appeared to him on the Damascus Road.[100] Similarly, Deissmann explains the faith-status of Peter and other apostles by the Christophanies they received.[101]

On this point Schweitzer is a good corrective to Deissmann, and to my own views. Schweitzer is at pains to point out that the experience of

---

[95]Ibid., p. 116. See Rom. 6.

[96]Ibid., p. 118.

[97]Ibid., Eduard Schweizer disagrees with this in *Bible Key Words* , pp. 67-69.

[98]Deissmann, *Paul*, pp. 135-136. (He terms it *Christ-Innigkeit*, in order to avoid the misunderstanding which might arise from the use of the term, *Christusmystik*.)

[99]Ibid., p. 142.

[100]Ibid., p. 128.

[101]Ibid., pp. 122-123.

"being in Christ" (and of Christ's "being in me") are not to be explained as individual, subjective experiences—which might be our temptation if we simply explain the phenomena on the basis of a Christophany. Rather "being in Christ" and its converse, "Christ in me," are both derived from the original conception of the corporeity of the Body of Christ, which grows out of the eschatologically determined belief in the Messianic Kingdom—a Spiritual Kingdom which is already present in the world, but which has not yet come publicly and in power. Only against the backdrop of such a "common denominator," the eschatological hope of the coming Kingdom, is union with Christ understandable as a collective and objective event,[102] which it undoubtedly was for Paul.[103] This counsel must be kept in mind, while accepting the view that Paul's understanding of the union with Christ (and his participation in it) grows out of his Damascus Road experience. In other words, the eschatological dimension of the Body was colored for Paul by his Christophany and conversion. As Paul repeats, again and again: "I have seen Jesus our Lord" (1 Corinthians 9:1); "He appeared also to me" (1 Corinthians 15:8); "I was apprehended of Christ Jesus" (Philippians 3:12); and (God) "revealed his son in me" (Galatians 1:16).

Each of these varied—and mystical (in the mystical-communion sense)— expressions show that the event on the Damascus Road was at the root of Paul's understanding of "being in Christ," for it was in that moment that Christ took possession of him, transforming him and calling him to be an apostle (Galatians 1:16ff.). Thus Deissmann can say: "All that can be called Christ-mysticism is the reaction to this initial experience."[104] This is the key, and the great contribution of Deissmann to the understanding of Paul: Paul is a reacting mystic, his Christ-union (and communion) arises from his response to the Divine initiative. Paul does not create his own ecstatic breakthrough to a new understanding of himself, or to an oceanic feeling of being at home in the universe (acting mysticism), but rather responds to a present energy that "grasps him" and takes possession of him, in the same manner that the Divine Spirit "grasped" the Old Testament prophets and moved them to prophecy (e.g., Jeremiah 11:1-5). Hence it was an "invasion" of the Divine Spirit that Paul experienced, the Spirit, that is the Spirit of Christ.

---

[102]A. Schweitzer, *The Mysticism of Paul the Apostle*, pp. 122-123.

[103]1 Corinthians 3:1; 4:18; 7:22; 15:17-18, 22; 2 Corinthians 5:17; Romans 8:1 and especially Romans 12:5—"We, though many are one body in Christ," with its parallels.

[104]Deissmann, *Paul*, pp. 130-131.

Schweitzer, writing of "the problem of Paul's mysticism" in *Paul and His Interpreters*,[105] says that while Paul is in no way influenced by the religious ideas of Hellenism, his thoughts about the Spirit are analogous to the conception of Stoicism. Stoicism taught that a "Spiritual substance" proceeds from God and permeates the universe, including corporeal organisms, and manifests itself in man as the rational soul. This "material conception" of the spirit is common to both Paul and Stoicism, Schweitzer maintains.[106] However, he clearly points out that in Stoicism the spirit is identical with the rational soul, while in Paul, the Spirit is introduced as something new alongside the "rational soul" and finally displaces it.[107] As Schweitzer put it in his "summing up" at the end of his review of the literature on Paul, "Paulinism and Hellenism have in common their religious terminology, but in respect of ideas, nothing."[108] Thus Schweitzer concludes that Paul's theology is actually an "eschatological mysticism":

> That Paul's mystical doctrine of redemption and his doctrine of the sacraments belong to eschatology is plain to be seen. The only question is in what way, exactly, they have arisen out of it. The future-hope, raised to the highest degree of intensity, must somehow or other have possessed the power of producing them. If the impulse, the pressing need to which they were the response, is once recognized, then Paulinism is understood, since in its essence it can be nothing else than an eschatological mysticism, expressing itself by the aid of the Greek religious terminology.

In apocalyptic thought sensuous and super-sensuous converge in such a manner that the former is thought of as passing away into the latter. Thus there is present in it the most general presupposition of all mysticism, since it is the object of the latter to abolish the earthly in the super-earthly. The peculiarity of the mysticism which arises out of apocalyptic is that it does not bring the two worlds into contact in the mind of the individual man, as Greek and medieval mysticism did, but dovetails one into the other, and thus created for the moment at which the one passes over into the other an objective, temporally conditioned mysticism. This, however, is only available for those who by their

---

[105]A. Schweitzer, *Paul and His Interpreters*, pp. 97-99.
[106]Ibid., p. 98.
[107]Ibid.
[108]Ibid., p. 238.

destiny belong to both worlds. Eschatological mysticism is predestinarian.

That a mysticism of this kind existed before Paul is not known. It may be conjectured that the conditions under which it could develop were not present until after the death and resurrection of Jesus.[109] This is a fair assessment of the background of Pauline Christ-mysticism. Since the living power that flows from the Spirit-Christ (resurrected Christ) flows into the believer, His state of being has become the believer's, so that they are, together, a new creation (2 Corinthians 5:17; Galatians 6:16).

We would qualify the assessment of Schweitzer by calling Paul a "Spirit- participation" mystic. We mean by this term that Paul thinks of himself, and all other believers, as part of the invisible Messianic Kingdom of God which has become visible — partially and frag-mentarily — in the church, the body of Christ, through the presence of the Spirit. We would also term Paul as "extrovertive mystic"[110] since his persuasion of participation in this reality ushers him into an active, ethical modality of life — in which he and other believers "walk by the Spirit." We would also call Paul a "reacting mystic," because, in Deissmann's phrase, Paul participates in *Christ-Innigkeit.*[111] Paul is responding to this "invasion" and "envelopment" of his personality — he did not initiate it, nor does he maintain it by any religious technique. Indeed, the Spirit is the necessary precondition of all religious activity, which is best seen in the necessity of the Spirit's presence for prayer to be possible, as seen in Romans 8. This is a "communion-mysticism" that grows out of the response (of the Elect) to grace; it is not a matter of religious achievement ("righteousness by the Law"). This means that Paul is an original combination of both the static (receptive) kind of mystic and the dynamic (activistic, ethically oriented) kind of mystic; the kind that Francis of Assisi undoubtedly was. But despite this activism, Paul is a "collectivistic mystic" rather than an "individualistic" one. Paul always speaks of the community of Christians as participants in the Spirit, based, without doubt, on the Messianic Kingdom concept of early Christian eschatology, as Schweitzer pointed out. And lastly, Paul is a "resurrection" mystic,

---

[109]Ibid., pp. 241-242. A. Schweitzer ends this famous survey of Pauline studies with these words: "It is the fate of the 'Little faiths' of truth that they, true followers of Paul, believing in the Spirit, walk secure and undismayed" (p. 249).

[110]The terms, "extrovertive"; "stoic"; "dynamic"; "rebirth"; "resurrection"; "individualistic" and "collectivistic" applied to "mystic" and used herein are drawn from W.T. Stace, *Philosophy and Mysticism* (Philadelphia: Lippincott, 1960).

[111]Deissmann, *Paul.* 135, note 4. See footnote no. 97 of this chapter.

which means a Risen, Spirit-Christ mystic. The Christian, according to Paul, enjoys a new mode of existence, the resurrection mode (Romans 6:1-11). For if we have been united with him in a death like his, we shall certainly be united with him in a resurrection like his (Romans 6:5).

This mode of existence, conceived in the environmental sense that underlies Paul's use, can be lost. This fact is made clear in Paul's teachings about sex-sins, in that Paul declares that he who "joins himself to the body of a prostitute" forfeits the relationship he has to the Body of Christ. "You cannot take the Body of Christ and join it to the body of a prostitute" (1 Corinthians 6:13-19). Indeed, Paul says that every other sin is outside a man's body, but a sin of fornication (or adultery) is a sin against his body. Thus the Pauline mysticism is a participation mysticism (based on many of the same "awarenesses" that function in the "magical" relationships between two people, such as attraction, love, repulsion, hate, etc.), that takes the union of the believer and Christ to be "an actual physical union."[112] This is further shown by the correspondence Paul draws between "being in Christ" and "being in the flesh." Therefore, it would be no surprise that Paul clearly describes the character of the believer's union with Christ as having the same character as the bodily union between man and wife ("the one-flesh" relationship of Genesis 2:24). As Schweitzer explains the ethical coordinates of this unity: "In the case of the morally blameless physical union between man and wife the connection with Christ continues through it; in the case of immoral intercourse the connection with Christ is broken by it."[113]

This same kind of response lies behind Paul's teaching that the unbelieving partner and the children of the union of a Christian and a pagan spouse will be sanctified by the believing partner (1 Corinthians 7:12-14).[114] Because the married pair belong corporeally to one another, and the believer belongs corporeally to Christ, the unbelieving partner and the children also become attached to Christ and susceptible of receiving the powers of the Spirit of Christ.[115]

From the analogies of the above passages, we can only conclude that union with Christ, for Paul, was conceived of in an environmental, spatial way. To participate in Christ's Spirit meant to enter (and live in)

---

[112]A. Schweitzer, *The Mysticism of Paul the Apostle*, p. 127. Paul Tillich, *Systematic Theology*, III (Chicago: University of Chicago Press, 1963), p. 122 (on "Magic").

[113]Ibid., p. 127.

[114]John C. Cooper, "Saint Paul's Evaluation of Women and Marriage," *The Lutheran Quarterly*, XVI, No. 4 (November, 1964), pp. 291-302.

[115]A. Schweitzer, *The Mysticism of Paul the Apostle*, p. 128.

a new realm, a new dimension that fills one's body, and in which the body dwells, on the analogy of air—in which we are immersed and which fills our lungs.[116] Such a conception is clearly the presupposition of the teaching about the "body of Christ," which is at the root of the doctrine of "being in Christ" and "in the Spirit." This relationship of the spatial metaphor of the "body" and the conception of new life "in Christ" is seen most clearly in the Deutero-Pauline literature:

> Put off your old nature which belongs to your former manner of life and is corrupt through deceitful lusts, and be renewed in the spirit of your minds, and put on the new nature, created after the likeness of God in true righteousness and holiness (Ephesians 4:22-24) "... the Head, from whom the whole body, nourished and knit together through its joints and ligaments, grows with a growth that is from God" (Colossians 2:19).

These passages by Paul's disciples quite well sum up the ecological, environmental nature of the communion-mysticism Paul preached. Obviously, he was influenced by the thought of his day, which as in the Stoics, thought of "spirit" in a "quasi-material" way.[117] We might think of this phenomena as the way in which Paul "mythicized" his experience of participation in the life of the Christ-Spirit, and of his fellowship with other Christians who similarly participated in him. Paul thus personalized, and made environmental (made social) his "spiritual experiences." It should be interesting to see how Paul Tillich, nineteen centuries later, "deliteralizes" the Pauline symbols and mythical framework, turning this mystical, organic mode of speech into insights into the ontological structures of reality.[118]

---

[116]"You are God's temple and . . . God's Spirit dwells in you." 1 Corinthians 3:16; 6:19; 2 Corinthians 6:16. The last passage, part of 2 Corinthians 6:14 - 7:2 may not be genuinely Pauline.

[117]On this whole topic, see J. A. T. Robinson, *The Body:A Study in Pauline Theology* (London: SCM Press, 1957).

[118] The occurrences of the phrases "In Christ," and "In the Spirit" and "In the Lord," in Romans, 1 and 2 Corinthians, Galatians, 1 Thessalonians, Philippians and Philemon are listed in the tables in the appendix.

2

THE DOCTRINE OF THE SPIRITUAL PRESENCE IN PAUL TILLICH'S SYSTEMATIC THEOLOGY

Introduction to the Tillichian System

The theology of Paul Tillich is a philosophical or ontological theology in which every doctrine, symbol, and concept is traced back to one of the structures of being itself. Yet, with this metaphysical foundation and structure, the Bible remains the primary source of revelation for Tillich. Where Luther, Barth and Brunner have spurned the aid of philosophy in the systematic task, Tillich has welcomed and made use of the entire history of philosophical thought in his theological writings. Thus in addition to the Bible, Tillich sees Church history, the history of Christian theology, and that great fund of the world's wisdom found in other religions (and in literature and art), as a general revelation. This is the chief distinguishing characteristic of Tillich's theology from that of most Protestant theologians. However, the differences can be stressed too harshly, for Tillich's theology is kerygmatic as well as apologetic. He sees the sources for theology in the history of Christian thought and in general revelation as useful sources only in so far as they are similar to the content of the original document which contains the record of the events on which Christianity is based, the Bible itself.

Tillich is an apologetic theologian in that he sees his task as one of making the Christian message intelligible to and acceptable to modern men.[1] He sees the human predicament as one in which men are hindered from receiving help from the eternal message of Christ by the obscure cast of many theologies and by the mythological form of most preaching. His desire is to interpret the great symbols of Christianity in terms of modern Existentialist philosophy, so as to make the power of Christ's message available to men today. The method by which Tillich does this is that of correlation, which means that Tillich gives the answers of Christian faith to the questions asked by modern men.[2] Basically, this correlative method is predicated on the need to harmonize the existence of two similar-but-different approaches to the discovery and elucidation of the situation and prospects of mankind, those of philosophy and theology.

Tillich's Theological Method
and Approach to
Theological Language

Tillich begins his system by declaring that we can only approach the understanding of Christian faith in an existential manner. God does not give answers to questions that men have not asked. Thus we must start where we are in our existential or life situation and pose the problems we face in this existence as questions, and only then turn to the revelation of God for the answer. In this task philosophy poses the questions and theology supplies the answers on the basis of the three sources of theological insight mentioned above, the Bible, theological tradition and general revelation. Tillich defines this method of correlation in the following way: "Philosophy is defined as that cognitive endeavor in which the question of being is asked on the basis of an analysis of the human situation, thus revealing the brokenness,

---

[1]Tillich seeks to make the Christian message intelligible and acceptable in the best sense, making it acceptable by the removing of all false offenses to the reception of the Gospel. Tillich declares that we must let the offense of the Gospel fall in the right place. See Paul Tillich, *Systematic Theology* (Chicago: Univeristy of Chicago Press, 1957), II, 107 ff.

[2]For a different interpretation of the method of corrolation, see Bernard M. Loomer, "Tillich's Theology of Correlation," *Journal of Religion*, XXXVI, No. 3 (July, 1956), p. 150.

ambiguities and problems of human existence."[3] Theology is based on revelation or the experience of men who have gained insights into the depths of the structures of being (which reveals itself to man).[4] Thus, those who have had such revelatory experiences have been transformed in the center of their being by becoming aware of Being's wholeness in the ecstatic depths of human reason. Such experiences supply the answers to the questions posed by philosophy. Therefore, Tillich starts with incompleteness, brokenness, and despair in the existentialist sense, and ends with completeness, wholeness, and a kind of "union with God" in the sense of classical Christian theology.[5] In order to have this correlation there must be a point of contact, and this contact is the structure of Being itself. For Tillich, man, nature and God are joined together in the structure of Being, indeed God is the structure of Being, the Ground of Being, although not being determined by that structure.[6]

Tillich clearly states that everything we say about God is symbolic except the statement that everything we say about God is symbolic. However, the phrase, "God is Being itself," may be considered literal, although even in such an abstraction there is a mixture of the symbolic (ecstatic) and the nonsymbolic (literal). This is true because these terms form the boundary line at which the symbolic and nonsymbolic modes of speech converge.[7] In all events, God is the inexhaustible depth within the structure of Being in which man and nature participate. But man has distorted the basic structures of Being by his sin, for becoming actual (existential) means becoming somehow separated from the Divine Ground and becoming distorted and alienated. Thus, there appears a "gap" between the essence of man and his existence (man's actuality). This gap, called finitude, alienation, brokenness, or sin, is overcome—and God and man are brought together—in Jesus as the Christ—the Bearer of the New Being, which is nothing else than unity with the Divine Ground, i.e., a re-establishment of the continuity between God and man by an "overcoming" of the discontinuities between them. In Jesus as the bearer of the New Reality the structure of Being is essentially exemplified even amid the existential distortions of

---

[3]Paul Tillich, *Biblical Religion and the Search for Ultimate Reality* (Chicago: University of Chicago Press, 1964), p. 5 (Hereafter cited as *BRSUR*.)

[4]"In relation to God, everything is done by God." Tillich, *Systematic Theology*, III, p. 135. Tillich calls this "the Protestant Principle." It expresses his idea of theonomy.

[5]Loomer, "Tillich's Theology of Correlation," pp. 150-151.

[6]Ibid., pp. 151-152.

[7]Tillich, *Systematic Theology*, II, p. 10.

it ("under the conditions of existence") in human history. Thus, Jesus is man as he is "meant to be"; here is man "transparent" to the depths of being-itself. Here is that unity with God for which all men (consciously or unconsciously) yearn, for as Augustine has said: "Thou has made us [men] for thyself, and our hearts are restless, till they rest in thee."[8] This last quotation from Augustine is quite enlightening, for the core of Tillich's thought, and the structure of his system, is largely a correlation between the analysis of modern existentialist philosophy and the teachings of classical Christianity (Augustine, Luther and Calvin) joined together with Scholastic and Idealistic philosophy (the so-called "Christian philosophy"), modified by Tillich's moderate Realism.

The Contents and Structure of Tillich's Ontological Theology

The structure of Tillich's ontological theology hinges on his vision of the eternal tension between Being and Non-Being. Tillich says that man's basic problem is that of Being and Non-Being. Tillich's concern for establishing an ontological foundation for his system (and for the Christian faith) is very clear in his refusal to rest at any point until he has laid bare the ultimate structures of reality, e.g., Being, Non-Being, Existence, Essence, Love, Power, Justice and the Logos. Then in each instance, Tillich seeks to relate the problems of the human predicament (as revealed by an existential analysis) to their ontological referent. He develops the "answers" of revelation to the "questions" raised by his existential analysis on this basis. Man exists pre-eminently among all creatures because he is aware of his existence and of the possibility of his own death, i.e., his own non-being. Man, as we know him, exists in anxiety—not fear—for fear has an object and is psychological—but man suffers from *angst*, which is ontological anxiety and has no objective referent but arises out of our awareness of our possible non-being. This is "the ontological shock" in which we become aware that there might be nothing rather than something. Everything in the system works out from this point.

God, according to Tillich, is the Ground of Being. In the symbolic language we are forced to use when speaking of God, God is the Creator of the Universe. In God alone is fullness of Being, for in Him all

---

[8]Augustine, *The Confessions* ii 4 in Augustine, *Confessions and Enchiridion*, ed. Albert C. Outler (Library of Christian Classics; Philadelphia: Westminster Press, 1955).

the ontological elements are perfectly balanced, whereas they are polarized, i.e., divided along the subject-object continuum, in man and nature. These ontological elements are the polarities of:

(1) Individualization and participation.

(2) Dynamics and form.

(3) Freedom and destiny.

Human lives are lived under these polarities, of which the most basic expression is that of the split between subject and object into I-Thou or I-it, which Tillich calls the basic ontological polarity of self and world.[9]

In the universe there are also categories that express the ontological situation. They are: time, space, casuality, and substance. In God all these elements and categories are perfectly in balance, but not so in the universe, where man lives in a condition which is not one of Being and not one of Non-being, but is a mixture of Being and Non-Being that is called finitude or existence.

The Place of the Doctrine of the *Spirit* in Tillich's Theology

Man alone of the creatures is aware of this ontological situation because he is a creature who lives on that level of reality called history. This means man alone is self-conscious, i.e., he has a completely centered-self and so can recognize the ontological structure of the world and to some extent transcend it. Only man has history, for according to Tillich, history in the proper sense takes place only in the dimension of spirit.[10] Thus history proper is human history for only man is a bearer of the spirit. Man alone bears the spirit because only man is free. Tillich's definition of man is finite freedom. Man is able to stand over against the world as a self, and through the power of the universals expressed in language, to have a world rather than to be in an environment, as in the case of animals. Man alone is capable of full participation in community (the realm of history, the spirit and of

---

[9]The above material is based on Paul Tillich, *Systematic Theology*, I (Chicago: University of Chicago Press, 1951), pp. 168-186.

[10]Ibid., III, p. 297.

culture) because only man is capable of full individualization. Similarly man is capable of having a destiny, because he alone can exercise his freedom fully, and one's destiny is the result of (among other things) one's existential decisions made in freedom. But for Tillich, life is a multi-dimensional unity and history is one of the dimensions of life.[11] In fact, it is the pre-eminent dimension. Life is multi-dimensional, each dimension signifying an encounter with reality in which the unity of life is seen above its conflicts and its ambiguity. These dimensions are always real, in every realm where reality is encountered; if not actually real, then at least potentially real. Life is a multi-dimensional unity, embracing the dimensions of the inorganic; the organic which embraces several sub-dimensions, the vegetative, the animal, and the psychic (or self-aware); and that of the spirit.

Life is defined as a polar concept, including within itself its opposite, death.[12] Ontologically viewed, life is the "actualization of being." In fact, life is ontological in its meaning, because it is the potential which is a "structural condition of all beings." Whatever lives, i.e., becomes actual, is involved in the conditions of actuality, finitude, conflict and estrangement, which make up the problem of life-ambiguity. This means that the essential cannot be actualized unambiguously under the conditions of existence, and thus a quest for unambiguous life emerges in the dimension of history — in man. Life, therefore, ambiguously unites the two main qualifications of existence, the essential and the existential. It is a "mixture" of elements of both. In this ambiguous mixture of essence and existence, Tillich sees the multi-dimensional unity mentioned above. Each dimension is potentially included in all the realms of life. A realm is a section of life where one dimension is actual and predominant while all the other dimensions are only potentially present. There is an organic realm, a vegetable realm, and animal realm, and a realm of the spirit, i.e., a historical realm. All dimensions, however, are actualized only in man as we know him, and the special character of this realm is determined by the dimensions of the Spirit and of history. Thus there is a graduation of value among the various dimensions. That which presupposes something else and adds to it is by so much the richer. When one considers the organic realm we find it characterized by self-related, self-preserving, self-increasing, self-continuing *Gestalten* ("living wholes"). In this realm, the psychic realm has evolved which actualizes within itself another dimension, the personal communal or spiritual dimension. This has happened, as far as

---

[11]Ibid., I, p. 67; ibid., III, p. 15ff.
[12]Ibid., pp. 1ff.

we can determine, only in man. Spirit is defined as the unity of power and meaning. The dimension of the spirit, which builds on the self-awareness, perception and intention of the psychic dimension, becomes related to the universals in perception and intention, and structurally is determined by reason (*logos*). This prepared the way for the appearance of a new dimension in life, the historical. It is impossible to pinpoint the time, place or historical group where this transition took place.

In the dynamics of life, the "historical dimension" is present in all other realms in an anticipatory way. But it comes to its full actualization only in man, in whom as the bearer of the spirit, the conditions for it are present. History is, in every realm, the dimension under which the new is being created. This "historical dimension," potentially present in all other dimensions, cannot be equated with history proper. History proper does not become actual until, through evolution, the inorganic, and animal realms provide the basis for the realization of the psychic realm of self-awareness which makes the realm of the spirit possible. There is no history where there is no spirit. History is "made" by acts of the spirit, morally and cognitively, and acts of the spirit constitute "leaps" which are possible only for a totally centered self, i.e., for a free self. Thus human history is the most comprehensive life process of all. Life, the actualization of potential being, reveals deep ambiguities, however. In order to describe the ambiguity of life under the historical dimension we must discuss the Basic Functions or Processes of life which Tillich discerns in the ambiguous self-actualization of life.

In life's process of self-actualization there are three processes:[13] (1) self-integration or "the movement from centeredness through alteration back to centeredness," (2) self-creation, in which life drives towards a new center; and (3) self-transcendence, in which finite life, by pointing beyond itself, is transcended. Actually there is one oscillating process of life, a going-out from the center of action, in such a way that the center is not lost, i.e., self-identity and self-alteration are ambiguously mixed. Thus the problems of the ambiguity of all life arise—under self-integration, the possibility of disintegration, death and disease; under self-creativity, problems of labor and struggle, under self-transcendence, the problems of profanization amd demonization. These are all examples of the struggle of Being and Non-Being. As God is the Ground of Being and Being is the power which overcomes Non-Being, the answer to the problem of the ambiguity of life is the presence of the Spirit in the world. The presence of the Spirit in the dimension of

---

[13]The following material is discussed ibid., III, pp. 30-106.

history is discussed under the symbol, the Kingdom of God.[14] The Kingdom of God answers the ambiguities of historical existence by resisting Non-Being.

The Polarity of Individualization-Participation

The function, self-integration, "the drive toward centeredness," is seen in history in the moral and political realms. There the ambiguities of empire and control, the drive towards a universal historical unity (empire), and a centered unity of a history-bearing group appear. Only in the historical dimension do the ambiguities of Justice appear.[15] The self-integrative function of life under the dimension of history shows the ambiguities of power. The relation of the Kingdom of God to this is that God is the power of Being, and the Spirit is the unity of power and meaning. Every victory of the Kingdom of God is a victory over the disintegrating consequences of the ambiguity of power. This ambiguity is based on the existential split between subject (self) and object (world), and its conquest involves a fragmentary reunion of subject amd object (love).

As self-integration is the Process of Life which under the dimension of history covers the political, then in so far as the centering and liberating elements in a structure of political power are balanced, the Kingdom of God in history has conquered the ambiguities of control.

The Polarity of Dynamics-Form

The function, self-creativity, in which life drives towards a new center, is seen in history as the realm of culture. Self-creativity expresses itself in the spiritual dimension as culture which is described as having several functions: the linguistic, the technical, the cognitive and aesthetic function called *theoria*, and the function of *praxis*, which is "the self-creation of life in the personal-communal realm"[16] The linguistic permeates *theoria* and the technical permeates *praxis*. However, *theoria* and *praxis* have their own sources of creation and destruction, i.e., their own ambiguities. *Theoria* is the act of looking at the encountered world in order to take something out of it into the centered self as a

---

[14]Ibid., pp. 297ff.
[15]Ibid., pp. 335-336.
[16]Ibid., pp. 62ff.

meaningful, structured whole. *Praxis* aims towards the realization of the essential nature with respect to societies and their problems. It seeks the good for man and true justice, seeking to realize man's potential being and thus create "humanity." The Kingdom of God conquers the ambiguities of this realm by balancing old and new insights into man's conditions and by fashioning creative solutions that direct man to the ultimate aim of history. Thus the ambiguities of revolution and reaction are overcome.

The Polarity of Freedom-Destiny

The function "self-transcendence" grows out of the polarity of freedom and destiny and creates the possibility and reality of life's transcending itself. Life strives in the vertical direction toward ultimate and infinite being. This vertical striving transcends both the circular line of centeredness and the horizontal life of growth. It is analogous to Aristotle's doctrine of all things moving by eros towards the unmoved mover. Self-transcendence expresses itself historically as Religion. One can speak about it only in terms which describe the reflection of the inner self-transcendence of things in man's consciousness.[17] Self-transcendence is contradicted by the profanization of life, which must also be described through the mirror of man's consciousness. The profane resists self-transcendence, and is present in every act of self-transcendence. Thus life transcends itself ambiguously. (Religion, the self-transcendence of life under the dimension of spirit, is essentially related to morality and culture. These three, religion, culture and morality, constitute the unity of the spirit, which must be separated in order to become actual.)[18] The essential ambiguities of self-transcendence are secularization or profanization by which religion desecrates the holy, and demonization, which occurs when religion elevates something conditional to unconditional validity. Religion always moves between the danger points of profanization and demonization. Tillich says that these ambiguities, under the dimension of history, are caused by the tension between the Kingdom of God realized in history and the Kingdom as expected. (The "third" stage as given and expected.)[19] Demonic consequences result from absolutizing the fragmentary fulfillment of the aim of history within history. It is the

---

[17]Ibid., p. 87.
[18]Note the dependence upon Hegel here.
[19]Tillich, *Systematic Theology*, III, p. 334ff.

task of the churches to keep alive the tension between the "now and not yet," between the consciousness of the presence and the expectation of the coming. When a sacramental church emphasizes social transformation, and an activistic church emphasizes the Spiritual Presence, then we see a victory of the Kingdom of God.

The foregoing description of the place of the doctrine of the Spirit in Tillich's over-all philosophical-theological position demonstrates the importance of "the Spirit" for his thought. We have not explicated the specifically theological development of the Spirit-Doctrine, to be sure, omitting all reference to Tillich's description of the working of the Spirit in the religious depths of man's life. To the specifically theological aspect of the doctrine of the Spirit we now turn. In this discussion we shall refer to the Spirit as "the Spiritual Presence," a phrase which serves to distinguish the religious usage of the term "Spirit" from Tillich's philosophical use of the term "spirit" or "Spirit" as a dimension of life.

The Spiritual Presence in Tillich's System

Tillich's Attempt to Revitalize the Concept of Spirit
in Modern Theological Discussion

Tillich has often remarked that part of his task has been to redefine the symbols of Christian faith in terms understandable to modern men. Part of this task has been Tillich's effort to salvage or revivify terms which have lost their keenness or relevance by overuse or by actual misuse in the past. Such a word is "spirit," which has been subjected to the illicit use of so-called "Spiritualists" and has taken on the connotation of the popular word "ghost," and has been rightly rejected, therefore, by serious religious thinkers. Part of Tillich's originality and of his contribution to theology has been his thorough-going effort to reclaim this Biblical and philosophical term for the constructive use of the modern religious person.

The Connection of Human Spirit
and Divine Spirit

In Tillich's teaching on the Spiritual Presences, "spirit" is used in a two-fold sense: (1) spirit (spelled with a lower case letter) which signifies the human spirit and which is used to name that function of life which characterizes man as man and which is actualized in morality, culture and religion; (2) Spirit (spelled with a capital S) which signifies the Divine Spirit or as Tillich prefers to say, "the Spiritual Presence." This is the manifestation of the depth of being or the Divine as the dimension of life which unites the power of being with the meaning of being. It stands for the actualization of power and meaning in unity. Insofar as we are aware, this actualization takes place only in man.[20] Of course, Spirit, like all other terms applied to God, is symbolic.[21] As a symbol it stands for the Divine power that is able to transform man in his centered self and to unite him both to the structures of his own being and to the structures of the community as well as to the Ground of his being, or God. This Divine power "grasps" the self and enables man to be transformed so as to be capable of receiving saving power.[22] Its characteristics are faith as against unbelief; surrender as against hubris; and love as against concupiscence.[23] Jesus as the Christ is the bearer of the Divine Spirit, and the New Being which is present in Jesus as the Christ may be spoken of as the Presence of the Spirit. Likewise, those who participate in the Christ receive a New Being through the Divine Spirit. The Spirit, then, is that aspect of God in which God goes out from himself in order to unite others with himself—Christ, man, the church.

Spirit as a Dimension of Life

Tillich holds that the spirit is a dimension of life.[24] The spirit comes into being in the realm of self-awareness (the psychological realm) and is actualized in man who is then called "the bearer of the spirit." Thus, the spirit is the dimension in which the forces of integration and creativity as well as of transcendence in the personal-communal dimension of life come into existence. The spirit is the power of life, the power of animation of the inorganic substratum.[25] Thus, spirit cannot be separated from body and is not to be confined to the intellect or mind. The spirit is the dimension of man in his totality, the peculiarly human realm. The spirit thus denotes the unity of the power of life and life in its meaningfulness. Power (Kraft) is basic to the meaning of spirit and Spirit. Tillich traces the root of the word "spirit" back to the Greek word, thymoeides, used by Plato, which means "spirited,"i.e., which

---

20Ibid., p. 111.
21Ibid.
22Ibid., p. 112.
23Ibid., pp. 129ff.
24Ibid., pp. 21ff.
25Ibid., pp. 17-21.

names the function of the soul which lies between rationality and sensuality. This function corresponds to the virtue of courage. Tillich considers this understanding of spirit to be very close to a genuine conception of spirit.[26]

The dimension of spirit appears only in man and is related to the Logos or Divine Reason. The Logos is included in the spirit (i.e., participation in the Logos), but the spirit is more than Logos, including also eros, passion and imagination. However, it is only through the Logos-structures (i.e., through reason) that the spirit can express anything.[27]

Because the spirit as the latest and all-embracing dimension of life comes to full actualization only in man, we speak of man as the bearer of the spirit. Man is such a bearer because the necessary preconditions for bearing the spirit are present in him.[28] This means that in man all the other dimensions, inorganic, organic and psychological, are transcended in a constellation of psychological factors that allow the personal center to appear. Tillich declares the "centered-self" in man to be transcendent over the psychological material which is necessary for thinking (as an activity). Such transcendence in man makes the cognitive act possible. The coming into being of human transcendence is the appearance of the subject-object relationship and as such is an act of knowing. This act of knowing (i.e., of recognizing the self-world polarity) is an act of the spirit. According to Tillich the personal center is not identical with any one of the psychological contents, but it is not another element added to them either. Rather, it is the subject of self-awareness, an organic spontaneous whole.[29]

In becoming actual itself, the psychological center transcends itself. This act of transcendence in seen in the moral act, wherein the centered-self actualizes itself by distinguishing elements and making decisions, thus, in its decision, transcending its elements. In its decision-making the centered-self acts in freedom, as a total reaction of a centered self which deliberates and decides. Such an activity is the life of the spirit. In referring to this activity, Tillich writes that the spirit is "life which cuts into life."[30] The norms for the values to be realized in the life of the spirit are not found outside life, but these criteria are implicit in life itself. Tillich says freedom and subjection to such valid norms equal

---

[26]Ibid., p. 23.
[27]Ibid., p. 24.
[28]Ibid., pp. 25-27.
[29]Ibid., p.27.
[30]Ibid., p.p. 27-28.

each other.[31] However, the norms of life are ambiguous because life basically is ambiguous since it unites essential and existential elements. The Logos structure of reality, the element of the essential nature of being present in all of life, is the source of values for the spirit acting in the centered-self. In attempting to express the norm which would make us realize something of the essential nature of man we encounter ambiguity, for to apply such a norm to a concrete situation is to take a risk and man must accept the possibility of failure when he attempts to concretize his values.

The relation between the Spirit and the spirit is said to be (in metaphorical terms) one of indwelling, in which the Spirit dwells and works in the human spirit. This "dwelling-in" implies the relation of the Creative Ground to the life of the creature. The Spirit does not rest within the human spirit but drives the spirit out of itself, i.e., the spirit is the dimension in which man is driven to transcendence by being grasped by ultimate concern.[32] The concept of "being driven" leads us to Tillich's doctrine of *ecstasy*. The conception of being "driven" or "grasped" is important, for ecstasy is an aspect of Tillich's conception of *revelation*.[33] However, nothing irrational is intended in this idea, for Tillich is quite clear that such an experience of ecstasy does not negate the structures of man's reason but confirms them.[34] In the Tillichian system the Spirit does not destroy the spirit. Clearly demonstrating his Pauline foundations, Tillich explicitly states that the unity of ecstasy and structure is classically expressed in Paul's doctrine of the Spirit.[35] Tillich says that Paul strongly emphasizes the ecstatic element in the experience of the spiritual presence. He identifies the Pauline formula, "being in Christ," as an expression not of psychological empathy with Jesus Christ but rather as involving an ecstatic participation in the Christ-who-is-the-Spirit, and thus the formula expresses the fact that one lives within the sphere of Christ's Spiritual Power.[36] The unity of ecstasy and structure means that the Spirit's Presence does not disrupt man's mental processes. The declaration that the Spirit works through rational means states Tillich's belief that ecstasy heals man's anxieties and needs.

---

[31]Ibid., p. 28.

[32]Ibid., pp. 111-112.

[33]Ibid., pp. 111; 147-150 (over-all discussion on pp. 106-159).

[34]Ibid. Also see Paul Tillich, "Systematic Theology," (Lectures at Union Theological Seminary, New York City, compiled by Peter H. Johns), p. 267.

[35]Tillich, *Systematic Theology*, III, p. 117.

[36]Ibid.

Human Life in the Spiritual Presence

The Marks of the Spirit's Presence

Once a man has been grasped by the Spirit and driven out of himself into a transcendent mode of life, we may speak of him as living under the Spiritual Presence. Tillich gives four principles that seem to be realized in such life in the Presence:

(1) Life in the Spiritual Presence leads man to increasing awareness: the man who is grasped by the Spirit becomes more and more aware of his existential situation. He recognizes its problems and ambiguities, and also recognizes possible answers to those problems. The answers may appear to such a man to be implied by the very posing of human problems as questions, as well by the actual answers offered by the Christian message.

(2) Life in the Spiritual Presence leads man to increasing freedom: The man who lives under the Spirit becomes more and more free from the moral law as commandment and specific ethical content. In increasing spiritual maturity such a man learns to live by the Spirit rather than the letter, or in Tillich's ethical terms, he acquires a "transmoral conscience."[37] By a transmoral conscience, Tillich means that one lives by grace rather than by rules. We live ethically not out of a sense of duty, but because we have been freed to become united with the Ground of our being, and so are now enabled to realize the inner law of our own being, i.e., to become what we are. To live "beyond morality," then, means to live out of a religious motivation rather than out of an ethical motivation. In such a state one lives under the power of the New Being and fulfills the law through creative love.

(3) Life in the Spiritual Presence leads man to increasing relatedness: The man who has been grasped by the Spirit increases in his faith and love so as to reach a mature self-identity beyond self-elevation and self-contempt. Such a man is enabled to relate himself creatively to the group because he has reached his goal in the search for identity. The man who has achieved such a mature sense of his own identity is the

---

[37]Paul Tillich, *Morality and Beyond* (New York: Harper and Row, 1963), pp. 65-81. Also see Paul Tillich, *The Protestant Era* (abridged; Chicago: University of Chicago Press, 1962), chaps. ix and x, pp. 136-160, "The Transmoral Conscience" and "Ethics in a Changing World."

possessor of "the courage to be," both to be as an individual and as a part of human society.[38]

(4) Finally, life in the Spiritual Presence leads man to increasing transcendence: The experience of transcendence is participation in the holy, or the devotional life of the man under the Spiritual Presence. This devotional life is not restricted to prayer or public worship, but includes that openness to the universe, that sense of oneness with the Ground of one's being that Tillich would call religion in the larger sense. By this he would mean devotion to the Ultimate.[39] It includes world-affirmation, but transcends this "yes-saying to life" by a commitment to the power of Being–Itself which continually struggles against Non-Being.

The above outline might be called Tillich's doctrine of the Christian life. However, the more basic question to be asked is how is the multidimensional unity of life, previously discussed, related to this experience of the Spiritual Presence? We must rule out any supranaturalism and reject any division of the spiritual life from the totality of man's life in the world. There is no dualism operative here, rather the spirit is a symbolic term that reflects the weakness of human language which requires us to speak in terms of a transitory dualism.[40] Tillich declares that in the human spirit's essential relation to the Divine Spirit there is not correlation but rather mutual imminence.[41] The answer to the question about the nature of this imminent relation is that the finite is potentially or essentially an element in the Divine Life. As Paul would say, "In him we live and move and have our being."[42]

The Phenomenology of the Spiritual Presence

In his phenomenology or description of the Spiritual Presence, Tillich primarily stresses that life is a unity and therefore the Spiritual Presence is universal in its scope. The Spirit is a meaning-bearing power which grasps the human spirit in an ecstatic experience, which experience, at least momentarily or fragmentarily, overcomes all the distortions and

---

[38]Paul Tillich, *The Courage To Be* (New Haven: Yale University Press, 1952), pp. 86ff. and 113ff.

[39]Tillich, "Four Principles Determining the New Being as Process," *Systematic Theology*, III, pp. 231-237.

[40]Ibid., p. 114.

[41]Ibid.

[42]Acts 17:28, Paul here quotes Epimenides.

limitations found in human life. This experience is not to be thought of as a miracle in the supernaturalistic sense, for it does not destroy the structure of man's spirit but contrariwise, heals and reunites the structures of the mind and of man's being in general by inspiration (a concept or term normally used by Protestants), and infusion (a concept or term usually restricted to Roman Catholic use). However, Tillich is clear in his use of the term "infusion" that the spirit is not a substance but is always personal in its effect.[43] On the other hand, Tillich is willing to revive the term "infusion," because Saint Paul does use the metaphor of the outpouring of the Holy Spirit.[44] This willingness to speak of the Spirit's "infusion" in the human spirit demonstrates that Tillich is always willing to be guided by Paul, especially on the topic of the Spirit. Tillich further reasons that the metaphor of infusion is justified on the basis of modern psychological discoveries of the unconscious and its significance for man's life. The work of Jung in reference to the archetypes or primordial symbols which arise from the unconscious to the conscious mind, has been quite influential on Tillich's thinking in this regard.

Tillich's Dependence on Saint Paul for his Doctrine of the Spiritual Presence

Tillich's dependence on Saint Paul is complete at the point of his development of the Spirit-Doctrine. Not only does he derive his conception of ecstatic participation in the Christ-Spirit from Paul (whose teachings were described in chapter one), but he also credits Paul with rejecting all tendencies to speak of spiritual ecstasy as breaking the mental structure of man. In this regard Tillich refers to Paul's rejection of glossolalia,[45] if such speaking in tongues disrupts the community, as well as Paul's rejection of other charismata (Spiritual gifts) if such gifts are not subjected to love.[46] Tillich is equally insistent that such ecstatic transcendence is not to be derived from the dynamics of human psychology. It is unfair and a misunderstanding to reduce Spiritual ecstasy to movements of the human psyche. The multidimensional unity of life provides the basis for such ecstatic experiences. It is, to be sure, only in the dimension of self-awareness that the psychological self can become the bearer of meaning, and thus the Spirit in enabled to

---

[43]Tillich, *Systematic Theology*, III, pp. 115-116.
[44]Ibid.
[45]1 Cor. 12.
[46]1 Cor. 13.

actualize itself only through the dynamics of self-awareness, under the biological conditions necessary for its organic development.

Tillich tells us ecstasy is the transcendence of the subject-object structure which liberates man in the dimension of self-awareness. It is not to be confused with intoxication but is to be seen as insight in which one is enabled to transcend the manifold differences of the objective world and to see the human situation under the light of eternity. It is to become aware of the Divine direction of life's process. Such ecstasy is best exemplified by a true prayer. Prayer is never to God as an object, but only to God as object and subject at the same time. Thus Paul is correct when he says that we can only pray to God who prays to himself — by the Spirit — through us.[47] Thus prayer is possible only if the subject-object structure is overcome in ecstasy.

The criterion by which we decide whether an extraordinary state of mind is spiritual ecstasy or mere intoxication is the rule that spiritual ecstasy manifests itself in creativity while intoxication displays no such result. In this development, Tillich apparently follows Paul's reasoning in 1 Corinthians 11-13 very closely.

Saint Paul and His Influences

If one were to raise the question of the *sources* of Tillich's doctrine of the content of the Spiritual Presence, it would not be hard to answer. Throughout Tillich's discussion of the Spiritual Presence, the Epistles of Saint Paul are clearly in evidence, directly behind the text.[48] For example, the entire discussion of faith and love is dependent upon Paul's hymn to love in 1 Corinthians 13. Tillich even goes so far as to attempt to show why love is greater than faith, which is the Pauline conclusion in that passage.[49] Again, Paul's discussion of the blame-worthiness of the Gentiles for their idolatry in Romans 1, is behind Tillich's insistence on the formal sense of faith as an ultimate concern which means, as he concludes, that every human being has faith in some degree. Tillich also is concerned to speak of the element of obedience in faith referring to Paul, Augustine, Aquinas and Calvin in support of this.[50] But most especially, in his insistence on the Divine Ground of salvation, that "in relation to God everything is by God,"[51]

---

[47]Romans 8.
[48]See chap. 1 and pp. 69-72 of chap. two of this study.
[49]Tillich, *Systematic Theology*, III, p. 138.
[50]Ibid., p. 132.
[51]Ibid., p. 132.

Tillich is clearly following Paul, Luther and his contemporary, Karl Barth. It is unnecessary to demonstrate further the fact that 1 Corinthians 13 forms the actual structure of the sub-section on "the Spiritual Presence manifest as love," for Tillich goes through that passage almost verse by verse in creating his doctrine. Of course, Tillich interweaves his moderate Realism and his interpretation of Platonic and other philosophical thought into his exegesis of Saint Paul, but Paul is the decisive foundation for his work. In an unpublished article, entitled "The Bible and Systematic Theology,"[52] Tillich recognized the problems involved in this kind of systematic approach to the elucidation of Christian doctrine.

The difficulty with which all systematic theology has to wrestle is the fact that the existential and the theoretical elements in philosophy interpenetrate each other and that, consequently, philosophical concepts may have religious implications which contradict the Biblical message they are supposed to interpret. This danger cannot be overcome by futile attempts to avoid philosophically defined concepts, but only by a religious analysis of the philosophical terminology and a critical awareness of the use of each concept in systematic theology.[53]

Tillich is willing to accept this risk since systematic theology is the methodological explanation of the Christian faith. The Bible, as the original document of revelation, is accepted as the primary source of such a theology in the material and authoritative sense, thus providing the basic content of theology. However, this does not exclude the use of other sources, such as church tradition, and content taken over from that general revelation found in the deposit of the world's wisdom created by philosophers and other religious traditions. The Bible's basic position as the foundation of such a systematic theology does not mean that the theologian must repeat Biblical statements in Biblical language, but to the contrary, the systematic theologian has to interpret the Biblical language in the terms and concepts of the time in which he works.[54] Tillich has courageously accepted this challenging task and in the opinion of this writer has carried through to significant conclusions with a feel for the inner meaning of the faith and a grace of style not often seen in theology.

---

[52]Paul Tillich, "The Bible and Systematic Theology" (a lecture delivered at Washington, D.C.). I am indebted to Dr. A.T. Mollegen of the Protestant Episcopal Seminary in Virginia for providing me with a copy of this unpublished manuscript.

[53]Ibid., p. 8.

[54]Ibid., p. 5.

Tillich has often been faulted for not being more Biblical in the sense of quoting the Biblical *sedes doctrinae*. To have done so in the context of the wide scope of his attempt at a systematic theology would have burdened it unnecessarily with passages that should be fairly obvious to any student of his system who is conversant with the Biblical material. Tillich has spoken of this problem in his unpublished "Personal Introduction to the Systematic Theology."[55] In this manuscript Tillich declared that he would have liked to have given the Biblical quotations with which he worked in each section of the system as well as references to the fathers, the creeds and to other theologians, but limitations of space prevented this.[56] Additionally, Tillich says that quotations have been proven to him to be of doubtful value unless used as material in an argument. Also, such quotations interrupt the flow of the discussion and actually mislead the reader in that they do not indicate the meaning they have in their original context, which is necessarily something different than the meaning they acquire in their new context.[57] Thus the relatively small number of quotations from Saint Paul does not disprove the Pauline character of Tillich's teaching concerning the Spiritual Presence. In actuality, Tillich refers to Paul by name a number of times throughout this entire section.

In our analysis of the Pauline teaching concerning the Spiritual Presence in chapter one, we pointed out that Saint Paul has a Spirit-Christ Christology and that although Paul is imprecise in his use of the term "Spirit," in the main it is used as a reference to the Risen, Glorified Christ. We have carefully pointed out there that Saint Paul connected his experience of the Spirit on the one hand to the manifestation of the Divine that came to him in the Damascus Road Christophany, and on the other hand to the experience of having Christ's power manifested to him in the corporate body of believers, the Body of Christ, or the Church. As we shall see later in this chapter, Tillich develops the conception of Spirit-Christology in his own system. Here again Tillich is following Paul.

Other Influences on Tillich's Doctrine of the Spiritual Presence

[55]The "Personal Introduction to the Systematic Theology," was unfortunately omitted from the published edition of Volume I, but has been preserved in manuscript by James Luther Adams in his collection of Tillich's papers at Meadville Theological Seminary, Chicago, Illinois.

[56]Ibid., p. 11.

[57]Ibid.

At this point, it is well to consider some of the influences of the theological past on Tillich's doctrine of the Spirit. Upon examination, we find that here, as in several other important places (as in the doctrine of the Trinity, and the doctrine of the Christ), Tillich reflects the influence of Schleiermacher.[58] We shall enlarge upon the relationship between Schleiermacher's theology and that of Tillich in a later section dealing with Spirit-Christology. Perhaps most important in its influence upon Tillich's doctrine of the Spirit is the German Idealism of Hegel[59] and the philosophical reaction of Schelling.[60] However, it is difficult to disentangle all the threads of philosophical and theological tradition in Tillich's Spirit Doctrine, because it, like the rest of his system, is like a river into which all the major streams of our Western intellectual tradition have come together, each stream bearing some of the silt and sand of the region from which it came.

From Schelling, the influence on the Tillichian concept of God is clear. The whole idea that in the God-head all the contrasting or polar elements are found in perfect balance is from Schelling. Schelling stressed that in God the contrasts of necessity and freedom, eternity and time, joy and suffering, finite and infinite, subject and object, are all in perfect tension.[61] This idea has passed into Tillich's system. Again, the unique (among the more prominent Protestant theologians) stress of Tillich on the element of negativity or nonbeing in God is from Schelling, who himself followed Jacob Boehme at this point.[62] This is a dipolar or panentheistic doctrine of God.[63] But more clearly in reference to the Spirit and its activity in the processes of life, is Schelling's stress (similar to Hegel) on the processive nature of God, that in Him there is

---

[58]Tillich, *Systematic Theology*, II, 150, "The similarity (to Schleiermacher's Christology) is obvious; but it is not identity"; and Ibid., III, 285.

[59]Note the references to Hegel *ibid.*, I, 9, 19, 56, 58, 72, 82, 86, 99, 165, 189, 233, 234, 256-266, 274-275; and Ibid., II, 23, 24, 25, 29, 45, 52, 72; and Ibid., III, 19, 22, 203, 255, 329, 330, 346, 353, 373, 374.

[60]*The Theology of Paul Tillich*, ed. Charles W. Kegley and Robert Bretall (Macmillan Paperbacks; New York: The Macmillan Co., 1961), pp. 10-11. Tillich often remarked in his seminars: "Schelling is my spiritual father."

[61]F. Schelling, *The Ages of the World*, trans. F. Bolman, Jr. (New York: Columbia University Press, 1942), pp. 95-99. Also see *Philosophers Speak of God*, ed. Charles Hartshorne and William L. Reese (Chicago: University of Chicago Press, 1953), chap. vii, pp. 233-243.

[62]Schelling, *The Ages of the World*, pp. 95ff.

[63]Hartshorne and Reese, *Philosophers Speak of God*, p. 4. See chap. I, "Ancient Quasi-Panentheism," and chap. seven, "Modern Pantheism."

an outgoing principle and a returning principle. In this process of transcendence the Spirit or the positive element in God overcomes the demonic, the negative element in the Divine abyss. Again, Schelling has given Tillich much material to use in stressing God's participation in everything that transpires in the universe. For Schelling, all history is an epic composed in God's Spirit. This epic has two parts, the first is the departure of humanity from its center and its centrifugal travel outward from the center (God), and secondly, its return in centripetal movement back to God.[64]

From Hegel, Tillich has gained that sense of what Hegel called the mysterious circle in religious experience, the fact that spiritual life objectifies itself and then turns back to itself, so that it comes full circle, thus enriching the self through this dialectical experience.[65] This movement, Hegel says, is necessary because there can be no love and no life without disunity and return to unity, for all that is was originally one. This dialectical relation also obtains within God where the Trinity of Father, Son and Holy Spirit appears as a process by which the original unity of life is divided and then restored.[66] Being–Itself, the Absolute Spirit, thus objectifies itself or "splits itself" by the begetting of the Son from the Father, and then reunites itself through the Holy Spirit, which is a reunion in love.[67] Here Tillich agrees with Hegel and both are dependent upon Saint Augustine who first so described the Trinity in his work, *On the Trinity*.[68] Tillich is particularly close to Hegel in holding the view that the Trinity is a living relation of living beings, a likeness of life in which Father, Son and Spirit are simply modifications of the same life, not opposite essences.[69] Again Tillich would agree with Hegel that the Holy Spirit is the active identification of the Absolute Spirit and his objectification is the externalization of the

---

[64]F. Schelling, *On Human Freedom*, trans. James Gutmann (Chicago: Open Court Publishing Company, 1936), a quote from Schelling's *Works*, VI, 57.

[65]G. F. Hegel, *On Christianity* (Harper Torch Books: New York: Harper & Bros., 1961), pp. 18; 160-161; 260.

[66]Ibid.

[67]*Hegel: Highlights*, ed. Wanda Oregnski (New York: Philosophical Library, 1960), p. 298; J. N. Findlay, *Hegel: A Re-examination* (New York: Collier Books, 1962), 140.

[68]Augustine, *Later Works*, ed. John Burnaby (Library of Christian Classics; Philadelphia: The Westminster Press, 1955), pp. 17-181.

[69]G. F. Hegel, "Absolute or Revealed Religion," in *The Phenomenology of Mind*, trans. J. B. Gaillie (New York: Macmillan Co., 1910), pp. 138-143; and in Findlay, *Hegel*, pp. 346-349, and Oregnski, *Hegel: Highlights*, p. 303.

Divine Word.[70] The influence of Hegel on Tillich's doctrine of the Trinity is clear, for in both Hegel and Tillich, God is the basic reality upon whom all things depend and who is the Absolute in whom all things root. For both, God's essential nature is Triune,[71] a Trinity of unity in a three-fold manifestation in which the Father is the eternal, self-identical and infinite (thesis); the Son is the finite expression of the infinite or the self manifestation of God (antithesis); and the Spirit is the reunion (or synthesis) of the infinite and finite and the world in God.[72] We may also note that for both Hegel and Tillich, finite reality subsists within the life of the Trinity. Because finite reality participates in the Trinitarian life, it becomes estranged from the Divine life when through becoming actual, it separates, in part, from the Divine. However, also because of this participation of the finite in the infinite, the finite is capable of being redeemed by the Divine. This conception, of the subsistence of the finite within the life of the Trinity, shared by Hegel and Tillich, differs from the orthodox Christian conception which does not speak of the life of the creature as contained within the Divine life. The influence of Hegel upon Tillich's thought is clear here, in this important insight into the aseity of God and the creature's paradoxical separation from and participation in the life of God.

It is fitting that we should consider the influences of the Medieval Mystics on Tillich's doctrine of the Spiritual Presence. This is the case because Tillich is not a naturalist, although he avoids the question-begging of supranaturalism. He declares that faith occurs within the structure and dynamics of the human spirit although faith is not created by the human spirit but by the Spiritual Presence. Man is conscious of the Spiritual Presence in him in that he is opened up to his possibilities by that Presence, and is enabled to accept it in spite of the infinite gap between the human and the Divine Spirit; and finally, man is enabled to expect a final participation in the transcendent union with the Divine, called unambiguous life.[73] Tillich here follows the mystics, Eckhart, Cusa, and Boehme. He deals with faith as a kind of independent reality

---

[70]Oregnski, Hegel: Highlights, pp. 304ff.

[71]Ibid., p. 298. "God is thus recognized as Spirit, only when known as the Triune, " and Tillich, Systematic Theology, III, pp. 283-294, esp. p. 204.

[72]Findlay, Hegel, pp. 346-351. Basically, Tillich agrees with Hegel in method, but differs from him in content, preferring Schelling's existentialism to Hegel's essentialism, see Paul Tillich, The Interpretation of History, trans. N. A. Rasetzki (Part I) and Elsa L. Talmey (Parts II-IV) (New York: Chas. Scribner's Sons, 1936), pp. 61ff.

[73]Tillich, Systematic Theology, III, pp. 130-134.

which is actual in all life processes, for it becomes actual at that point where one experiences the grasp of ultimate concern in that one becomes aware of the unity of subject and object (of God and man) in ecstasy.[74]

Jacob Boehme (1575-1624) is a genuine background source for Tillich's doctrine of the Spirit. Boehme taught the paradoxical fact that there is an element of identity as well as of non-identity between the human spirit and God, because for Boehme, the Divine is a dimension of depth—a quality of being above the split between subject and object—which can be sensed in every area of life and is not to be considered a special area in itself "out there."[75]

From Nicolaus Cusanus (1401-1464), Tillich receives much more than materials for the doctrine of the Spirit. Cusa's career reminds us of Tillich's, as he made war on superstition, and tried to advance the scientific investigation of the physical world. Like Tillich, he stood at the boundary line between theology and philosophy, and between the Middle Ages and the Renaissance. Cusa gives Tillich the basic operational notion of the coincidence of opposites in God. Cusa recognized that there was no sharp limit drawn between the Divine and natural spheres but rather a continuity between them. In the midst of the particulars of life, Cusa sought to understand all differences by reference to their common unity, although the knowledge of the absolute unity of all things is available to man only through mystic intuition. This is essentially the concept of *participation* which plays such a large role in Tillich's system. And like Tillich, Cusa believed that we could give no name to God since all that we say about him is symbolic. Nor can we take the attributes ascribed to God literally. Yet within all this, the infinite remains the measure and ideal of the finite, for God is the unity of all things. In him all contradictions come to rest.[76]

In regard to the Spirit, Cusa held that the Holy Spirit is the infinite nexus or web of interrelations which holds the universe of nature together. The Spirit is the bond which cements all things in this world together and which holds the Trinity together in unity.

From Meister Eckhart (1250?-1329), Tillich received his emphasis on epistemology. This idealistic mystic taught that the soul is essentially rational and that knowledge is the primary relation in the world. For

---

[74]Ibid., p. 134. Tillich declares this approach is in line with Pauline thought.

[75]Paul Tillich, *The Theology of Culture* (New York: Oxford University Press, 1964), chap. two, "The Two Types of Philosophy of Religion."

[76]Wilhelm Windelband, *A History of Philosophy*, I (Harper Torch Books; New York: Harper & Bros., 1958), pp. 345-347.

Eckhart, the good is rational and for him there is a unity of thought and being. For being and knowledge are one, which is echoed and made an important part of Tillich's system. For Eckhart, God is the Ground of Being, or the *Urgrund*. He lies beyond the separation of subject and object in knowledge. However, this God reveals himself as Triune for he knows himself and this knowing is his creating. Thus there is an element of self-revelation in God—The Logos—which is a fundamental principle in Tillich's system also. In Eckhart's thought there is no creation out of nothing, but a continual unfolding, a going outward of God, and a continuing collapsing into or returning to God. That is to say, there is an eternal creating and an eternal ending for Eckhart.

On the other hand there is a doctrine of creation out of nothing in Tillich. In *Systematic Theology*, Volume I,[77] Tillich speaks of the phrase "creatio ex nihilo"and says that "the first task of theology is an interpretation of these words."[78] Tillich says that this doctrine is Christianity's protection against any kind of ultimate dualism. There cannot be two ultimates; thus Tillich affirms that God finds nothing "given" to him which influences him in his creation or which resists his purposes. Additionally Tillich says that the doctrine of creation out of nothing stresses that the creature has a "heritage of non-being," which means that "being a creature includes both the heritage of non-being (anxiety) and the heritage of being (courage)."[79] Tillich goes on to declare that the doctrine of creation out of nothing guards us against thinking that the tragic character of existence is rooted in the creative Ground of Being, and secondly, it stresses the element of non-being in the creature which leads to the natural necessity of death and the potentiality of the tragic element in life. Tillich concludes his discussion of this doctrine by saying that the formula *creatio ex nihilo* expresses the relation between God and the world."[80]

Eckhart teaches that God is all, and whatever things are, they are only in so far as they are expressions of God. By way of coming to knowledge, man's spiritual essence which Eckhart calls his "spark," is freed from the husks of sense and returns to its created ground, thus the goal of all life is knowledge of God. Since this knowing is being it means that man becomes a part of God. But this movement back to God is not self-initiative, not done by man's own action, it is the act of God

---

[77]Tillich, *Systematic Theology*, I, pp. 252-254.
[78]Ibid., p. 253.
[79]Ibid.
[80]Ibid., p. 254.

in man.[81] This is quite parallel to Tillich's idea of man's fragmentary participation in the New Being now and of man's transcendent unity with the Divine in unambiguous life under the impact of the Spirit, and of man's eventual elevation to the positive in the Kingdom of God beyond history in Tillich's system.[82]

The Media of the Spiritual Presence
Pan-Sacramentalism

Tillich discusses the effective presence of the Spirit in terms of The Word and Sacrament of traditional theology. He agrees with the sacramental concept; in fact, he enlarges the sacramental concept to include all personal and historical events in which the Spiritual Presence is effected. Tillich has actually created a pan-sacramentalism.[83] For him the Sacramental sign or objective event is older, more primordial than the spoken word. Tillich is quite willing to state that objects can become vehicles of the Divine Spirit.

Tillich bases his pan-sacramentalism on the multi-dimensional unity of life, although he rejects the Roman Catholic sacramental system as well as the ultra-Protestant, anti-sacramental position. For him, the Spiritual Presence cannot be received without a sacramental element. Thus he attempts to unite Protestant principle and Catholic substance. Tillich says the sacramental materials are symbolic in that they point beyond themselves to the Divine, and participate in the power of that which they symbolize. The material of a sacrament is intrinsically related to what it expresses, e.g., the water used in Baptism symbolizes washing.[84]

The Spiritual community is bound to definite media of the Spiritual Presence and yet these media must be subject to the criterion of Jesus as the Christ. Nothing out of harmony with this revelation can be a sacrament. Also, the sacramental act must refer to the historical or doctrinal symbols related to the life of the Christ.[85]

---

[81]Windelband, *A History of Philosophy*, I, pp. 334-337.

[82]Note the relevance of St. Bonaventura's "The Triple Way, or Love Enkindled" in *The Works of Bonaventura*, Vol. I, *Mystical Opuscula*, trans. Jose de Vinck (Paterson, New Jersey: St. Anthony Guild Press, 1960), to Tillich's conception of man's participation in the New Being under the grasp of the Spirit, which is marked by the creation of faith and love in man.

[83]Tillich, "Nature and Sacrament,"*The Protestant Era*, pp. 94-112.

[84]Tillich, *Systematic Theology*, III, p. 123, and *Protestant Era*.

[85]Tillich, *Systematic Theology*, III, p. 123.

The Word of God

The Word of God, i.e., the word which becomes the vehicle of the Spiritual Presence, is not limited by Tillich to the Bible. The Word is used by the Spirit just as sacramental media are used. Any word can be the Word of God if it so grasps the human mind in such a way that it creates an ultimate concern for it. On the other hand, no word is a Word of God unless it is a Word of God for someone. Additionally, no word can be the Word of God if it contradicts the faith and love which are the work of the Spirit and which is the New Being manifested in the Christ.[86]

Tillich discusses the so-called inner word which has played such a large part in the "spiritual movements" in Christianity. He admits that the spirit-movements of Protestantism have influenced him, especially in this part of the system, but he rejects the concept of inner word, saying that if God (so to speak) speaks to us, this is not an inner word, but rather the Spirit grasping us from outside—or really from a position which transcends inside and outside. Inner and outer mean nothing when we speak of God's relation to man.[87]

Tillich agrees with the reformers who were opposed to spirit-movements because they were afraid that the criterion of all revelatory experiences—the New Being—would be lost in the immediacy of the Spirit. Tillich says the Reformers were correct in binding the Spirit to the Word, to the Biblical message of the Christ.

The Content of the Manifestation of Spirit in the Spirit: Faith and Love

For Tillich, faith and love are but two aspects of one spiritual or ecstatic experience, the transcendent union which comes into being when the Spiritual Presence comes into the human spirit. This transcendent union is the quality of unambiguous life.

Faith is the state of being grasped by this transcendent unity of unambiguous life; love is the state of being taken into this unity. Thus faith logically precedes love, although neither can be present without

---

[86]Ibid., p. 125.
[87]Ibid., p. 127.

the other. Faith, for Tillich, is the state of being grasped by an ultimate concern,[88] while love is a state of being grasped and filled with a drive toward reunion of the separated existing individual with the Ground of his Being and with all other individuals.[89] Faith is thus the state of being grasped by the ultimate in being and meaning, which is that to which self-transcendence aspires. This is a formal definition, and in this sense everyone has faith. The material concept of faith, for Tillich, as a Christian, is that faith is the state of being grasped by the Spiritual Presence or by the New Being which are interchangeable terms in Tillich's system. Tillich claims that faith, defined as being opened by the Spirit to the transcendent unity of unambiguous life, is a universally valid definition—good for all religions—despite its Christian background.[90]

This state of being grasped by the Spirit is not a matter of knowledge attained within the subject-object structure of reality; thus it is not subject to verification. Faith is not to be thought of as the result of the will to believe, or as a feeling state, either, although there is an element of obedience and of passionate feeling within faith.[91] Tillich is quite willing to admit that there is an emotional element in the faith state. He defines it as the oscillation between the anxiety of finitude and the ecstatic courage which overcomes the anxiety by taking it into itself in the power of that transcendent unity which brings the experience of unambiguous life when one is grasped by the Spirit.[92] One might think of Paul's word that he desired to depart and be with Christ, but he felt it better to remain with his disciples to be their guide.[93]

---

[88]Ibid., p. 130 and Paul Tillich, *Dynamics of Faith* (Harper Torch Books; New York: Harper & Bros., 1957), pp. 1-29.

[89]Tillich, *Systematic Theology*, III, p. 134 and Paul Tillich, *Love, Power and Justice* (new York: Oxford University Press, 1960), pp. 18-34.

[90]Tillich, *Systematic Theology*, III, pp. 131 and 139. Also see Paul Tillich, *Christianity and the Encounter with the World Religions* (New York: Columbia University Press, 1963).

[91]Tillich, *Systematic Theology*, III, pp. 132-133.

[92]Ibid., p. 133, and Tillich, *The Courage To Be*, pp. 160-163, where Tillich calls this "The Courage of the Reformers." (The "in spite of," p. 161.)

[93]Philippians 1:23-24.

The Spiritual Presence
Manifest as Love

Love is the state of being taken by the Spiritual Presence into the transcendent unity of unambiguous life. Love is actual in all the functions of the mind and has its roots in the innermost core of life itself. Love is the drive towards the reunion of the separated—Tillich says this is ontologically, and, therefore, universally, true. Love is effective in all three life processes:
(1) In self-integration—love unites in a center,
(2) In self-creativity—love creates the new, and
(3) In self-transcendence—love drives beyond everything given to its ground and aim.[94]
Tillich says this ontological drive towards an unambiguous reunion of separated individuals towards participation in each other, through participation in the transcendent unity, is *agape*, which is the creation of the Spiritual Presence. This transcendent unity overcomes the ambiguities of life. These ambiguities are rooted in the separation and inner-play of essential and extential elements in being. However, in the transcendent union all separated elements are reunited, which removes the conflicts and ambiguities of the life processes so that actual being becomes the true expression of potential being. This potential being can be realized only after estrangement, contest and decision. In this reunion ambiguous life is raised above itself to a transcendence it could not achieve by its own power. This union therefore, is the answer to the question implied in the processes of life and in the function of the spirit. In love there is an element of emotion which is the participation of the centered whole of a being in the process of reunion whether in anticipation or fulfillment. This drive for reunion, the eros element in love, belongs to the essential structure of life and is found throughout all the various dimensions of life. As emotion it is experienced as blessedness in man. Without this emotional quality we would not experience agape, for agape contains the Divine symbol of blessedness.[95] Love as faith is a state of the whole person. As in Plato, eros functions by creating knowledge of a person's emptiness as over against the fullness of that which is to be known. In Aristotle we have a clear symbol of the reunion quality of eros in that eros drives all the matter of the universe toward actualization in the form. Thus love

---

[94]Tillich, *Systematic Theology*, III, p. 134.
[95]Ibid., p. 136.

includes knowledge of that which is loved, not in the sense of analysis, but in the sense of *Verstehen,* or participating knowledge which changes both the knower and the known. As the urge toward the reunion of the separated, love includes all the many qualities known as love, *philia, eros, epithymia* amd *agape.* This means that love is one under all its manifold forms and is actually the inner dynamic quality of life. However, only agape in an ecstatic manifestation of the Spirit and is possible only in unity with Faith. In this respect, agape is equivalent to the New Being. Agape may indeed be used to characterize the Divine life itself symbolicly and essentially.

The Manifestation of the Spiritual Presence in Historical Mankind

The question arises as to the place in historical mankind in which the New Being as the creation of the Spiritual Being is manifest. Tillich answers this by saying that the Divine Spirit's invasion of the human spirit does not occur in isolated individuals but in social groups. Tillich, of course, bases this idea of the Spirit's operation in social groups upon Hegel and Schleiermacher.[96] It is the group that is spirit-bearing and history-bearing in Tillich's system. However, the manifestation of the Spirit and/or the creation of the New which is the mark of historical progress, is not done in some kind of collective experience or group decision, but actually is accomplished by the grasping of an individual by the Spirit within the group.[97] The conditions for such a state of being grasped, however, are made possible only by that individual's participation in the life of his social group, be it tribe, nation, or church. This is the case because all the functions of the human spirit, moral self-integration, cultural self-creation, and religious self-transcendence are conditioned by the social context of the I-Thou encounter.[98] Man is

---

[96]Ibid., p. 139. For the influence on Tillich's idea of the Spirit's working in social groups, see F. Schleiermacher, *The Christian Faith* (Harper Torch Books; New York: Harper & Bros., 1963), II, para. 121, 560ff. Also pp. 569 and 574. For the influence of G. F. Hegel, *The Philosophy of History* (New York: The Colonial Press, 1899), "Introduction," pp. 17ff., esp. pp. 38-48.

[97]Tillich, *Systematic Theology,* III, p. 134. "The rise of personalities and movements which fight against ... demonization of these symbols." Tillich amplified this is his Seminars at the University of Chicago, 1963-1965.

[98]Ibid.

constituted as man by the context of interrelations which is the living nexus of an historical group.

The Spiritual Presence is manifested in all history but history itself is not the manifestation of the Spiritual Presence.[99] There are marks by which the Spiritual Presence indicates its presence in a group. (1) The presence of symbols in both *theoria* and *praxis* through which the group expresses its openness to the Spirit's impact, and (2) there is the rise of personalities and movements which fight against the universal tragedy of the unavoidable profanization and demonization of these religious symbols.[100]

Tillich cites the Old Testament history of Israel and Judah as a familiar example of the struggle of the prophets against the profanization of Yahweh religion, and the transformation of the group under the Spiritual Presence manifest in them.[101] However, Tillich declares that "mankind is never left alone,"[102] for the Divine Spirit breaks into all history in revelatory experiences which have saving and transforming character. Thus there is always New Being in history in a fragmentary sense, since the participation in the transcendent union of unambiguous life is always partial, never complete. Tillich here quotes Paul who speaks of the anticipation of the possession of the Spirit,[103] for the fulfillment of transcendent union is an eschatological concept. However, even these fragmentary participations are salvatory and healing for even such a fragment points unambiguously to the Divine Power it represents.[104] Thus throughout history the New Being does conquer the ambiguities of life in time and space.[105]

We pass over Tillich's discussion of the general Spiritual Presence seen in the world religions other than Judaism and Christianity, noting only that the Spirit does make his presence felt wherever men are grasped by an ultimate concern. We come now to the most important single section of Tillich's Spirit-Doctrine, his elucidation of the Synoptic Gospels' Spirit-Christology, under the heading "The Spiritual Presence in Jesus as the Christ."

---

[99]Ibid.
[100]Ibid.
[101]Ibid., pp. 139-140.
[102]Ibid., p. 140.
[103]Ibid.; Philippians 3:12-14.
[104]Tillich, *Systematic Theology*, III, p. 140.
[105]Ibid., p. 141.

Spirit-Christology:
The Spiritual Presence
In Jesus as the Christ

For Paul Tillich, the one unambiguous, undistorted, clear and final manifestation of the Spiritual Presence is seen in Jesus as the Christ.[106] In Him, the Divine Spirit was present without distortion, not in a fragmentary, but in a radically clear and decisive way. In Jesus as the Christ, the New Being has appeared in history as the criterion of all spiritual experiences in the past and in the future, both within and without the church. His spirit was completely grasped by the Spiritual Presence, or was possessed by the Divine Spirit. This Spirit-possession makes him the Christ, the decisive embodiment of the New Being for historical mankind.

Tillich correctly observes that the earliest Christian tradition as found in Mark was one that interpreted the disciples' experience with Jesus by reference to a Spirit-Christology. For example, Saint Mark begins by speaking of Jesus being grasped by the Spirit at his Baptism.[107] Again and again, Jesus has ecstatic experiences which demonstrate the presence of the Spirit of God in him, e.g., the Spirit drives Jesus into the wilderness,[108] leads him through the temptation experience,[109] gives him knowledge of the inner motives of men and gives him power to cast out demonic powers and heal the body and mind of those who come to him.[110] According to the Synoptic writers, the Spirit is decisively present with Jesus in every moment of his career, in the ecstasy of the Transfiguration experience, in the suffering in the Garden, and in the certainty that comes to him that this is his *Kairos*, or "hour" for going through the suffering of the cross.

Tillich says that the doctrine of Jesus' procreation by the Spirit in the legend of the Virgin Birth is the consequence of the disciples' reflection upon the problem of how the Divine Spirit was able to find a vessel so completely open to its presence. He declares that this legend is justified in that here must have been a teleological predisposition in Jesus to become the bearer of the Spirit without limit. He says that this is justified by insight into the psychosomatic level at which the Spiritual

---

[106]Ibid., pp. 144-149.
[107]Mark 1:9-10 (also 1:8).
[108]Mark 1:12.
[109]Mark 1:13.
[110]Mark 1:21-26.

Presence works. But he rejects the legend in so far as it limits Jesus' full humanity in that it rules out a human father.[111] Tillich asserts that the doctrine of the multidimensionality of life answers the question of the psychosomatic basis of Jesus' predisposition to be the Bearer of the Spirit without such an ambiguous conclusion. Tillich goes on to explain that Jesus manifested the two marks of the Spirit's Presence, faith and love. Little interpretation is needed to demonstrate the presence of self-sacrificial love in Jesus. Jesus embodied the principle of *agape* in his being and radiated it into the world which had known it only ambiguously before him.[112]

Despite the rarity of reference to Jesus' faith in the Bible, Tillich declares that Jesus certainly did manifest faith in the sense of being grasped by the Spiritual Presence. The faith of the Christ is his state of being continuously grasped in an unambiguous way by the Spiritual Presence. Understood in this way, the faith of the Christ is clear, for the Spirit never leaves him, he is always supported by the transcendent union of unambiguous life.[113]

Tillich says that the Spirit-Christology of the Synoptics imply that it is not the spirit of the man Jesus of Nazareth that makes him the Christ but that it in the Spiritual Presence of God in him that possesses and drives his individual spirit.[114] This, Tillich says, is a salutary insight for it guards us against a Jesus-theology such as developed in Pietism or in recent theological liberalism. Tillich says Paul supports his position when Paul (2 Corinthians 3:17a) declares that "the Lord is the Spirit," and goes on to say that we do not know the Christ according to his flesh, but only as the Spirit who is alive and present (2 Corinthians 5:16). This saves Christianity from a legalistic subjection to an individual as an individual.[115]

The other implication of Spirit-Christology is that Jesus as the Christ is the keystone to all Spiritual manifestations in history. He is not an isolated event, but has an organic relation with past and future manifestations of the Spirit. Thus, Jesus as the Christ is unique but not isolated. He is the center of history and the criterion by which all other Spiritual manifestations are to be measured and judged.[116] Tillich concludes that the Spiritual Presence in history is essentially the same as

---

[111]Tillich, *Systematic Theology*, III, pp. 144-145.
[112]Ibid., p. 145.
[113]Ibid.
[114]Ibid., p. 146.
[115]Ibid., and 2 Corinthians 5:16-17.
[116]Tillich, *Systematic Theology*, III, p. 147.

the Spiritual Presence in Jesus as the Christ.[117] Wherever God reveals himself, he is the same God who decisively has revealed himself in the Christ.

The meaning of the assertion that Jesus is the criterion for all manifestations of God both "before" and "after" him, does not mean "before" a certain year in history, like 30 A.D. Rather the term "before Christ" means "before an existential encounter" with the New Being in Christ, and the term "after Christ" means after such an existential encounter—understood in the sense of being confronted by Christ and asked to make a decision about him. The Spirit who created the Christ within Jesus, says Tillich, is the same Spirit who prepared mankind and who continues to prepare mankind for the encounter with the New Being in him.[118] This means that there are men living in every age, who live "before Christ," since they have not yet encountered the New Being in him.

Paul's Influence on
Tillich's Spirit-Christology

It is at the locus of Tillich's explanation of the exact relation of the Spirit of Jesus as the Christ and the Spiritual Presence, or Holy Spirit, that Tillich most clearly shows the significance of the Pauline Spirit-Christology upon the formation of his doctrine of the Spiritual Presence. Tillich clearly elects to follow the stream of Spirit-Christology which Paul incorporates in his teaching and which comes to clear expression in such passages as 2 Corinthians 3:17a, where Paul says "the Lord is the Spirit." The Pauline material for the formation of this Spirit-Christology has been discussed in chapter one of this study. Briefly, 2 Corinthians 3:18, "the Lord who is the Spirit," and Romans 8:2, 8:9-10, and Philippians 2:1, state Paul's explicit identification of the Risen Christ and the Spirit. However, as was seen in the discussion in chapter one, Paul did not exclusively limit his identification of the Holy Spirit to the Risen Christ, for he also refers to the Holy Spirit as a separate expression of the Godhead as well as using the term "Spirit" in rather imprecise ways.[119] But the point to be made here is that Tillich has chosen to follow the quite primitive Spirit-Christology recorded in the Synoptic Gospels and which is basic to the central Pauline idea of

---

[117]Ibid.
[118]Ibid.
[119]See chap. one of this book.

communion with Christ, in his development of the doctrine of the Spiritual Presence. For Tillich the Spiritual Presence equals the New Being and the New Being equals the quality of a revelatory experience wherever and whenever it occurs.[120] Thus, although Tillich has declared that the principle of the Logos is foundational for his thought, he has elected to follow a Spirit-Christology rather than a Logos-Christology, and has indeed developed what might be called a non-incarnational Christology that comes very close to being the kind of Adoptionistic Christology taught by the ancient Syrian Church, which is most clearly seen in Paul of Samosata.[121] However, Tillich is in the tradition of modern theology on this point, for his view of Jesus as the Christ is very close to that of Schleiermacher.

Tillich and Schleiermacher

The most direct influence of Schleiermacher on Tillich's thought is, of course, the Spirit-Christology of both, and the emphasis in both theologies upon the redemption of men through the Spiritual Presence in the community of the Christian Church. In both Tillich and Schleiermacher, Christ is the bearer of a new reality whose life and influence creates a new community. This new community, the church, is the arena of the Spirit's work where men are brought into a closer relationship to God and are formed in the image of Christ. According to Schleiermacher,[122] Jesus had an unhindered potency of God-consciousness, and yet Christ is not a breaking-in of the Divine into the world, but rather Christ carried to completion that God-consciousness which God implanted in the human race as a developmental force. According to Schleiermacher, Christ should be considered more as the result of a new creative divine act than as the entrance of the divine into the world of man. Thus Christ is the ideal man, who differs from other men in that his God-consciousness was absolutely clear and fully committed at every moment. The basic principle which both Tillich and Schleiermacher share is the conception that the divine can only exist in man in terms of the perfection of man and not as a nature imposed upon or added to the perfection of humanity. Therefore, Schleiermacher says that in Christ the creation of man reached completion for the first time. Schleiermacher is also a factor in Tillich's formulation of the

---

[120]Tillich, *Systematic Theology*, III, p. 140.

[121]*Paul Tillich in Catholic Thought*, ed. T. A. O'Meara and C. D. Weisser (Dubuque: The Priory Press, 1964), pp. 295-296. (Hereafter cited as *PTCT*.)

[122]Schleiermacher, *The Christian Faith*, pp. 93-96 and 381.

concept of the New Being borne by Jesus as the Christ, for in Schleiermacher, Jesus as the Christ is also the norm of theology and the criterion of all other revelations, for in Schleiermacher's view of Christian doctrine everything in Christianity is related to the redemption accomplished by Jesus. In Christ, believers are taken into the power of God, challenged to a higher life and put in fellowship. Of course, Schleiermacher said all this on the basis of the inner experience of the believer, i.e., upon what is drawn out of the Christian's religious consciousness. In Schleiermacher, everything we say about God in simply a description of states of our religious consciousness, and thus we might say in Tillichian terms, is symbolic. Schleiermacher did not use ontology in his elucidation of Christian doctrine, for in the time in which he wrote the category of Being was not available to him. But for Tillich, coming after the close of the long development of German Idealism and of existentialism and working with a strong Platonic and Augustinian (as well as Hegelian) bent, the category of *das Sein* (Being) was available and seemed most desirable as the mold in which to cast the development of his system. Additionally, the rise of existentialism during the decades in which Tillich developed his Systematic Theology pointed out the need for a system that would take "essence" as seriously as "existence."

For Tillich, Jesus as the Christ is the norm of theology and the criterion of all other revelatory experiences. He is never to be transcended.[123] In him eternal God-manhood came into existence, or as Tillich says, we might say "eternal manhood," thus making Schleiermacher's influence on his system very clear.[124] For Tillich, the Christ is the Bearer of the New Being. He is this in the totality of his being and not in any part of it. This means that Jesus is a human being who realized the eternal God-man unity under the conditions of existence (in space and time, in estrangement and alienation, in ambiguity and distortion) and thus became eternal God-man or essential man. Schleiermacher's view of Jesus as the original image of what man essentially is, is logically equivalent to Tillich's formulation. Tillich says that he differs from Schleiermacher in that for him Christ exemplifies the New Being under the conditions of existence, and yet

---

[123]Tillich, *Systematic Theology*, III, p. 148; and ibid., II, pp. 93-96, and ibid., I, p. 137. (Jesus as the Christ is the *telos* and criterion of every revelation.)

[124]It must be noted that Tillich has maintained that Schleiermacher is not a direct influence on his Christology. See Ibid., II, p. 150.

Schleiermacher also speaks of Jesus as entering the corporate life of mankind which is characterized by sinfulness.[125]

For Tillich, Jesus, by his ultimate concern and obedience, realizes his essential unity with the Ground of Being, and manifests that being (the Spirit or the New Being) in a personal life in history. Thus Jesus becomes Jesus as the Christ. The saving work of the Christ was done by his total participation in man's existential estrangement and his victory over that estrangement. The subjection to existence is expressed for Tillich in the symbol of the cross of Christ; the conquest of existence is expressed in the symbol of the Resurrection of the Christ.[126]

In both cases (in Tillich and Schleiermacher) there is no real incarnation in the traditional or orthodox understanding of that symbol, i.e., in the sense that God became man. Rather the Christ is the perfect expression of manhood. Thus Schleiermacher called Jesus the original image of man or the first perfectly created man, and Tillich calls Jesus essential God-manhood, and says that this is equivalent to essential man. Thus, for Tillich, the Christ is the unity of the finite and infinite. No harsh conclusion should be drawn as to the faithfulness of either Schleiermacher or Tillich to the Biblical witness, for it is Tillich's intention to speak truthfully of all the varied strands of interpretation of the event, Jesus the Christ, which are found in the New Testament, and Schleiermacher does on occasion speak of Christ as the Divine essence in humanity.[127] While neither may be precisely incarnational in the sense of the ancient creeds both attempt to present the meaning of the manifestation of God which was decisively present in the life of Jesus, who is called the Christ.[128] It is interesting to note that the influence of the first great modern theologian is most evident on Tillich just here in regard to the interpretation of the Christ-event, which is the center and norm of any attempt at creating a Christian systematic theology.

---

[125]Alexander T. McKelway, *The Systematic Theology of Paul Tillich*, (Richmond: John Knox Press, 1964), p. 165, note 8. (Hereafter cited as *STPT*.) See Tillich, *Systematic Theology*, II p. 150. The reference to Schleiermacher is found in Schleiermacher, *The Christian Faith*, II, para. 104, subsection 2, 453 (also see, para. 100, pp 425ff. and para. 104, pp. 451ff; para. 101, 2, p. 422 is also informative).

[126]Tillich, *Systematic Theology*,II, pp. 153-165.

[127]Schleiermacher, *The Christian Faith*, II, para. 100, 425ff.

[128]*Contra* the conclusions of McKelway (*STPT*, p. 168), and of O'Meara (*PTCT*, pp. 295-296).

The Spiritual Presence
and the New Being
in the Spiritual Community

Tillich clearly states that Jesus would not be the Christ if he were not received as the Christ.[129] It is the spiritual community of the church which performs this receptive function. Thus the creativity of the Spiritual Presence in mankind has three parts:

(1) In mankind as a whole in preparation for the central manifestastion in Christ;

(2) In the Divine Spirit's central manifestation in Jesus as the Christ;

(3) In the manifestation of the spiritual community under the creative impact of the Christ-event.[130]

Tillich is insistent upon the point that the Christ would not be the Christ without those who receive him as the Christ. Christ could not have brought the New Being without those who have accepted the New Being in him and from him. Those who have accepted Christ as Christ and thus accepted the New Being in him are called the Spiritual Community. Tillich does not call the Spiritual Community "the Church" because "Church" is involved in the ambiguities of religion and the Spiritual Community, since it shares in the New Being, is at least potentially able to conquer the ambiguities of life including those of religion. Tillich is willing to call the Spiritual Community the "Body of Christ" and the "Assembly of God" because these terms express the unambiguous quality of life created in those who have received the New Being by reason of their participation in the Spiritual Presence. Thus we may speak of the Spiritual Community as being unambiguous, since it exemplifies the New Being. However, it has only a fragmentary or potentially unambiguous nature, an unambiguousness in anticipation of the Kingdom of God that comes only beyond history. This unambiguous quality is fragmentary because it has now appeared under the conditions of existence, in space and time, while it—in this existence—conquers man's estrangement and life's ambiguity.

Tillich speaks of the Spiritual Community as being Spiritual also in the sense which Luther designated by his use of the terms "invisible," "hidden," "open to faith alone." This means that the Spiritual Community is visible only to faith, as Saint Paul observed: only the

---

[129]Tillich, *Systematic Theology*, III, p. 149.
[130]Ibid.

Spirit can discern the Spirit (1 Corinthians 2:11-12).[131] Although the Spiritual Presence is invisible, Tillich affirms that it is none the less real, just as the New Being was hidden in Jesus but was nevertheless unconquerably real in him.

The relationship of the Spiritual Community to the churches is a dialectical one, i.e., one of identity and non-identity. It is not to be identified with the churches in their manifest form although it is to be found within them as well as outside of them in what Tillich calls the latent church.[132] The relation of the New Being in Christ to the New Being in the Spiritual Community can be seen by reference to several stories recorded in the New Testament. The most important is the story of Peter's confession that Jesus is the Christ, and Jesus' reply that such a recognition is the work of the Spiritual Presence within Peter and not the result of ordinary experience. Here Tillich closely follows Saint Paul's declarations in Romans 8. As Tillich says, "It is the Spirit grasping Peter that enables his spirit to recognize the Spirit in Jesus which makes him the Christ.[133] And further, "As the Christ is not the Christ without those who receive him as the Christ, so the Spiritual Community is not spiritual unless it is founded on the New Being as it has appeared in the Christ."[134]

The Pentecost story gives evidence of the Spiritual Community's character. Tillich discerns five elements in the symbolic meaning of the story:

(1) The Spiritual Presence's character is ecstatic and thus creates an ecstatic Spiritual Community in which ecstasy and structure are united. Pentecost demonstrates an ecstasy united with faith, love, unity and universality. Tillich says that without ecstasy there is no Spiritual Community.

(2) The Spiritual Community manifests faith in that an ecstatic experience reassured the disciples after their certainty was almost destroyed by the Crucifixion. Tillich says without the certainty of faith there is no Spiritual Community.

(3) The Spiritual Presence manifest at Pentecost created love which expressed itself in mutual service to all men, neighbors and strangers, and especially to those in need. Tillich says there in no Spiritual Community without self-surrendering love.

---

[131]Ibid., p. 150.
[132]Ibid., pp. 152-155.
[133]Ibid., p. 150.
[134]Ibid.

(4) The Spiritual Presence at Pentecost created unity in that it united different individuals and traditions and gathered them together for the sacramental meal. Tillich says there is no Spiritual Community without the ultimate reunion of all the estranged members of mankind.

(5) The Spiritual Presence at Pentecost created universality as seen in the missionary drive of the disciples. Tillich says the New Being would not be the New Being if mankind as a whole, and even the universe itself were not included in it. This conception of the universality of the Spiritual Presence is clearly reflected in Tillich's application of the idea of the multi-dimensional unity of all life. He says there would be no Spiritual Community without openness to all individuals, groups and things and the drive to take them into itself.[135]

The Pauline as well as Lucan (or, i.e., the theology of Acts) basis of the doctrine of the universality of the Spiritual Presence is seen in Tillich's assertion that the marks of the Spiritual Community are derived from the symbolic image of Jesus as the Christ which is known as the Body of Christ. The Body of Christ metaphor is taken directly from 1 Corinthians where Christ is said to be the Head and the Spiritual Community is called His Body.[136] Tillich says the body of Christ metaphor applied to the Christian Community means that the Divine Spirit is the Spirit of Jesus as the Christ and that the Christ is the criterion to which every spiritual claim must submit.

The Spiritual Community Is Its Latent and Its Manifest Stages

For Tillich, the Spiritual Community is determined by the appearance of Jesus as the Christ but it is not identical with the Christian churches. On the other hand, there is a question about the Spiritual Community's relation to the manifold religious groups which appear in the history of religion.[137]Tillich says that wherever there is the impact of the Spiritual Presence, there is revelation and salvation and thus the creation of the Spiritual Communlty. However, since the New Being which appears in Christ is the central manifestation of the Divine Spirit, the appearance of the Spiritual Community must differ in its preparatory period (before the reception of Jesus as the Christ) and in its

---

[135]Ibid., pp. 150-152.
[136]1 Corinthians 12:12-27.
[137]Tillich, *Systematic Theology*,III, pp. 154-155.

appearance after such reception. The community before the reception of the Christ Tillich calls the latent church, and the community after that reception he calls the manifest church.[138] Here Tillich shows some similarity to Schleiermacher in that Tillich will speak of the visible and the invisible church, but for Tillich the concept of the visible and the invisible church is not the same distinction as that which he wishes to make by the terms, latent and manifest.

The two distinctions overlap. The qualities of visibility and invisibility must be applied to both the latent and the manifest church.[139] For Tillich, the visible church is the social group made up of individual Christians joined together in an organization which shows all the characteristics of ambiguity seen in life in general.[140] Thus he agrees with Schleiermacher who spoke of the mutable or invisible church which is a mixture of the church and the world.[141]

On this basis Tillich speaks of the paradox of the churches, saying we must speak of them both sociologically and theologically. The invisible church is the true Spiritual Community, the Body of Christ, which has its impact upon its members in faith and love, creating the transcendent union of unambiguous life, partially and fragmentarily among men. These include artistic, educational and political movements, and certain individuals who manifest the Spiritual Presence.[142] The invisible church is the latent form of the Spiritual Community which Tillich, in his broad, culture-affirming manner, identifies as the latent church in Western humanistic culture. The Spirit is certainly ecstatically present in this latent church and to that degree revelation and salvation are there. At least potentially such groups are open to the reception of Jesus as the Christ,[143] although the ultimate criterion of the manifestation of faith and love of the Christ is lacking. Tillich sees the latent Spiritual Community in the people of Israel, in Islam, in the ancient Greek philosophical schools and in many aspects of the great Asiatic world religions.[144] He says that in all of these groups there are elements of faith in the sense of an ultimate concern, and there are elements of love in the sense of a transcendent reunion of the separated. But the Spiritual Community is still latent since the ultimate

---

[138]Ibid., p. 152.
[139]Ibid., pp. 152-155 and pp. 165-172, "The Paradox of the Churches."
[140]Ibid., p. 165, "The Sociological Aspect of the Church."
[141]Schleiermacher, The Christian Faith, II, para. 148-150, 676ff.
[142]Tillich, Systematic Theology, III, p. 153.
[143]Ibid.
[144]Ibid., p. 154.

criterion, the faith and love of the Christ, has not yet been received by these groups.[145]

On the other hand, the manifest church is the bearer of the Spirit in preaching and sacraments. The church is holy because of the working of the New Being within it, although its holiness can be demonized.[146] Its members are Holy because they want to belong to the church and have received the New Being in spite of their unholiness. The church is one, holy and Catholic or universal, because it is the community of faith and actualizes the Spiritual Community in a real way, although none of these aspects can be empirically seen. The marks of the church, unity, love, and universality are never completely realized, but are fragmentary and anticipatory under the limits of time and space, although they are unambiguous under the impact of the Spirit, and as such are the criterion for all religious groups.[147] However, in the churches the Spiritual Community exists as the invisible spiritual essence within them. It is interesting to note that for Tillich the manifestation of faith, love, unity and universality is the content of what he means by speaking of the holiness of the Spiritual Community. The driving, dynamic force within the universe, and within the Divine Life itself, is the power of love, seen in the churches because of the Spiritual Community which is the invisible essence in them, which drives toward the reunion of all separated beings in the eternal Ground of Being.

The Spiritual Community and the Unity of Religion, Culture and Morality

In Tillich's system that transcendent union of unambiguous life in which the Spiritual Community participates includes the unity of the three functions of the life of the human spirit, religion, culture, and morality. Under the Spirit's impact, man's basic inner structure which was formed essentially in a unity of these three functions, and then distorted and broken by the conditions of existence, is restored by the healing presence of the Spirit within the Spiritual Community.

---

[145]Ibid.
[146]Ibid., p. 155.
[147]Ibid., pp. 156-157.

Religion is not a special function within the Spiritual Community, for in it all the actions of man's spiritual life are grasped by the spirit.[148] The Spirit grasps all reality, every situation, and is the depth of all cultural creations, placing them in relation to their ultimate ground. Religion in the narrow sense does not exist here, and there are no religious acts because every act done under the driving force of the Spirit is an act of self-transcendence. Culture is the form of religion, and religion the substance of culture whenever the Spiritual Community is realized, even though it is realized only fragmentarily or momentarily. Tillich says this hidden unity of religion and culture struggles within mankind to prevent their separation. In the Spiritual Community morality functions to constitute persons (egos) as persons in their encounter with other persons.[149] Here religion in the broad sense unites with morality, for the term "Spiritual Community" points to the personal-communal character in which the New Being appears. Thus the moral imperative is unconditional here because it expresses man's essential being and it means that we affirm what we essentially are. The act of faith and the act of accepting the moral imperative unconditionally are really one act.[150]

Tillich is at his Pauline and Lutheran best in affirming that the motivating power behind the moral imperative is grace and not law.[151] He reasons that the Spiritual impact is pure grace and nothing can establish the moral personality and community but that transcendent union brought about by the Spirit.

For Tillich, then, the Spiritual Community is manifest and hidden in like manner as the New Being is both manifest and hidden in its expressions, and it creates New Being in the history of man, and indirectly in the universe as a whole. The Spiritual Community is open only to the eyes of faith, only manifest in its hiddenness, for as Paul said in Romans 8, only that which is Spiritual can discern the Spirit, or as he said elsewhere, no one can call Jesus "Lord" who does not have the Spirit.[152]

---

[148]Ibid., pp. 157-161.
[149]Ibid., p. 158.
[150]Ibid., p. 159.
[151]Ibid.
[152]Ibid., p. 160; Romans 8:26-27 and 1 Cor. 12:3. (Also, 2 Cor. 5:16-17, and 1 Cor. 2:14-16.)

Can Tillich's Doctrine of the Spiritual Presence
Adequately Convey the Biblical Conception
of the Presence of the Spirit?

Cyrillus of Jerusalem has written:

> The grace of the Spirit is truly necessary if we want to deal
> with the Holy Spirit; not that we may speak adequately   about
> Him — for that is impossible — but that we may pass through this
> subject without danger, by saying what the divine Scriptures
> contain.[153]

This section is intended as an exploration of the adequacy of the
Tillichian formulation of the traditional Christian doctrine of the Holy
Spirit. Does Tillich's conception of the Spiritual Presence convey to
people of the twentieth century the same essential meaning which the
fourth century creedal formula conveyed to people of that day when it
confessed:

> I believe in the Holy Spirit, the Lord and Giver of Life who
> proceedeth from the Father and the Son, who with the   Father
> and the Son together is worshipped and glorified; Who spake
> by the prophets?[154]

Tillich on the Possibility of
Speaking of God

The point of departure for an investigation of Tillich's adequacy in
conveying the meaning of the Biblical conception of the Spiritual
Presence must begin with an understanding of Tillich's conception of
the phrase,"I believe in God." As Tillich has thoroughly explained in
Systematic Theology, Volume I, and as we have already discussed in the
earlier part of this chapter, in his conception, God is not a being along
side other beings but is rather the source, structure or Ground of Being
itself.[155] On the other hand we must observe that Tillich's doctrine of
God is so framed as (in his view) to preserve all of the values of the
Christian idea of God. Tillich is very clear that whenever we speak of

---

[153]H. Berkhof, *The Doctrine of the Holy Spirit* (Richmond: John Knox Press,
1964), Preface.
[154]*The Nicene Creed*, Third Article.
[155]Tillich, *Systematic Theology*, I, 235ff.

God we speak in symbolical terms, except for the root statement that God is Being Itself. Tillich has varied somewhat in his discussion of this point, in one place declaring that the only non-symbolic statement about God that can be made is this: "The statement that everything we say about God is symbolic."[156] However in the same place Tillich declares that we may speak of man's ultimate concern, of man's quest for God, in nonsymbolic terms, such as calling God the Infinite, the Unconditional or Being Itself. Tillich says that these terms designate the boundary line at which the symbolic and non-symbolic modes of speech converge. The statement that "God is Being Itself," "The Infinite" and "The Unconditional" are non-symbolic, according to Tillich, while every statement about "God" beyond these three is symbolic. We must distinguish here the various meanings of the term "symbol." We are speaking only of religious symbols. A statement, therefore, about a religious symbol is *univocal in reference* to the religious symbol itself. Of course, every statement is made up of word-symbols, and is, on the literary level, symbolic. In this instance we intend to convey only Tillich's belief that God is the *prius*, the foundation of everything that is, and thus to speak of God as Being-Itself is to speak univocally of God. Beyond the point of speaking of God as Being Itself or the Unconditional, every statement about God, however, becomes symbolic in that such statements as "The Almighty," "The Power of Being," refer to the Divine in terms derived from finite reality. Tillich only accepts the statement that God is Being Itself as being a direct or univocal statement.

In this writer's investigation of Tillich's philosophical view of what is and what is not symbolic when applied to God, a certain development of thought has been uncovered. Before 1957, when *Systematic Theology*, Volume II was published, Tillich would have said very precisely that there is one non-symbolic statement about God—the only such statement—namely, that God is Being Itself. Tillich discusses this in his "Reply to Interpretation and Criticism" in *The Theology of Paul Tillich* (published in 1952), where he defends himself against the criticism of Charles Hartshorne and John Randall.[157] In this discussion Tillich admits that the structure of being, although it is rooted in being as such, is not identical with it and that "ground" and "power" of being are symbolic in that they use elements of being in order to circumscribe Being Itself. However, he affirms in this discussion that he does not believe that "Being-Itself" is symbolic. He defends this as a literal statement on the

---

[156]Ibid., Introduction, II, p. 9.
[157]Kegley and Bretall, *The Theology of Paul Tillich*, pp. 333-336.

grounds that every philosophy offers an implicit or explicit answer to the question: "What does the word 'is' mean ?"[158] This is the same kind of reasoning that Tillich uses in his identification of the basic "quest" of ontology and theology in his *Biblical Religion and a Search for Ultimate Reality*, first published in 1955.[159]

The movement of Tillich's thought concerning symbolic and non-symbolic statements about God can be illustrated by another reply of Tillich to a criticism of his position, this reply being the concluding chapter of *Paul Tillich in Catholic Thought* (published in 1964).[160] In this reply to his critics (in this case the critics are Kenelm Foster and George McLean) Tillich defends his doctrine against the charge that there is a pantheistic trend in his thought. Tillich admits that he has spoken of a "pantheistic element" in every adequate doctrine of God, declaring that he must say this as a corrective against the semi-deistic theism of much Protestant thought. He strikes at his critics by saying it is odd that this pantheistic element should be be criticized by Catholics whose tradition implies that God is *ipsum esse* (Being Itself). Tillich goes on to reject the assertion of George McLean that Tillich calls God "the essence of all things."[161] Tillich declares that to speak of God as the essence of all things would be to dissolve God into the essence of the world and remove his qualitative transcendence. Tillich continues by saying that the pantheistic element is necessary, however, as a corrective to many theologies that emphasize only God's freedom, for to attribute freedom to God demands that we attribute necessity also. Tillich's word for necessity is destiny, and in his system God is spoken of as having a destiny as well as man. In conclusion Tillich declares that "God transcends the polarities of freedom and destiny (as well as all the other polarities), as he transcends essence and existence."[162]

In the last analysis, Tillich's doctrine of God requires the acceptance of the literalness of this one affirmation about God, "that God is Being Itself." In *Biblical Religion and the Search for Ultimate Reality* (the materials contained in BRSUR were delivered as lectures in 1951 but not published until 1955 and republished in 1964), Tillich reaffirmed his belief in the essential unity of the "absolute" of philosophy and the "absolute" of theology. This clearly states Tillich's belief in the identity of Being and God. In this reaffirmation of his belief that God is Being

---

[158]Ibid., p. 335.
[159]Tillich, *BRSUR*.
[160]*PTCT*, pp. 307-309.
[161]Ibid., p. 308. Compare with p. 79.
[162]Ibid., p. 308.

Itself (although he is not to be identified with the structures of being, nor with essence, but to be understood as transcending essence and existence), Tillich returns to his clearest expression of his doctrine of God, the expression that "*Deus est esse . . .* the certainty of God is identical with the certainty of Being itself: God is the presupposition of the question of God."[163] This quotation is taken from Tillich's famous lecture on "The Two Types of Philosophy of Religion, published in *Theology of Culture*[164] (published in 1959), which is an even later expression of his views than *Biblical Religion and the Search for Ultimate Reality.* However the whole drift of the essays in the *Theology of Culture* is a renewal of those elements in philosophy and theology that were the passions of Tillich's life. As Tillich says in the forward to this volume, the title "Theology of Culture" is an abbreviation of the title of his first published speech, "Uber die Idee einer Theologie der Kultur." The expression of opinion found in Tillich's lecture on the philosophy of religion is the basic one that must be followed in any interpretation of his thought about God.[165] We are cognizant of Tillich's formal definition of his position in *Systematic Theology,* Volume II, where he declared that "the only nonsymbolic statement about God is that everything we say about God is symbolic."[166] This formal definition is not a full expression of Tillich's theological position, so the language of "Two Types of Theology of Religion" serves as the basis of this investigation and, thus, I will interpret Tillich as teaching that man may make one literal, affirmative statement about God, i.e., that God is Being Itself that transcends the split between essence and existence.[167]

---

[163]Tillich, *Theology of Culture*, pp. 15-16.

[164]Ibid., pp. 10-29.

[165]See John C. Cooper, "The Necessity of Ontology in the Hermeneutic Task" (Paper delivered before the 1966 meeting of the Southern section of the American Academy of Religion at Decatur, Georgia), pp. 7-12. Also see "The 'New Hermeneutic' and Metaphysics," in *The Bucknell Review*, Vol. XIX, Spring, 1971, No. 1, pp. 125-140.

[166]Tillich, *Systematic Theology*, II, p. 9.

[167]Ibid., I, p. 235.

The Relationship of Tillich's
Doctrine of the Spiritual Presence
to Tillich's Conception of God

Since God is identified as *Esse Ipsum Subsistens* (subsistent Being Itself) in Tillich's theology, and since we can only speak of God as personal in a symbolic way, according to Tillich, it follows that Tillich's conception of the Spiritual Presence has a philosophical or ontological basis. Tillich speaks of Spirit as being a dimension of life which unites the power of being with the meaning of being. Tillich defines the Spirit as the actualization of power and meaning in unity.[168] In Tillich's thought this actualization of power and meaning in unity occurs only in man, for man is a unity in which all the dimensions of life, the organic, the inorganic, the psychic and the spiritual are present. According to Tillich man is conscious of being determined in his nature by spirit as a dimension of his life. This dimension called "spirit" is the dimension in which man employs his creativity and produces the artifacts and ideas that make up human culture. Because of this experience of Spirit, Tillich holds that it is possible to speak symbolically of God as Spirit and of the Divine Spirit.[169]

As we have discussed earlier in this chapter, Tillich makes an effort to re-establish a tradition of speaking of the human spirit and the Divine Spirit, an effort made necessary by the debasement of the term Spirit in pseudo-religions and by the loose usage of popular theologians. For Tillich, his identification of the spirit as a dimension of life and his definition of man's creativity in cultural affairs as the activity of the human spirit makes it possible for him to speak in an intellectually consistent way about the spirit and the Spirit.

Tillich develops his conception of the Spiritual Presence in chapter ii of Part IV of his *Systematic Theology*.[170] Throughout this chapter we are impressed by Tillich's frequent references to the Epistles of Paul. In his development of the doctrine of the Spiritual Presence, Tillich says that the relation between the Divine Spirit and the human spirit is to be metaphorically identified by the statement: "The Divine Spirit dwells and works in the human spirit."[171] This word "in," used metaphorically, is made to bear all the weight of the problems of speaking of the

---

[168]Ibid., III, p. 111.
[169]Ibid.
[170]Ibid., pp. 111ff.
[171]Ibid., p. 111.

relationship of the Divine to the human. This relationship of man and God is identified by Tillich as the relationship of the conditioned to the unconditioned, of the creature to the creative ground from which it comes.[172] Thus we can see that Tillich uses the conception of the Spirit metaphorically to "close the gap" between the Ground of Being Itself and the creature, man, who is grounded in the Divine Ground while being separated from the Divine on the psychological and spiritual level by estrangement, anxiety and guilt.

Tillich says that the experience of becoming aware of the presence of the Spirit as the Divine Ground which underlies that dimension of man's life (which Tillich calls spirit) is the experience of ecstasy. Ecstasy is man's experience of being "driven" into a successful act of self-transcendence, of being grasped by some ultimate and unconditional concern. It is this successful act of self-transcendence (perhaps best seen in the overcoming of anxiety through the courage to be one's self, or perhaps seen in the act of self-transcendence that occurs in the arts when one creates something that is culturally new) that unites in man both the power of being and the *meaning* of being. The spirit is thus the dimension of life in which value and meaningfulness arise for the human mind.

Tillich and Heidegger

At this point we recognize Tillich's indebtedness to the Existentialist philosopher, Martin Heidegger. Heidegger, himself educated in Roman Catholic theological thought, was one of the chief revivers of ontological investigation in the twentieth century, having written a study of Duns Scotus in the light of Husserl's phenomenology and a famous study of *Sein und Zeit* (Being and Time).[173] Many other commentators have recognized the connection of Heidegger's ontology and Tillich's theology, including Alasdair MacIntyre[174] and J. Heywood Thomas.[175] While MacIntyre, writing from the point of view of an English Language Philosopher, calls the relationship with Heidegger "unfortunate,"[176] Thomas apparently approves of this connection.[177] Thomas reports:

---

[172]Ibid.

[173]*A Critical History of Western Philosophy*, ed. D. J. O'Connor (New York: The Free Press, 1964), pp. 509, 522ff.

[174]Ibid.

[175]J. Heywood Thomas, *Paul Tillich* (Richmond: John Knox Press, 1966), p. 3.

[176]O'Connor, *A Critical History of Western Philosophy*, p. 522.

Though it was only a year he spent there, Marburg has left its mark on Tillich. There he met with existentialism in its twentieth-century form. His reaction he describes thus: "I resisted, I tried to learn, I accepted the new ways of thinking more than the answer it gave." In some ways it was not a new way of thinking—at any rate, Tillich regards himself as having been prepared for it by three things—his familiarity with Schelling, his knowledge of Kierkegaard and the contact he had had with "the philosophy of life."[178]

Tillich's relationship to Heidegger, therefore, is not accidental, but is a conscious relationship which Tillich cultivated in order to achieve a new way of thinking. As the quotation from Thomas and as our investigation of the sources of Tillich's doctrine of the Spirit (discussed earlier in this chapter) have indicated, this new existential way of thinking was related to Tillich's over-all way of looking at the world which was largely determined by his study of Schelling and the German Idealists. Tillich, like Heidegger, begins from and tries to go beyond a Husserlian concept of Philosophy. Tillich believes that in analyzing the structure of the categories of thought, as Husserl did, the philosopher is driven to recognize that these are the categories of a finite being, and to recognize further an unconditional ground behind that thought and its objects.[179]

Heidegger and his discussion of man's mode of existence in the world (*Dasein* or "being there") is congenial to Tillich's thought because of Heidegger's own dependence upon Kierkegaard and Saint Augustine who are both influential on Tillich's over-all theological position. MacIntyre, in his criticism of Heidegger, has suggested that Heidegger's account of *Dasein* is a blend of Kierkegaard's insights given in *The Concept of Dread* and *Either/Or*.[180] For Heidegger "Dasein ist Sorge," i.e., *Dasein* is care or concern. It is being-concerned-with. But what characterizes our concern is our finitude and the way in which our being is consumed in the moment-to-moment passage of time. *Dasein* is open towards the future and confronts possibilities that fill it with anxiety or dread. This anxiety can only be overcome by facing one's existence in its totality, and this means to face the fact of one's own death as the limit of possibility. This is the kind of reasoning found in Saint Augustine and especially in Kierkegaard. It is no longer, in Heidegger's philosophy, a discussion of anxiety alone, however, but a systematic ontology which founds itself upon man's sense of being in the world and faced with the necessity of decision-making. MacIntyre notes that this ontology differs from Kierkegaard's in that in Heidegger's description God is not mentioned.[181] We can not conclude from this that Heidegger is an atheist, however, for he has repudiated the charge with great indignation.[182] We might observe that in the hands of Tillich the concept of *Dasein* and the ontology of Heidegger has God related to it *again*, thus bringing Heidegger's development of man's situation in the world back into line with the Christian conceptions of Kierkegaard and other more theologically oriented existentialist thinkers. It is the contention of this writer that Tillich makes use of Heidegger's ontology in his development of the spirit as the dimension of life in which man employs his creativity to create culture.

Tillich and Karl Jaspers

Tillich is also indebted to another of the towering figures of modern European Existentialist philosophy, Karl Jaspers, for materials which he works into his description of the dimension of spirit. The chief conception taken from Jaspers seems to be that of Jaspers' description of man's existential situation. Jaspers has written:

We are always in situations. Situations change, opportunities arise. If they are missed they never return. I myself can work to change the situation. But there are situations which remain essentially the same even if their momentary aspect changes and their shattering force is obscured; I must die, I must suffer, I must struggle, I am subject to chance, I involve myself inexorably in guilt. We call these fundamental situations of our existence ultimate situations. That is to say, they are situations which we cannot evade or change. Along with wonder and doubt, awareness of these ultimate situations is the profound source of philosophy. In our day-to-day lives we often evade them, by closing our eyes and living as if they did not exist. We forget that we must die, forget our guilt, and forget that we

---

[181]Ibid.
[182]Ibid.

are at the mercy of chance. We face only concrete situations and master them to our profit, we react to them by planning and acting in the world, under the impulsion of our practical interests. But to ultimate situations we react either by obfuscation or, if we really apprehend them, by despair and rebirth: we become ourselves by a change in our consciousness of being.

Or we may define our human situation by saying that *no reliance can be placed in worldly existence.*[183]

The term that immediately catches our attention here is Jaspers' phrase "ultimate situations " which is the English translation for the German term *Grenzsituation.* Tillich's liking for the expression "an der Grenze," i.e., "on the boundary," is well-known. Tillich has often spoken of his entire life and thought as being "on the boundary" between Philosophy and Theology, between Idealism and Marxism, and between Europe and America. He has also demonstrated the significance of the conception of *Grenzsituation,* which should be translated "boundary situation" rather than "ultimate situation" in his description of faith as "ultimate concern." For Jaspers, *Grenzsituation* is also a central concept, designating the inescapable realities in relation to which alone human life can be made genuinely meaningful. Ultimate situations can not be changed or surmounted; they can only be acknowledged. As Jaspers has also written,

In ultimate situations man either perceives nothingness or senses true being in spite of and above all ephemeral worldly existence. Even despair, by the very fact that it is possible in the world, points beyond the world.

Or, differently formulated, man seeks redemption. Redemption is offered by the great, universal religions of redemption. They are characterized by an objective guarantee of the truth and reality of redemption. Their road leads to an act of individual conversion, This philosophy cannot provide. And yet all philosophy is a transcending of the world, analogous to redemption.[184]

---

[183]Karl Jaspers, "On the Philosophical Life" in *Value and Man,* ed. L. Z. Hammer (New York: McGraw-Hill, 1966), pp. 429-430.
[184]Ibid., pp. 430-431.

The parallels between Jaspers and Tillich seem obvious. The human condition analyzed by Jasper leads man to recognize *Grenzsituation* in which man must simply acknowledge that either he comes to an ultimate concern because of the indication of true being that lies "beyond the world" or else his life is simply destined to end in nothingness.

*James Luther Adams on
Tillich's Concern for "Meaning"
(the Concern of the Spirit)*

In Heidegger and Jaspers, Tillich finds the materials he needs to discuss the meaning of life in a way that is at once philosophical as well as theological. James Luther Adams, in his reflective discussion of Tillich's *Philosophy of Culture, Science, and Religion*, declares that for Tillich "meaning is the characteristic concern of the human spirit, and hence it is, for Tillich, the foundation of his whole system."[185] In making the problem of the meaning of life central to his system, Tillich shows his concern with the direct confrontation of life which is the spirit of existential philosophy.

In making his observations about the importance of the conception of the meaning of life for Tillich's system, Adams declares that Tillich is employing philosophical categories that are common to Heidegger and Jaspers, Barth and Brunner, as well as to Dilthey, Brentano, Hartmann and Husserl.[186] Adams further observes that Tillich sharpens and clarifies the concept of meaning by relating it to his whole philosophy of spirit and being.[187] Here we have come full-circle, for we have now returned to the place of the spirit in Tillich's system. However, we return with a richer idea of the antecedents and relations of the concept of spirit as Tillich uses it, particularly in its relationship to modern existential thought. Against this background we are able to say several things about Tillich's doctrine of the spirit that will make it more possible to compare it with the thought of the early Christian theologian, Saint Paul.

---

[185]J. L. Adams, *Paul Tillich's Philosophy of Culture, Science, and Religion* (New York: Harper and Row, 1965), p. 56. Adam's footnotes this observation by referring to Tillich's *The Interpretation of History*, p. 38.

[186]Adams, *Paul Tillich*, pp. 56-57.

[187]Ibid., p. 57.

In Tillich's *Systematic Theology*, spirit (*Geist*) is the concept that denotes the dynamic power of creativity in man. "It is not to be identified with reason or with creative intellect; it is rather in between the two. . . . It is dependent on thought and being. Spirit is the self-determination of thought in the realm of existence.[188] Spirit has freedom as its presupposition, for only on the basis of freedom can something valid be realized. Spirit is oriented, therefore, in the realm of meaning. Spirit is oriented to the realm of meaning where individuality expresses itself by living in and beyond reality, by accommodating itself to the nature of being but also by giving to being a novel expression.[189] Thus in the realm of spirit man is conscious of an unconditioned meaning which is present in every particular meaning and this uncon-ditionedness of meaning is itself not a meaning, but the ground of meaning.[190] On this basis we are able to see that in the dimension of spirit man encounters *Grenzsituation* or ultimate situations which point beyond themselves to the ground of meaning just as surely as man's awareness of his finitude becomes the occasion for his sense of the infinite which is the ground of his being. In the realm of the spirit one meets an unconditional demand for meaning in his life, for "Spirit is only present where existence is impregnated with the unconditional demand that gives it validity.[191] Therefore the creative spirit in the dimension of spirit brings together individuality and infinity, concreteness and universality.[192] We are able then to understand on this basis why Tillich can maintain that "In spirit the meaning of being fulfills itself."[193]

It is this insight of Tillich's that in the dimension of spirit we have the unity of the power of being and the meaning of being that brings the meaning of being itself to fulfillment that James Luther Adams calls the "principal assumption of metalogic, the paradoxical imminence of the transcendent."[194] On this level of metalogic or metaphysics, we are, of course, dealing with symbolic concepts.[195] Tillich has discussed this

---

[188]Ibid.

[189]Ibid., p. 58.

[190]Ibid., p. 59.

[191]Ibid., p. 137. This sentence is a quote from *Das System der Wissenschaften* . . ., p. 91.

[192]Adams, *Paul Tillich*, p. 137.

[193]Ibid., p. 147. This sentence is a quote from *Das System der Wissenschaften* . . ., p. 102.

[194]Adams, *Paul Tillich*, p. 166.

[195]Ibid., p. 165.

symbolic nature of metaphysics lm his *Das System der Wissenschaften nach Gegenstanden und Methoden,* [196]where he says:

The goal of metaphysical knowledge is the unity of the concept of being and the concept of meaning; that is, a system that is the same time a universal Gestalt and a universal framework of meaning. The approach of metaphysical knowledge is the unity of apprehension of form and import, of the scientific and the aesthetic view, of the perception of being and the understanding of meaning. The method of metaphysical knowledge is the contemplation of the unconditioned import in the conditioned forms, which in the philosophy of the Renaissance was designated as the contemplation of the *coincidentia oppositorum* . . .[197]

From this description of Tillich's efforts to understand the conception of spirit as a dimension of life which is relevatory of the ground of being itself and which expresses the meaning that is implied in being, we may conclude that Tillich is trying to give us a philosophical concept based on those elements of nineteenth and twentieth century philosophy which he considers most useful to Christian theology. Tillich is not trying to explain spirit in terms of this world only, but is attempting to express the paradoxical fact that the transcendent is imminent in the world that man inhabits. We might say that he is attempting to give us a theonomous philosophy of the spirit. This conception of theonomy, or the apprehension of the Divine and ultimate loyalty to the Divine, is based on Tillich's insight that God is not one more object alongside other objects in the universe but is the *Esse Ipsum Subsistens* (subsistent Being Itself) which transcends the split between essence and existence. As such Tillich's conception of the spirit is an attempt to "let God be God,"[198] and to reverence the majesty and holiness of the Divine which man encounters in the *Grenzsituation* of human life. "Through his conception of meaning Tillich interprets thought and spirit as manifestations of an infinite and inexhaustible reality which in its ultimate character is referred to as the unconditionally real and the unconditionally valid."[199] Thus Tillich can

---

[196]Paul Tillich, *Das System der Wissenschaften nach Gegenstanden und Methoden* (Göttingen: Vandenhoeck und Ruprecht, 1923).

[197]Ibid., P. 133.

[198]Philip Watson, *Let God Be God,* (London: Epworth Press, 1954).

[199]Adams, *Paul Tillich,* p. 183.

say "Metaphysics is alive so long as the holy import of its creations is retained, so long as the sacramental element is preserved."[200] This consideration, that is, Tillich's desire to rationally understand the presence of the unconditioned, one might say, of the Holy in human life, makes it clear that there is no desire in Tillich to give a non-theological description of the "Spirit." Tillich is concerned to interpret theological statements about the Spirit in ways that are adequate to modern men who are impressed by the descriptive power of existential philosophy. He is concerned to make the experience of the Spiritual Presence "available" for men of the twentieth century, which certainly must have been the concern of the Biblical writers in their efforts to speak of the Holy Spirit. In brief, it seems to this writer that it is perfectly legitimate to compare Tillich's doctrine of the Spiritual Presence with the Pauline teachings concerning the Holy Spirit.

A Comparison of Paul's Teachings about the Spirit with the Teachings of Paul Tillich

The investigation of Saint Paul's teachings about the Spirit in chapter one revealed that Paul's theology is neither systematic nor wholly consistent. The results of that investigation demonstrated that Paul is not a conscious ontologist. Paul's conception of God is essentially that of late Judaism, in which God is thought of as a personal being, who reveals himself, who makes covenants with men, and who is at once imminent in the world and transcendent over it. Thus it would appear that we could not compare Paul and Tillich. However, this need not be the case since the first century Paul and the twentieth century Paul Tillich are so full orbed in their approach that there is a portion of each one's "theological circle" which overlaps the other. The point of contact lies in the fact that both men present an existential theology, as indeed Brunner and some other modern theologians do also.[201] Saint Paul offers us a bipolar theology, having at one pole the message of Christ preached, and at the other pole the situation in which the hearer lives, wants and questions. Thus Paul's message on the Spirit, as on other topics, is given the form of a dialogue between the needs of the

---

[200]Ibid., p. 235. Adams quotes this sentence from Tillich's *Religion-philosophie*, pp. 820-821.

[201]Ibid.; the evaluation of Saint Paul's usage of the phrases "in the Spirit" and "in Christ", chapter one. Also see the constructive analysis in chapter two.

Christian community and the historical traditions about Christ Jesus, supplemented by personal mystical experiences with the Risen, Spiritual Christ. The passage in 1 Corinthians 12-14 is illustrative of this insight. Without more weight on Tillich's teaching than is warranted, we can conclude from the analysis of his doctrine of the Spirit given above, that Tillich's treatment of the Spirit is also existential, bipolar, or as Tillich himself would say, is the result of correlation. I would also say that Tillich's doctrine is the result of a consistent attempt to be faithful to the Pauline answers to the problems of Paul's time as they are found in his Epistles.

The second major constellation of considerations that must be faced when examining the adequacy of Tillich's formulation of his Spirit-doctrine to the full expression of the Pauline witness, is whether Tillich's ontological interpretation conveys essentially the same meaning to men of our day as Paul's mystical and social interpretation did in his day. The insight that Paul's interpretation of the meaning of the manifestation of the Holy Spirit was personal and social rather than ontological, can be gained from the fact that the Pauline text for the treatment of the Spirit's presence is 1 Corinthians 12:7, "To each is given the manifestation of the Spirit for the common good." This passage expresses the social basis of Paul's interpretations just as 1 Corinthians 12:3 expresses the personal interpretation of the Spirit's presence, "No one can say 'Jesus is Lord' except by the Holy Spirit."

However, without the slightest intention of performing a verbal sleight-of-hand, we conclude that *within the social interpretation of the Spirit's Presence given by Paul, there is an ultimate ontological reference.* The ontological reference in Paul's doctrine of the Spirit lies in his use of the originally Stoic metaphor of the *Soma*, the Body and its several members discussed in chapter 1.[202] The *Soma* metaphor was derived by Stoic philosophers to describe the construction of the universe and its binding structures. The universe, in this line of reasoning, is the Body of God and the individuals that make up the social universe are component parts of the Divine body. It is from this much used Pauline metaphor that we can draw the clearest parallel between the teachings of Paul and those of Paul Tillich. We will discuss this and other

---

[202]1 Cor. 12:12-31, Rom. 12:4, Gal. 3:28, Col. 3:11, Eph. 2:13-18, Eph. 1:23, 4:12, Col. 1:18, 24, Eph. 5:30, Rom. 12:5. The Concept of the Body of Christ has its background in the common Hellenistic Doctrine of the *Soma* used by Plato, Josephus, Xenophon, Philo, Seneca, Marcus Aurelius, and other ancient writers. See Robinson, *The Body – A Study in Pauline Theology* (London: SCM Press, 1957), p.59, n. 1.

important connections between Paul and Tillich here, leaving a detailed examination of the relation between Paul and Tillich in regard to the Spirit for chapter four.

Analysis and Conclusions

On the basis of Table 6 (in the appendix) showing the relationship of Tillich's thought to that of Paul, we may draw the following conclusions:

(1) The Tillichian doctrine of the Spiritual Presence is based on his view of God as being the Ground of Being. Therefore, we must accept the fact that Tillich's interpretation is ontological and stated in terms of his fundamental principle, the multi-dimensional unity of life. Thus, the Spirit is identified as a quality of life, a manifestation of the Divine Ground. Paul, on the other hand, speaks in personal terms and usually refers to the Spirit in a personal way. This basic difference between Paul and Paul Tillich must not be thought of as an insurmountable block between Tillich's theology and the Biblical language used by Paul and the rest of the New Testament writers, but must be accepted as the price demanded by the "pole called Situation." Because Tillich has developed his Spirit doctrine in a systematic and an ontological way (quite different from Paul except in regard to the body of Christ idea), this does not mean that Tillich has rejected the Pauline message. Quite the contrary, Tillich is attempting to render the meaning of what Paul taught in terms understandable to modern sophisticated persons.

We look in vain for the traditional language about the Spirit in Tillich's theology. Not that some of it is not included — some is. But Tillich has deliberately refrained from merely repeating what Paul has said, [203]and has striven to state what people experience when they are grasped by the presence of God so that people today who are not open to literal language used in reference to God may be able to understand what Paul is saying, and perhaps to be open to the same experience of the Spirit.

Tillich has often been criticized for his use of ontological language in the construction of his Systematic Theology. Many critics deny that modern men can understand and be grasped by such a terminology. Some critics have said that Tillich only makes the Christian message intelligible by his correlation of ontology and existentialism to a small group of highly educated people who are already interested in religion. However, this is not necessarily the case. While it is true that ontology

---

[203]Tillich, *Systematic Theology*, Preface, II, viii.

has not been in fashion in the twentieth century, there are signs that philosophy may be returning to ontological considerations. Such books as Mortimer Adler's *The Conditions of Philosophy*[204] and P. F. Strawson's *Individuals*,[205] which is a work done by a language philosopher, point in the direction of a recovery of ontological thinking in the second half of the twentieth century. In this movement towards a recovery of ontology we believe Tillich's philosophical theology to be a constructive influence.

The kind of interpretation which Paul Tillich has given in his three volume *Systematic Theology* is not only an ontological interpretation, but also an existential interpretation, a fact that we will illustrate and discuss at length in chapter three. We may anticipate what will be said there at this point by offering the following "key" to Tillich's hermeneutical approach. In Tillich's attempt to point out ways in which modern, secular man may continue to use "God-language" without falling into the pitfalls of literalism on the one hand and of insensitivity to the meaning of religious language on the other, Tillich seeks to meet two basic needs of a modern theology. These two basic needs are the statement of the truth of the Christian message, and the interpretation of this message for every new generation. Tillich's "key" is: "The meaning of a Biblical symbol (or myth) is interpreted for our age when it is transposed into an ontological statement, and transposed into an existentialist statement (in terms of the present situation)."[206]

Guyton B. Hammond in his excellent study of the thought of Tillich and Erich Fromm, *Man in Estrangement*,[207] has pointed out that Tillich's dialogue or correlation has been carried on mainly with one general trend of modern thought, existentialism. However, Hammond admits that this one trend is an important one. Hammond sees existentialism and Tillich's modern ontology as both being rooted in the Hegelian insight concerning the dialectical property of life.[208] In this insight Hammond is quite correct, as we have demonstrated in an earlier section of this chapter.[209] Furthermore, as Tillich's theology is heavily indebted to the philosophical works of Heidegger and Jaspers, it would

---

[204]Mortimer J. Adler, *The Conditions of Philosophy* (New York: Atheneum, 1965).

[205]P. F. Strawson, *Individuals* (London: Methuen, 1959).

[206]See chap three of this book.

[207]Guyton B. Hammond, *Man in Estangement* (Nashville: Vanderbilt University Press, 1965).

[208]Ibid., p. 134.

[209]See chap two, pp. 75-76

seem that Tillich's ontological approach is in the main stream of continental philosophy. The fact that the theological position of Rudolf Bultmann is dependent upon Heidegger, and despite that rather obscure philosophical background, revolutionized Biblical theology and Biblical interpretation after 1941, tends to point out the usefulness of and acceptability of an ontological theology in the twentieth century. While it may be granted that some parts of Tillich are difficult to read, it is also true that many other theologians who are not ontologically inclined are equally difficult to understand. The charge that Tillich's ontology per se makes him unavailable to modern men is not borne out by Tillich's popularity among students in American colleges and universities over several decades.

(2) If we do not reject out of hand this ontological, systematic approach, and read Tillich with an appreciative awareness, it may be that the doctrine of the multi-dimensional unity of life can help us to see the wonder and the tragedy of what it means to be a man. Once we allow such an approach we see that Tillich includes in his discussion of the Spiritual Presence all the salient features of the Pauline Doctrine:

The Spiritual Presence is God present to man. The Spirit comes (in traditional language) from God. The Spirit is pure grace. The experience of being grasped by the Spirit makes man whole and drives him to self-transcendence. It is an experience of healing, or salvation.

The marks of the Spirit are faith and love just as in Paul. The Spirit unites man to man and man to God. Under the impact of the Spirit a holy community is established. This holiness is not the result of the keeping of the law or of man's own good will or good works but is the result of being in-dwelt by the Spirit who in the Spirit of God, the ground of holiness. Thus, Tillich teaches a Spirit ethic or an ethic of love that is clearly true to Paul and to Luther.

Tillich's dependence upon Paul is clear on any reading of his doctrine of the Spirit. His system has used Paul's letter to the Corinthians (especially 1 Corinthians 1-3 and 12:13) as a guide in developing his doctrine of the Spirit. The concept of ecstasy is straight out of Paul. The idea of faith as a gift of the Spirit is Pauline. Tillich especially uses Paul's idea in Romans 8:26-27, that the Spirit helps us to pray, saying that every true prayer takes place under the impact of the New Being or the Spiritual Presence.

But the methodological and structural similarity of Paul and Paul Tillich is most clearly seen in Tillich's development of Paul's teaching about the Body of Christ. Of course, Paul was not a philosopher, but in his use of the common Stoic concept of *Soma*, Paul grounded his Spirit-Christology in ontology. Some commentators have felt that Paul's use of the *Soma* concept has meant that he has passed from speaking of the risen Christ and the work of the Spirit in metaphorical terms to ontological usage. George Johnston said, "Such a conception is on the verge of passing beyond the stage of metaphor, if it has not yet done so."[210]

Tillich is faithful in developing the doctrine of the Spiritual Presence on the basis of the Pauline teaching; faithful to what Paul himself said, and to the implications of what Paul has written. Paul's passage in Romans 12:4-13 (4-5,11) could be straight out of Tillich's description of the Christian life lived under the impact of the Spirit: "For as in one body we have many members, and all the members do not have the same function, so we, though many, are one body in Christ, and individually members one of another ... Never flag in zeal, be aglow with the Spirit, serve the Lord."

---

[210]George Johnston, *The Doctrine of the Church in the New Testament* (Cambridge: Cambridge University Press, 1943) p. 90.

3

THE HERMENEUTIC OF PAUL TILLICH

Introduction: What Is Hermeneutic?

The traditional term "hermeneutics" has been defined as "the art and science of interpreting ... authoritative writings ... [1] However, in the mid-twentieth century the art and science of interpretation has grown into a much more complex undertaking than the determination of principles of exegesis and practice in the "art" of applying them to the authoritative documents of Christian theology. This conception of the place of interpretation in theology arose out of the influence of Heidegger in philosophy and the problems that came upon the theological scene with the advent of Bultmann's method of demythologization. The interest in the problems of interpretation was so completely different from the older attempts at the establishment of principles of interpretation that a new term was coined to name it. The modern hermeneutical undertaking, which began in 1954, with the publication of *Hermeneutik* by Ernst Fuchs,[2] has been widely designated as *hermeneutic* (in the singular), a direct transliteration of the German term *Hermeneutik*. This difference in name is continued in the discussion of the movement by James M. Robinson and John B. Cobb, Jr., entitled *The New Hermeneutic*.[3] The selection of a singular noun for the name of

---

[1]Dagobert D. Runes (ed.), *Dictionary of Philosophy* (Paterson, New Jersey: Littlefield, Adams & Co., 1962), p. 126.

[2]Ernst Fuchs, *Hermeneutik* (Bad Cannstatt: R. Millerscttön, 1954).

[3]James M. Robinson and John B. Cobb, Jr., *The New Hermeneutic*. New Frontiers in Theology Vol. II (New York: Harper & Row, 1964).

this method of interpretation may seem to be a small detail to include in an introduction to the meaning of hermeneutic, but it is actually highly significant for an understanding of the modern movement in theological interpretation. The term 'hermeneutic" is derived from the words of Heidegger who defends the use of the singular in such names as "logic" and "ethic," as well as "hermeneutic," on the grounds that such terms are adjectives in the original Greek that modify the unexpressed noun *episteme* or knowledge.[4] In all events, when Gerhard Ebeling's German works[5] and the works of Ernst Fuchs[6] were translated into English, the translators elected to use the singular form of the English equivalent of *Hermeneutik*, and the translator's practice has been adopted by most English-speaking theologians. The presence of the singular noun "hermeneutic" in a title today readily identifies the content of the book or article in question as being in the post-Heidegger, post-Bultmann tradition.[7] We might sum up the approach of the New Hermeneutic, as opposed to the older conception of the discipline, by speaking of the "ontological turn in hermeneutic ...," which means that the newer approach has abandoned the search for a special art or method of interpretation and now "makes the theory of understanding into a central philosophical problematic."[8]

Heinrich Ott in his article, "Language and Understanding,"[9] declared that he considered the problem of hermeneutic the most important question in contemporary theology. According to Ott, this problem does not involve the necessity of a theologian's election of some position for or against the hermeneutic of another theologian, but the recognition of the fact that a theological position concerning interpretation "does not actually yet exist."[10] Thus Ott concludes that "the decisive issue that divides the theologians is whether or not one has grasped the hermeneutical problem *as such*, i.e., whether one has been sufficiently impressed by its inevitability."[11] Ott is referring, of

---

4Ibid., Preface, p. ix.

5Gerhard Ebeling, *Word and Faith* (Philadelphia: Fortress Press, 1964).

6Fuchs, *Hermeneutik*. Also Ernst Fuchs, *Zur Frage nach dem Historischen Jesus* (Tubingen: Mohr, 1960).

7Robinson and Cobb, *The New Hermeneutic*. See James M. Robinson's article, "Hermeneutic since Barth," pp. 1ff.

8Ibid., p. 77.

9Heinrich Ott, "Language and Understanding," *Union Seminary Quarterly Review*, XXI, No. 3 (March, 1966), p. 275.

10Ibid.

11Ibid.

course, to the concept of hermeneutic which sees the theory of understanding as itself the central philosophical (and theological) problem.

The New Hermeneutic

When we survey the theological literature lf the past half-century, we find that we have experienced a theological revolution that turns upon the problem of hermeneutic. The large number of books and articles published in Europe and America since 1954, make it apparent that hermeneutic is one of the most vital theological issues of the twentieth century.[12]

The works of Karl Barth, Emil Brunner, Rudolf Bultmann, Paul Tillich and especially the philosophy of Martin Heidegger, called forth a new and vital hermeneutical reflection in Germany and America. The most important source of the theological interest in hermeneutic was the so-called "New Hermeneutic" school of Ernst Fuchs and Gerhard Ebeling. These two men have established another way of looking at the problem of theological interpretation, based on the philosophy of Heidegger which considers existence as linguistic.[13]

James M. Robinson has written the most helpful introduction to this movement in hermeneutic in his essay, "Hermeneutic Since Barth": [14]

> It is a central recognition of the new hermeneutic that language itself says what is invisibly taking place in the life of a culture .... Language in the new hermeneutic is not viewed as an objectification behind which one must move in establishing the understanding of existence objectifying itself therein. It is indeed not man at all who is expressing himself in language, rather it is language itself that speaks ... "The basic thing about a text is not what the author intended to express in words by following up a given point of view, rather, basic is what wills fundamentally to show itself and have its say prior to or apart from any subjective intent ..."

> The subject matter of which language speaks is primarily being. It is men's very nature to harken to the call of being. "Man is actually this relation of cor-'respond'-ence, and only

---

[12]Robinson and Cobb, *The New Hermeneutic*, pp. 15-19.
[13]Ibid., p. 55.
[14]Ibid., pp. 1ff.

this." In this way language is located at the center of man's nature rather than being regarded primarily as an objectification of an otherwise authentic self-understanding. For man's nature is defined as linguistic, in that his role is to re-speak, to re-spond, to an-swer, the call of being.[15]

These quotations amply illustrate the "ontological turn" of reflection upon the problem of interpretation and also illustrate the influence of Martin Heidegger upon the discussion. It is Heidegger's influence that has caused the problem of *language* to come to the fore in continental theological thought. Under his influence the problem of hermeneutic becomes the asking of the question, "What is understanding?" and the related question, "How does a given text become intelligible?" These two questions are seen by the practitioners of the New Hermeneutic as practically identical.[16] Of course, we might observe that such a practical identification of "understanding" and the "intelligibility" of a text means that the New Hermeneutic practitioners limit "understanding" to its relationship to a given text. This conception of "understanding" does not include other forms of understanding such as those which function in science, mathematics and the every-day area of "common sense."

The New Hermeneutic school understands language as itself interpretation, not just the object of interpretation, for it sees the whole theological enterprise as a "movement of language, from the word of God attested in Scripture to the preached sermon in which God speaks anew.... "[17] The movement of language discussed by Ebeling and Fuchs is the action of translating scriptural texts by reference to what they call "the hermeneutical structures of man's existence." These hermeneutical structures include man's use of language (which is primary for the establishment of his *being* human) and man's sense of his historicity, which the European thinkers call man's "place in historic life."[18] We might understand man's "historicness" as the "place" where the text is to be put if it is to begin to speak to us, i.e., to be interpreted for us. This rather difficult concept has been put in homely terms by Fuchs who says, "Put a cat before a mouse and the cat gets into action and shows what a cat is."[19] Thus the New Hermeneutic, linguistically is

---

[15]Ibid., pp. 37, 46-47. They are here quoting Helmut Franz, "Das Wesen des Textes," *Zeitschrift für Theologie und Kirche*, LIX (1962), p. 190.

[16]Ott, "Language and Understanding," p. 276.

[17]Fuchs, *Zur Frage nach dem Historischen Jesus*.

[18]Robinson and Cobb, *The New Hermeneutic*, pp. 70ff.

[19]Ibid., pp. 53-54.

seen as a structure functioning in much the same way as ontology does in the hermeneutic tasks performed by Augustine, Thomas Aquinas, and in the twentieth century, by Paul Tillich.[20] On the other hand, there is something pragmatic, or empiricistic, about Fuchs' illustration that reveals Fuchs' essentially practical, non-metaphysical interests.

Gerhard Ebeling, in contrast to Fuchs, attempts to visualize the connection of his Heideggerian conception of language and the traditional concerns of ontology. Ebeling calls for further theological reflection upon the connection of theology and reality, calling the problem of theology and reality "the basic theological question."[21] In this regard, Ebeling declares that he does not accept the old proofs for God's existence which once provided the connection of theology and reality, claiming that the reality of God is known only by God's revelation to faith. However, Ebeling demands that theology take upon itself the ontological task in the terms of Barthian personalism. The result of such an ontological investigation, according to Ebeling, will be a concept of reality which is based not on an objectification of the structures of being but on man's historic encounter with God. Indeed, Ebeling holds that such an investigation will reveal that reality is best understood as linguistic rather than as being. Fuchs also agrees with much of this emphasis, often speaking of the word which proceeds all relations. Fuchs calls his ontologically-understood movement of language a "language event" (Sprachereignis), and Ebeling refers to his ontological language structure as a "word event" (Wortgeschehen).[22] This new approach to hermeneutic must be declared ontological in a basic sense because it assumes that "the subject matter of hermeneutic is the relation between the interpreter and the text he is studying.[23] We might conclude that for Fuchs and Ebeling the religious encounters which are spoken of in the theologies of Barth and Brunner have become the basis of a new kind of ontology, which tell us about the

---

[20]See Tillich, *Systematic Theology*, I, 19-20, "The Necessity of Ontology in Philosophy; also vol. II, "The Use of the Concept of Being in Systematic Theology," 10-12.

[21]"The New Testament and the Problem," by Ernst Fuchs, quoted in Robinson and Cobb, *The New Hermeneutic*, p. 141. Tillich gives a fuller ontology of subjectivity and linguisticality in I, 173: "According to Parmenides, the basic ontological structure is not being but the unity of being and the word ...." That is, the discovery of those conditions or presuppositions which are structurally basic to an understanding of the world. See Ebeling, *Word and Faith.*, pp. 199ff.

[22]Robinson and Cobb, *The New Hermeneutic* , p. 59.

[23]Ibid., p. 75.

genuine realities in which man is constituted as man. In other words, man is made man by his participation in the sphere of language, not by his exemplification of some structures of being. On this view revelation does not reveal something about being as such, but reveals something to man about the activity in which he is constantly engaged, the use of language. In the terms of the New Hermeneutic, revelation gives man a word to which he must respond in faith or unbelief. We must observe that it is difficult to understand just what Ebeling can mean by saying that reality is better understood as linguistic rather than as objective being. Basically, both Ebeling and Fuchs seem to believe that the only reality man knows he knows through the medium of language. Apparently these thinkers are willing to exchange the traditional categories of being, essence and existence for expressions of the linguistic modes in which man refers to ultimate reality and to existence. Both Fuchs and Ebeling desire to speak "ontologically," but their "linguistic ontology" appears to be incomplete, even truncated compared to that of Tillich.

The Radical Theology

On the other side of the theological spectrum from the New Hermeneutic school is the most radical expression of the modern sense of the problem of religious language and its interpretation, the Radical Theology, popularly known as the Death-of-God Theology. This movement is best exemplified by the works of William Hamilton[24] and Paul van Buren,[25] although it has its most extreme formulation in the

---

[24]William Hamilton, *The New Essence of Christianity* (New York: Association Press, 1961); Thomas J.J. Altizer and William Hamilton, *Radical Theology and the Death of God* (New York: Bobbs-Merrill Co., 1965). In this section we refer to the "Death of God" Theologians as "Radical Theologians" because of the connection given to the two titles in the United States by the book *Radical Theology and The Death of God*. We recognize that there are some British theologians who have also been designated as "radical theologians" (such as John A. T. Robinson), but are deliberately restricting the discussion of "Radical Theology" here to its American expression. See also John Charles Cooper *The Roots of the Radical Theology* (Phila.: Westminster Press, 1967) and *Radical Christianity and its Sources* (Philadelphia: Westminster Press, 1968). Altizer announced his "Death of God Theology" as a visitor to the joint seminar of Tillich and Eliade at the University of Chicago—a seminar for which I served as recording secretary for Tillich and Eliade in the Spring 1965 semester.

[25]Paul van Buren, *The Secular Meaning of the Gospel* (New York: Macmillian Co., 1963).

works of Thomas J. J. Altizer.[26] The background of this radical movement has been documented by the religious sociologist Gabriel Vahanian.[27]

Altizer took his graduate degrees at the University of Chicago in the field of History of Religions. His speciality is Eastern Religion with an emphasis on mysticism, but in later years he turned to the study of English literature, especially of William Blake. He spent much of his career at the State University of New York at Stoney Brook. He published *Oriental Mysticism and Biblical Eschatology, Mircea Eliade and The Dialectic of the Sacred,* and, in 1966, *The Gospel of Christian Atheism.* Altizer is the most famous of the so-called God-is-Dead theologians because of his unique style and flare for unusual statements. In his second book, he wrote, "we must recognize that the death of God is a historical event: God has died in our time, in our history, in our existence. Insofar as we live in our destiny, we can know neither a trace of God's presence nor an image of his reality."[28] In his 1966 work, Altizer wrote: "If there is one clear portal to the twentieth century, it is a passage through the death of God, the collapse of any meaning or reality lying beyond the newly discovered radical imminence of modern man, an imminence dissolving even the memory or the shadow of transcendence."[29]

Altizer clearly throws down a challenge to those theologians concerned with the problem of hermeneutic because the kind of self-understanding of man he represents denies the relevance of the authoritative documents of the Christian faith to the situation of modern man.

William Hamilton was a young Baptist theologian teaching at Colgate-Rochester Divinity School. Prior to his radical period, he produced several lay-oriented studies of the New Testament. His background is that of Neo-orthodoxy. While Altizer was influenced by Tillich and Eliade, Hamilton was influenced by the humanitarian emphasis of Albert Camus. This influence can to seen in Hamilton's emphasis upon Christ as an example for interpersonal relationships and his reduction of Christianity to Christ-like ethics. Most of Hamilton's

---

[26]Thomas J. J. Altizer, *The Gospels of Christian Atheism* (Philadelphia: Westminster Press, 1966). Also, *Mircea Eliade and the Dialectic of the Sacred* (Philadelphia: Westminster Press, 1963); and *Oriental Mysticism and Biblical Eschatology* (Philadelphia: Westminster Press, 1961).

[27]Gabriel Vahanian, *The Death of God* (New York: George Braziller, 1961).

[28]Altizer, *Mircea Eliade . . . .*, p. 13.

[29]Altizer, *The Gospel of Christian Atheism,* p. 22.

radical elements stem from his reading of the socially concerned French Existentialist, Albert Camus. Hamilton also reflects the influence of Jean-Paul Sartre.

Hamilton most fully expressed his views in his short work, *The New Essence of Christianity.*[30] In this work he holds that men no longer are able to accept belief in a transcendent deity or to believe in traditional theology. Thus the theologian must "reduce the area of belief and lay hold on those few things of which we can be certain." Those few things include our obligation to love one another and to recognize the tragic situation in which modern man finds himself. Hamilton agrees with Camus who once said that it is better to give a cup of milk to a child in need than to say a million Masses. Hamilton declares that the modern experience of the death of God now summons man to follow Jesus who was a "man for others" — a truly good man who lived only for the good he could do for other men.

Hamilton is also greatly influenced by the young Lutheran martyr and theologian, Dietrich Bonhoeffer, who was hanged by the Nazis for his opposition to Hitler. The influence of Bonhoeffer's "Religionless Christianity," combined with the search for social justice called for by Camus, explains Hamilton's reduction of Christianity to ethics and the honoring of the "historical Jesus." Hamilton changed his views several times and it is not clear whether he thinks that God is simply absent and will soon reappear or whether God never really "existed," or whether God somehow has "died."

The third member of the "Radical Theology" school, Paul van Buren, formerly taught at the Episcopal Seminary in Austin, Texas, but since publishing his book, *The Secular Meaning of the Gospel,* moved to Philadelphia's Temple University. Basically, van Buren is a modern language philosopher. In this book, he applied the techniques of philosophical analysis to the creeds of the church and to the New Testament. After doing this he concluded that any language about God as being alive or dead is meaningless." In this assessment, van Buren reveals his indifference to the development of Language Philosophy, for while the earlier linguistic analysis would have come to a similar conclusion, the newer Ordinary Language Philosophy might not. The Ordinary Language Philosophers would see theological language as perfectly meaningful among believers, while the earlier language philosophers would have judged theological language by standards appropriate only to the physical sciences. Van Buren says that once we understand that "God language" is symbolic we also see that nothing is

---

[30]Hamilton, *The New Essence of Christianity.*

left for us to believe or reject, when we analyze it by the means of Language Philosophy. This is no great loss, however, for the radical theologians say that modern men are quite able to "live without the God hypothesis." We modern men do not need God to meet our needs or solve our publems, for we have science to solve them for us.

Van Buren, like Hamilton, proceeds to reduce Christianity to admiration for the historical Jesus who was a kind, unselfish man, open to the problems of other men. We Christians today ought to follow Jesus' example, for in such loving conduct life could be far happier and richer than it is living by other standards.[31]

Assessment of the Radical Theologians

The God-is-Dead theologians have carried the logic of the position that what men say about God is purely and simply descriptive of man's own self-understanding (and a part, one might say, of a 'language-game"), expressed in purely symbolic language, to the inevitable extreme of denying that the "language of transcendence" has any referent whatsoever. Thus out of a sense of honesty, religious language must be dropped. Such a crisis over religious language differs considerably from the older theological discussion of the 1930's and 1940's. The older controversy about "God-language" consisted in the claim of the Biblical theologians, Barth and Brunner, that one can interpret the Scriptures in personal terms, because God has revealed himself in a person, Jesus Christ; while Tillich and Bultmann, denied that this was enough, but maintained that the personal categories of the Bible were mythological and symbolic. The situation in the late '60s was quite different, however. The New Hermeneutic school represents a shift toward the left in which Fuchs and Ebeling defend preaching from the Scriptures in personal and familiar (e.g., "family") terms because they believe man is made man just by his use of language. They then disclaim any need for a wider interpretation. To this poetic (and rather sentimental) position, Hamilton and van Buren reply that the theologian can speak only of things that are immediate in their reference and "God" is not a part of man's experience in the "God is dead" view. Hamilton and van Buren are concerned about how we are to speak in theology, too, and they decide to show an honesty and sincerity which admits that the theologian has very little (if any) more light to shed upon the troubles of the world than any one else.[32] Thus,

---

[31]Van Buren, *The Secular Meaning of the Gospel.*
[32]Hamilton, *The New Essence of Christianity*, p. 25.

the answer of the God-is-dead school to the problem of hermeneutic is to maintain that we can say nothing about God. This answer undercuts the debate over whether our God-language is literal or symbolic, reduces the area of what is believed, and lays a firm hold on "those few things which are certain." For Hamilton these few things boil down to a confession that Jesus is Lord and a call for a "style of life" (best seen in marriage) which will express genuine Christian values.[33]

The "God is dead" theology seems to be quite different from the New Hermeneutic, and yet both movements arise from a common background, the Bultmannian demythologizing attempt—carried to a radical extreme not desired by Bultmann himself.[34] Again, both movements are theological reactions provoked in some manner by the rise of modern Language Philosophy, or its Middle European ancestor, Logical Positivism. However, the most direct influence on Fuchs' and Ebeling's position is Bultmann's interpretation of the famous dicta of Heidegger that "Language is the house of being,"[35] rather than the "Language Philosophers." But if we couple these philosophical influences to the breakdown of the radically transcendent theology of Karl Barth and Neo-orthodoxy, against which Hamilton and van Buren are revolting, then the God-is-dead theology appears. Hamilton writes of the revival of transcendent theology in our time and cuttingly points out its short-comings. As in the History of Religions analysis, it would appear that the God who is defined as "too high" ultimately disappears (the *dei otiosi* phenomena).[36]

---

[33]Ibid., p. 30.

[34]See R. Bultmann, "New Testament and Mythology," in *Kerygma and Myth*, ed. Hans Werner Bartsch (Harper Torchbooks; New York: Harper & Bros., 1961), p. 43. Also Karl Jaspers and R. Bultmann, *Myth and Christianity* (New York: Noonday Press, 1962); and R. Bultmann, *Jesus Christ and Mythology* (New York: Chas. Scribner's Sons, 1958), esp. chap v, pp. 60ff. And yet Bultmann gives one the impression that the myth needs to be "eliminated." (See Bultmann, "New Testament ..., p. 10.)

[35]This phrase is from *Brief uber den "Humanismus,"* quoted in William J. Richardson, S. J., *Heidegger, Through Phenomenology to Thought* (Hague: Martinus Nizhoff, 1963), pp. 528, 535; cf. Pp. 629-633.

[36]Hamilton, *The New Essence of Christianity*, pp. 35ff. On this entire matter, see William Hamilton, "The Death of God Theology," *The Christian Scholar*, XLVIII, No. 1 (Spring, 1965), 27-48. For the *dei otiosi* phenomena, see Mircea Eliade, *The Sacred and the Profane* (Harper Torchbooks; New York: Harper & Bros., 1961). Also see John Charles Cooper, *Radical Christianity and Its Sources* (Philadelphia: Westminster Press, 1968).

Basic to both the New Hermeneutic and the God-is-dead theology is the preference of both for an existentialistic, phenomenological description of man's situation and his self-understanding.[37] Although we may speak of an "ontological turn" in hermeneutics, the New Hermeneutic school would restrict ontological interpretation to a discussion of man's linguisticality. On the other hand, William Hamilton would rule ontology out—along with any language about God, since he has decided to subscribe to "religionless" Christianity, in which there is to be no reference to God as the fulfiller of needs or solver of problems. Meanwhile, Paul van Buren would rule out both ontology and God-language as impossible, because of the modern, secular way of looking at things which does not take God into account. Basically, van Buren thinks of Christianity as being about man, and not about God. Altizer, on the other hand, has adopted Hegel's ontology, but he has modified it so that he is able to say once there was a God, but there is a God no longer as He annihilated Himself in the death of Jesus Christ.[38] Altizer declared that the death of God means the radical imminence of God in the world, especially in the body of humanity. Thus Altizer will not speak about God as the Ground of Being, but speaks of the Christ we can see in every human face.

Assessment of the New Situation in Hermeneutical Studies

It is clear from our investigation of the New Hermeneutic school of Ebeling and Fuchs, as well as from the comments of Heinrich Ott, that hermeneutic is indeed one of the major concerns of twentieth century theology. However, hermeneutic has shifted its content from the older conception of its role as the delineation of a set of doctrines or principles of interpretation to an understanding of itself as the methodological approach to the investigation of understanding per se as a philosophical problem.

Ott and the other exponents of the New Hermeneutic are saying that the phenomenon with which hermeneutic is concerned is that of translation. This is not the problem of translation of a foreign language

---

[37]Tillich, *BRSUR*, pp. 15ff. (Tillich's argument against Logical Positivism.) One clear connection between the two schools, New Hermenuetic and "God-is-dead," is the influence of Diefrich Bonhoeffer. His importance for Hamilton and van Buren is evident throughout their works, and his significance for Ebeling can be seen in *Word and Faith*, chap ix, pp. 282-287.

[38]Hamilton, "The Death of God Theology."

into one's own language, but of interpreting a historically conditioned thought (e.g., a Biblical idea) into another thought (e.g., a modern form of that idea, such as a "translation" into an existentialist vocabulary), which is supposed to be one and the same thought. This conception of hermeneutic means that the interpreter must constantly ask himself if he really understands the Biblical thought and does he really carry the thought over into its "modern" form. [39]

In this movement of the content and aim of hermeneutic as a theological science, we can discern the influence of twentieth century existentialism, both in its inspiration and development. In other words, the New Hermeneutic shift represents an acceptance of the existentialist ontology of Martin Heidegger which investigates the mystery of language and sees language as being somehow "the house of being." This shift of interest has been called an "ontological turn," and indeed it is a turn toward ontological concerns, although it is a kind of ontology quite different from that pursued by more traditional theologians or by the existentially influenced systematic theologian, Paul Tillich.

The so-called Radical Theology of Altizer, Hamilton, and van Buren apparently has no need for a hermeneutic, either ancient or modern. It would appear that the Radical Theology is willing to take its models from the secular life of the twentieth century and pattern its teachings upon the altruistic elements of modern society. Thus it would seem that the Radical Theology would have no need for a set of principles of interpretation of authoritative texts, or for an assessment of man's self-understanding in terms of language. On this view, the Radical Theology is the expression of such a self-understanding of man, patterned on man's technological and sociological advances rather than upon an investigation of man's language. This view of the Radical Theology seems tenable, but incorrect. A better view of the Radical Theology seems to be that the Radical Theology is no more able to establish itself without an ontology and a hermeneutic than any other kind of theology. Thus I see the Radical Theology of Hamilton and van Buren as implicitly, if not explicitly, expressing an ontology of naturalistic materialism that sees the ultimate principle of the universe as being matter in motion, from eternity, without beginning or end. In this materialistic ontology, consciousness, mentality and spirituality are incidents which have been produced by the motion and interaction of material phenomena, which therefore are transitory and have no lasting significance. Thus there in no need in such an ontology to suppose that life can only come from that which is living, or the personal can only

---

[39]Ott, "Language and Understanding," p. 281.

arise from that which in some sense is personal itself. Life arises as a happenstance of the eternal brute movements of a universe of matter, and cannot be considered as the "aim" of the universe's "history." Thus this ontology dictates the conclusion that there is no God. God is but a figment of the imagination of the fragile mind of man, a projection of man's inner wishes and hopes without ontological substance. Since Altizer speaks of the God who once was, but who died in Jesus' death on the cross, we do not imply that this ontology is his.

It is clear that Altizer does not wish to confess a materialistic ontology. Altizer says there once was a God but there is no longer — except for the "divinity" we see in Jesus which is identified with the forward moving process of human unity in the world. Even William Hamilton falters before the atheistic decision, and speaks of "waiting for God," although he is not very clear in expressing what he means by this statement. But regardless of the reservations of these theologians, a materialistic ontology is the background of a theology that declares that God is dead, even if the radical theologian does not consciously affirm such an ontology.

The hermeneutic of the God-is-dead school, on the other hand, shares much of the same material as the existentialist-oriented linguistic hermeneutic of Ebeling, Fuchs, and Ott. Basically, the God-is-dead theology is the expression of the radically new self-understanding of modern man. This self-understanding is more than modern man's sense of history and his recognition of the evolutionary development of the human race, of human social institutions and of philosophical and theological ideas. The self-understanding of the Radical Theology begins with the historical self-understanding that delimits a modern mind from the traditional mind sets of earlier eras, and builds on the historical self-understanding by recognizing man's potentiality for completely mastering the physical world — including outer space and other worlds beyond our own — through the application of the scientific and technological developments of the past 150 years. In other words the self-understanding of the Radical Theology is the self-understanding of the secular scientist or technician who believes in the possibility of human progress and is optimistic about the possibility of humanity overcoming all the problems (that are logically capable of a solution) that face the human race. It is this note of confidence, so like the philosophies of the nineteenth century, and so unlike the era of existentialism that undercut the foundations of the older liberal theology, that characterizes the Radical Theology. In Hamilton's words, the death-of-God theology represents a "new optimism."[40] Because of the liberal self-confidence that undergirds the Radical Theology, it must reject the ontologies and hermeneutic of other theological systems. Quite clearly the new theology must reject the hermeneutic of Paul Tillich, which is based upon an existentialist evaluation of the human condition that reveals humanity's need of "answers" drawn from the Christian tradition. Tillich certainly does use the answers of religion as "solutions of problems" in a way that can only be rejected by the death-of-God theologians.

Thus, it is at the basic level of the function of ontology in hermenutic that Tillich's systematic theology speaks to the problems raised by the radical movement in Christian thought. We now turn to a discussion of Tillich's attempt to demonstrate the need for ontology in hermeneutics.

Tillich's Demonstration of the Need for Ontology in Hermeneutic

Tillich's fundamental position with regard to the need for ontology in hermeneutic is clearly set forth in his *Systematic Theology*, where he declares: "Since knowing is an act which participates in being or, more precisely, in an 'ontic relation,' every analysis of the act of knowing must refer to an interpretation of being."[41] Accepting this epistemological principle, we suggest that unless our statements about the meaning of the New Testament message and of man's self-understanding have a *fundamentum in re*[42] which is recognized and made explicit—then our interpretations and proclamations will simply float in the air without any demonstrable rootage in any level of reality, either empirical (ontical) or ontological. "Free floating" in this way, our interpretations either are credited by us with some mystical validity ("life is linguistic"; "love guarantees itself") or they are subjected to arbitrary pragmatic tests that do not fit and cannot prove their validity or non-validity (e.g., "If there is a 'God, why does not he rule out evil?"). Once the ontological root of our theological statement is cut, it is to be expected that the extent and content of theology will wither, collapse and become smaller—as is the case in both the New

---

[40]William Hamilton, "The New Optimism from Prufrock to Ringo," *Union Seminary Quarterly Review*, XXI, No. 2, Part2 (January, 1966): 187-198.

[41]Tillich, *Systematic Theology*, I, 19.

[42]Cf. Sidney Hook (ed.), *Religious Experience and Truth* (New York: New York Univeristy Press, 1961), pp. 6-7. (Tillich on the establishment of the referent symbols.)

Hermeneutic and the God-is-dead theology. Unless there is at least one sense in which we can speak of God and of the things of our religious faith in non-symbolic, denotative ways, so that we can say, "This is an affirmative content-filled statement—this is what we mean by 'God,'" than the entire "superstructure" of theological and religious discourse is severed from any level of reality; and is, in sober fact, meaningless.[43] There must be a principle of limitation that "fixes" and establishes the justification of and the referent of that symbolic and mythological language we use about God, or else the stuff of theology is floating smog that hinders our seeing reality aright, instead of an aid to the meaning of life. If there is not an ontological basis for the symbolic language of religion, then the strong, cold wind of philosophic honesty should blow away "God-language." If the symbol "God" does not participate in any reality beyond the sphere of language, if it is completely symbolic, or only operational in the sphere of linguisticality, with no denotative referent outside the sphere of linguisticality whatsoever, then "God is dead."[44] We suggest that the reintroduction of the ontological dimension into both the hermeneutic and the systematic theological task by Paul Tillich [45]is the only method of making God-language meaningful for ourselves and for those we teach. In support of Tillich we submit that it is neither necessary nor desirable to give up what is, after all, the classical tradition in theology.

Tillich on Myth, Symbol, and Deliteralization

In order to discuss the hermeneutical principles at work in the theology of Paul Tillich, we must first investigate the kinds of presuppositions and methods which are used by Tillich in the establishment of his theological position. We will begin our

---

[43]See F. B. Dilley, "Theism and Metaphysical Proof," *Metaphysics and Religious Language* (New York: Columbia Univerity Press, 1964), p. 117.

[44]*The Collected Works of Nietzsche* (New York: Modern Library, 1937). It is of interest to me that G. F. Hegel first used the expression "God is dead" in *Philosophical Theology*, in the section "Revealed Religion," *Phenomenology of Mind*, trans. J.B. Baillie (New York: Macmillan, 1910), p. 762, where Hegel credits the phrase to one of Martin Luther's hymns.

[45]Tillich is not alone in demanding an ontological hermeneutic; ontology has been reintroduced into philosophy and theology generally by Charles Hartshorne and others following Alfred North Whitehead. See Tillich, *BRSUR*, pp. 16ff; and Tillich, *Systematic Theology*, I, 167, on the justification of process philosophy and its limitations.

investigation of Tillich's hermeneutic therefore with a discussion of Tillich's conception of myth, of symbols and of the problem of the demythologization of the scriptural text. In this study we must attend to Tillich's conception of religious language and symbolic language, and investigate his assessment of the role of myth in religious discourse. Finally, we will go on to investigate Tillich's actual interpretations of several key Christian doctrines such as Creation and the Christ. From the insights gained in this investigation, we shall attempt to specify the hermeneutical principles which are at work in Tillich's theology.

In speaking of the significance of a Biblical word or symbol for Paul Tillich's Systematic Theology, it is not enough merely to document what "doctrines" are presented in the Scriptures (e.g., in Saint Paul), and to document the fact that some such "doctrine" appears in the theology of Tillich. There are several reasons why such an approach is impossible. These include: (1) the obvious fact that nineteen and a half centuries separate Paul, the Apostle, and Tillich, the philosophical theologian; (2) Tillich's own statement that he is a self-conscious philosopher (ontologist) as well an an apologetic theologian, whereas Paul is not; and (3) the theological insight that Tillich is deliberately retranslating the symbols of the "eternal message" of the church into forms that are claimed to be more "available" — because more relevant and intellectually respectable — to the people of our day.

The last difference between Tillich and Saint Paul is perhaps the most important consideration for our study of Tillich's hermeneutic. Tillich's retranslation is taking place in his system on several levels. On the deepest ontological level, the retranslation takes place by means of Tillich's identification of several important Biblical symbols (e.g., the Fall, sin, the Christ) with an ontological explanation of human existence. The retranslation also is involved in Tillich's conscious "deliteralizing" (not precisely the same as demythologizing) of the ancient Christian symbols (e.g., Salvation and Resurrection).

The above considerations therefore make it *ipso facto* impossible to identify the Tillichian presentation in a comparative manner with the Biblical presentation. Such a comparison would be a mistake because it would be based on the assumption that there is but a simple "borrowing" going on that is understandable (in Tillich's system) in Biblical terms — point for point — without remainder.

This consideration leads us to an awareness of the importance of a knowledge of Tillich's hermeneutical principles for the precise understanding of what he means by his use of a Biblical or traditional symbol. Only if we have such an understanding of his hermeneutic can Tillich be understood correctly, for it is precisely in this way that he wants to be understood.[46] A theology of "recital"[47] without reference to the changed situation of mankind is not what Tillich conceives to be the task of the systematic theologian. This means that many factors external to the text must be taken into account in positing his rules of interpretation.

Because of the differences between Saint Paul and Paul Tillich, and because of the necessity of a thorough knowledge of Tillich's hermeneutical principles, we must discuss the following areas by way of prolegomena before attempting to identify Tillich's hermeneutical principles: (1) Tillich's conception of myth and symbol; (2) Tillich's conception of the role of myth in religious discourse; (3) Tillich's technique of "deliteralization," as distinct from Bultmann's program of "demythologization"; and (4) Tillich's view of the relationship of the historical events of the Biblical accounts to the Christian "eternal-message" which elicits our faith-response.

In order to identify and establish Tillich's hermeneutical principles, we will use his treatment of the myth of Creation and Fall and the Christ-myth as illustrations. A major question throughout this investigation will be "How does 'ontologizing' 'deliteralize' a myth, in Tillich's view?"

For Tillich, the symbol is the basic language-term of religion and the myth is the proper form of religious language in conveying human apprehensions of the Divine depths of life. One cannot have religion without myth, and to completely demythologize religion—if such a process was possible—would be destructive of the value of Scripture and make religious speech impossible. As Tillich expresses himself in *Systematic Theology*, Volume II:

> This is the problem of the systematic knowledge of God. If God as the ground of being infinitely transcends everything that is, two consequences follow: First, whatever one knows about a finite thing one knows about God, because it is rooted in him as its ground; second, anything one knows about a finite thing cannot be applied to God, because he is, as has been said,

---

[46]*Ibid.*, Preface, II, viii. "... I cannot accept criticism as valuable which merely insinuates that I have surrendered the substance of the Christian message because I have used a terminology which consciously deviates from the biblical or ecclesiastical language. Without such a deviation, I would not have deemed it worthwhile to develop a theological system for our period."

[47]George Ernest Wright, *God Who Acts: Biblical Theology as Recital* ("Studies in Biblical Theology," No. 8; Chicago: Alec R. Allenson, Inc., 1952).

"quite other" or, as could be said, "ecstatically transcendent." The unity of these two divergent consequences is the analogous or symbolic knowledge of God. A religious symbol uses the material of ordinary experience in speaking of God, but in such a way that the ordinary meaning of the material used is both affirmed and denied. Every religious *symbol* negates itself in its literal meaning, but it affirms itself in its self-transcending meaning. It is not a sign pointing to something with which it has no inner relationship. It represents the power and meaning of what is symbolized through participation. The symbol participates in the reality which is symbolized. Therefore, one should never say "only a symbol." This is to confuse symbol with sign. Thus it follows that everything religion has to say about God including his qualities, actions, and manifestations, has a symbolic character and that the meaning of "God" is completely missed if one takes the symbolic language literally.[48]

Tillich goes on to state that the only point at which a non-symbolic statement about God can be made is this: "The statement that everything we say about God is symbolic."[49] Of course, we may speak of man's ultimate concern, of man's quest for God, in nonsymbolic terms, such as saying that God is infinite, the Unconditional, or Being Itself. But even in these abstract terms there is a mixture of the symbolic (ecstatic) and the non-symbolic (rational), i.e., these terms form the boundary line at which the symbolic and the non-symbolic modes of speech converge.[50] In recent years, however, Tillich has moved to the position of saying that there is and must be one non-symbolic statement about God, i.e., that God to Being Itself.[51] Approaching the problem

---

[48]Tillich, *Systematic Theology*, Intorduction, II, p. 9.
[49]Ibid.
[50]Ibid., p. 10. Tillich has written in *Symbol and Wirklichkeit*, (Gottingen; Vandenhoeck and Ruprecht, 1962), p. 1. (Translated excerpts are my own.) "The Meaning and Justification of Symbols": "Religious symbols need no justification when their meaning is grasped. For their meaning is that they are the language of religion, the only language in which religion can immediately express itself. Concerning religion one can also make assertions in philosophical or theological concepts, or one can seek to comprehend religion in artistic pictures (representations). But the religion itself can express itself only in Symbols or in complexes of symbols, which we call myths if they are joined together into a unity."
[51]Kegley and Bretall, *The Theology of Tillich.*, p. 335.

from another side, the psychological, Tillich speaks of man's ultimate concern in terms of man's quest for God.[52]

"Man's ultimate concern must be expressed symbolically, because symbolic language alone is able to express the ultimate."[53]

Tillich goes on to explain how he uses the term "Symbol." Symbols have one characteristic in common with signs; they point beyond themselves to something else. However, a sign may be replaced quite arbitrarily as it represents only a "convention" in human communication. This replacement is impossible in the case of a symbol because:

The symbol participates in the reality in which it points. E.g., the flag participates in the power and dignity of the nation for which it stands. An attack on the flag is an attack on the group who acknowledges that flag.[54]

But more than this, the symbol opens up levels of reality which otherwise are closed for us. E,g., a "picture and a poem reveal elements of reality which cannot be approached scientifically."[55] And correlative with this: the symbol also opens up dimensions and elements of our soul which correspond to the dimensions and elements of reality. E.g., "A great play . . . opens up hidden depths of our own being. Thus we are able to receive what the play reveals to us in reality."[56]

Symbols cannot be produced intentionally — they grow out of the collective unconsciousness and cannot function without being accepted by the unconscious dimension of our being.[57]
And it follows from this that:
As symbols cannot be invented, then like living beings, they grow old and die. They grow (appear) when the situation (the *kairos*, the proper moment), is ripe for them, and they die (disappear) when the situation changes. But this "death" is not brought on by scientific criticism. The symbol dies when it can

---

[52]Tillich, *Systematic Theology,* I, pp. 204ff.
[53]Tillich, *Dynamics of Faith,* pp. 41-54.
[54]Ibid., p. 42.
[55]Ibid.
[56]Ibid., p. 43.
[57]Ibid.

no longer produce its response in the group where it originally found expression.[58]

Why cannot man's religious concerns be expressed directly, but only in symbols? Tillich's answer is that everything which is a matter of ultimate concern is capable of being made into a god. This is true of the nation, of money and of success. In this way concepts designating ordinary realities become idolatrous symbols of ultimate concern.[59] Concepts, e.g., that of the "nation," are transformed into symbols because of the nature of faith, which is characterized by ultimacy. But, "that which is the true ultimate transcends the realm of finite reality infinitely."[60] Thus no finite reality can express the ultimate directly, and, whatever we say about God must be symbolic, because that which we say points beyond itself while participating in that pointed-to reality. Therefore, Tillich demands that we never say, "only a symbol,"[61] for that reveals an attitude that confuses a symbol with a sign. For Tillich, religious belief can only come to expression in symbols, for only the symbol can express the ultimacy and the transcendence implied in religious faith.

The Role of Myth in Religious Language

Symbols do not occur in isolation, however, but united together in "stories of the gods," or *mythos* – the Greek term from which the English word "myth" is derived. Essentially, Tillich agrees with Bultmann in describing the myth as a story of the divine expressed in terms of this world—"speaking of the other side in terms of this side" [62]—yet, Tillich's emphasis is somewhat different. He writes: "This is the world of the myth . . . *man's ultimate concern symbolized in divine figures and*

---

[58]Ibid. Cf. Martin Heidegger, *Being and Time*, trans. J. MacQuarrie and Edward Robinson (New York: Harper, 1962), pp. 52ff.

[59]Tillich, *Dynamics of Faith*, p. 44.

[60]Ibid.

[61]Ibid., p. 45.

[62]Bultmann, *Kerygma and Myth*, pp. 10-11, especially, footnote on page 10: "Myth is an expression of man's conviction that the origin and purpose of the world in which he lives are to be sought not within it but beyond it." Also see John Charles Cooper, "Mythology and Religion," *Discourse*, VII, No. 2 (Spring, 1964): 129-139.

and actions. Myths are symbols of faith combined in stories about divine-human encounters."[63]

Tillich explains that the myth is present in every act of faith because faith's language is the symbol. This is the case because the myth is but a system of related symbols (a "story of the gods"), woven together out of the materials of our every-day experiences. Myths put the Divine into the framework of time and space (although the ultimate is beyond time and space), and divide the Divine into several figures (or gods), removing ultimacy from each of them but without removing the claim of each god to ultimacy.

Tillich tells us that each great religion contains a criticism of myth within itself, drawing this criticism from the above mentioned nature of myth itself. Thus myths are undergoing a continual critique, one mark of which is the rejection of the "division of the divine into 'gods' and the movement toward monotheism." But the criticism doesn't stop there, for monotheism, too, needs "demythologization."[64] Whenever monotheism adopts a personal, anthromorphic way of speaking about God, then that convention must be criticized also.

Tillich's Conception of "Deliteralization"

Tillich, characteristically, both affirms and denies that which is represented by Bultmann's program of "demythologization." As Tillich's program identifies all the stories of divine-human interactions in the Bible as mythological, Bultmann's program must be affirmed, for he points out the necessity of recognizing a symbol as a symbol and myth as a myth. But this program must denied if it attempts to remove the symbols and myths altogether. Tillich says that the attempt to remove all myth (if it were ever made) would be a failure, as symbol and myth are "forms of the human consciousness," always present in every age. It is only possible to replace one myth by another; it is not possible to remove the myth from man's spiritual life.[65] The attempt to remove all symbolic speech about God from religion in the "Death-of-God" theology has thus provoked Tillich's rejection of this new development of radical theological thought.[66]

We must observe here that what Tillich means by "deliteralization" is precisely what he affirms in demythologizing — the specification and

---

[63]Tillich, *Dynamics of Faith*, p. 49. (My italics.)
[64]Ibid., p. 51.
[65]Ibid., p. 50.
[66]Ibid.

identification of various figures and events in the Bible as symbols, and the description of various narratives in the Bible as mythological. Once one has pointed out the symbolic and mythological nature of these Biblical elements, he has "deliteralized." The person who does this, therefore, now understands a myth as a myth and, thus, for him, the myth is "broken."[67] It is "broken," but not discarded, which is the element of denial in Tillich's assessment of "demythologizing."[68]

Tillich claims that Christianity, by its very nature, denies any unbroken myth, because of the meaning of the First Commandment: "The affirmation of the ultimate as ultimate and the rejection of any kind of idolatry."[69] In this assessment, Tillich is right. Tillich concludes:

> All mythological elements in the Bible ... should be recognized as mythological, but they should be maintained in their symbolic form and not be replaced by scientific substitutes. For there is no substitute for the use of symbols and myths: they are the language of faith.[70]

In the *Theology of Culture*,[71] Tillich discusses the nature of religious language, particularly the nature of religious symbols.[72] He writes:

> Religious symbols do exactly the same thing as all symbols do—namely, they open up a level of reality, which otherwise is not opened at all, which is hidden. We can call this the depth dimension of reality itself. The dimension of reality which is the ground of every other dimension and every other depth, and which therefore, is not one level besides the others but is the

---

[67]Tillich goes on to discuss "literalism," the attitude which takes the myth in its immediate meaning, and distinguishes two stages of it—the natural or primitive (society) or childlike (individual) which is justified; and the conscious stage, in which men's doubts about myth are repressed by ecclesiastical and/or political power. This forcible repression is not justifiable, for it may break a mature mind in its personal center, splitting its unity and hurting its integrity. *Ibid.*, pp. 52-53. (Bultmann has no desire to discard myth, but wishes to "interpret" it also.)

[68]Ibid., p. 51. See Bultmann, *Jesus Christ and Mythology*, p. 18.

[69]Tillich, *Dynamics of Faith*. Tillich defines "breaking the myth" as "by making *conscious* [my italics] its symbolic character," on the same page, 51.

[70]Tillich, *Theology of Culture*, pp. 53-67.

[71]Ibid., pp. 58ff.

[72]Ibid., p. P. 59.

fundamental level, the level below all other levels, the level of being itself, or the ultimate power of being. . . .

The dimension of ultimate reality is the dimension of the Holy.[73]

Symbols, drawn from the material world around us, can function in this way because "everything that is in the world we encounter rests on the ultimate ground of being."[74] Everything in reality can impress itself as a symbol for a special relationship of the human mind to its own ultimate ground and meaning.[75] Tillich points out that this possibility of everything in the world functioning as a symbol has the concomitant danger of demonization. That is, since a symbol participates in the reality (the "Holy") to which it points, although not itself being the "Holy," the human mind has the tendency to replace the Holy with the symbol—thus becoming idolatrous. Idolatry is nothing else than such an absolutizing of symbols of the Holy.[76]

Quite germane to this discussion of Tillich's conception of how myth and symbol ought to be handled in theology is his identification of the levels of religious symbols.[77] There are two basic levels in the religious symbol, the transcendent level, which goes beyond the content of the physical, empirical reality we encounter, and the imminent level, which we find within our physical encounter with reality.

Tillich tells us that within the transcendent level, of which the basic symbol is God himself, there is a duality of meaning: There is a non-symbolic element in our image of God—that he is the Ground of Being, Ultimate Reality; and there is a highly symbolic element in that we say he is the highest and most perfect being. Although the term Being-Itself is *not* symbolic,[78] to speak of God in personal language *is* symbolic— although it is altogether necessary to speak of God in this way—else we

---

73Ibid.
74Ibid.
75Ibid., p. 60.
76Ibid., pp. 61ff.
77Ibid., p. 61. Tillich also analyzes symbols into "integrative" and "disintegrative" symbols, see Paul Tillich, "Symbols and Knowledge," *Journal of Liberal Religion*, II, No. 4 (Spring, 1941), pp. 202-206. See Hook, *Religious Experience and Truth*, pp. 5-6.
78This position explains why Tillich rejects the ontological argument for God's "existence." See *ibid.*, pp. 15-16. See the article by Norman Malcolm in Alvin Plantinga (ed.), *The Ontological Argument* (Garden City, NY: Doubleday Anchor Books, 1965), pp. 136-171.

could not pray to him. As Tillich says, "He who is the Ground and Source of personality is not less than personal."[79]

Tillich goes on to point out that the attributes of God, such as love, mercy, etc., are symbolic—being taken from our own experiences. This is also true of our speaking of the acts of God, such as "he has sent His son." This is obviously symbolic language, for if taken literally it becomes absurd.[80] God is beyond all temporality, and does not move from place to place in space, nor is he subject to causality. This symbolic mode of speech must be pointed out for: "If the Incarnation is taken symbolically, it is a profound expression, the ultimate Christian expression, of the relationship between God and man in the Christian experience.[81] But taken literally, the concept of Incarnation is an absurdity, and is rightly rejected.

Perhaps the most difficult problem involved in Tillich's discussion of the symbols used in religious discourse is found just here in connection with his understanding of levels of meaning in religious symbols. The transcendent level of the symbol, which expresses the connection of symbols in the Divine to the non-symbolic element in man's conception of God (that is, that God is Ultimate Reality or Being-Itself), is much clearer than Tillich's discussion of the immanent level of the symbol. Basically, the immanent level in a religious symbol, according to Tillich, is the level which we find within our encounters with reality. These encounters with the Divine on the imminent level involve the many scriptural reports of theophanies or manifestations of the Divine under the conditions of existence in time and space. On this level would be placed the evaluation of Jesus Christ as the Incarnation of God. Tillich is especially polemical against Christian theologians who seem to consider the concept of the Incarnation as a uniquely Christian insight or doctrine.[82] Tillich equates the concept of Incarnation in Christianity with the mythological stories of the Greek and the Hindu religions that speak of various gods assuming the shape of animals or man in order to fulfill their purposes. Quite clearly Tillich is not inclined to accept a traditional idea of the Incarnation of Christ. As we shall see later in this chapter, Tillich describes Christ as a "bearer of the New Being," that is, as one who is open to the unconditioned Ground of Being, not as one who "incarnates" the Divine in himself. For Tillich, the Christ is the Christ just because he self-empties himself in such a manner that men

---

[79]Tillich, *Theology of Culture*, p. 63.
[80]Ibid.
[81]Ibid.
[82]Ibid.

may see through him to the Unconditioned which lays its claim upon human life.

In connection with Tillich's discussion of the imminent level in the religious symbol, he deals with the primitive doctrine of "Mana, " the belief that a mystical power permeates all reality. This doctrine he sees as more than the idea of Incarnation, because it is a belief that the Divine is present imminently in everything as a hidden power and yet is not confined to the imminent level, but transcends it so that it is very difficult to know and can be grasped only through sacramental symbols or rituals.

In Tillich's symbolic interpretation of the Christ, Jesus Christ is interpreted sacramentally. In this view, Jesus is seen as a human being, a part of concrete reality that has become the bearer of the holy in a unique way under special circumstances. Basically, God is everywhere and present to everything, but he is not known because of the estrangement of the human personality under the conditions of existence. However, in Christ (and in other sacramental realities such as the Lord's Supper) the Holy or the unconditioned Ground of Being is made known because the Christ and the sacramental elements are negated (that is, emptied of their surface, phenomenal, sense-content) and the unconditioned Ground of Being is allowed to "shine through." In all these cases, that which is the reality to which the symbol, including the Christ, points is the unconditioned Ground of Being (primitively referred to as "Mana"), and hence everything but this unconditioned ground is a symbol. Thus if we were asked if "Being-Itself" is a symbol, we would have to say, "No, it is not, although the words are symbols." That to which we refer as the ultimate reality (God) is not a symbol, although everything else we say about God: that he is a person, that he has attributes, that he acts, that he becomes Incarnate, that he is present in sacraments, etc., is all symbolic. In Tillich's view, any other belief than this leads us into idolatry, for in any other approach we seek to absolutize some segment of concrete reality such as "personality" or "activity" and refer to it as God. Tillich's interpretation of the Commandment forbidding images means for him that only that which transcends every concrete expression as the creative ground of all that exists can be worshipped as God.

Summary

In our discussion of Tillich's approach to the problems of the presence of myth and symbols in our religious tradition, we have seen that Tillich believes that the very nature of Christian faith demands that we recognize myth as the proper form of religious language. Myths come into being as systematically developed linguistic constructs of basic religious insights based on experiences with power-bearing elements and events called symbols. The symbol is the basic element of religion because a symbol functions in two ways. First of all, it is concrete and has existential warmth, as in the case of a being or a piece of bread; and secondly, it points beyond itself to that which transcends it ultimately, because that transcendent quality is the creative ground out of which it arose. The symbol points to this creative ground by the process of negating its own particularity and peculiarities. This is most clearly seen in the events of the life of Jesus called the Christ, in that Jesus humbled himself and emptied himself of all that was personal in order to allow Ultimate Reality to "shine through" his death on the Cross. This function of symbols and symbolic acts is made possible because if God is the Ground of Being, then we have an ambiguous and yet disturbing experience when we face any concrete thing. First, since God is the Ultimate Reality, anything we know about this concrete thing we know about God also. But secondly, since God is not the concrete thing and transcends it as the quality of ultimacy out of which it has come, then whatever we know about this concrete thing we cannot say we know directly about God. However, this situation does not leave us at an impasse, but by the very disturbing nature of the symbol we sense that it points beyond itself—since it is not grounded in itself—to the Unconditioned—which is to say, to God. It follows from this insight that in every discussion of the Divine our religious language will be formed by reference to symbols and hence be "symbolic," although not completely symbolic since the basis of our symbolic speech is grounded in the one nonsymbolic element in our idea of God, that is, that God is the Ultimate Reality.

We may well ask what is the relationship between "Word-symbols" and "entity-symbols" in Tillich's theory of symbols? How are events and persons, bread and wine related to the symbolic terms that are used to refer to them? It is quite clear that theological doctrines are "word-symbols, " and that Tillich's Christology, for example, is constructed of word-symbols, although Jesus himself is an entity-symbol, different from the words used to speak of him.

Tillich has not really made the distinction between "Word-symbols" and "Entity-symbols" very clear. His entire discussion of symbols has a resultant vagueness, particularly in reference to the "word-symbol." Tillich's discussion of "entity-symbols" seems to be better developed, although the relationship of the entity (e.g., a flag) to that which it "points to" (e.g., a nation) is not discussed beyond the point of referring to the participation of the "entity-symbol" in its "referent," by mention of the "entity-symbol's" power of arousing a response in the historical group in whose midst that symbol arose and lives.

Perhaps Tillich developed the "entity-symbol" element in his theory of symbols more fully than he did the "word-symbol" element because of his pan-sacramental sense. Tillich's pan-sacramentalism, which sees the possibility of any entity becoming a sacrament, a bearer of the holy, is developed in his essay, "Nature and Sacrament."[83] Tillich's pan-sacramentalism, is, of course, a part of his "belief-ful realism, " which seeks the power and meaning of nature within and through its objective physical structures. Tillich's fondness for the concrete symbol, for the entity-symbol as over against the description of the entity-symbol (e.g., Christ) in word-symbols might also explain his frequent reference to the "picture" of Jesus as the Christ which is mediated by the New Testament. Bernard Martin[84] has criticized Tillich's discussion of the "picture" of Jesus as the Christ as being a very selective and a highly personal reading of the New Testament sources.[85] Perhaps the constant reference to "picture," is a kind of concretization of the word-symbols used in the Gospels to describe the event of the Christ, indicates Tillich's deep interest in art, the realm of entity-symbols. However, Tillich is aware of the danger of idolatry in the use of concrete symbols, and clearly warns that only that which transcends every concrete expression can be worshipped as God.

In "Nature and Sacrament," Tillich asserts that words can be understood as having the natural power to be the bearer of the power of meaning (i.e., the holy). This realistic interpretation of "words" is affirmed by Tillich, who declares that words have "... a power through which they can become bearers of a transcendent power ..."[86] But in the last analysis, we must observe that while the materials for a definite description of the relationship between the "word-symbol" and the "entity-symbol" are present in Tillich's works, Tillich never develops this important point. We might suggest that the relationship of "word-symbol" and "entity-symbol" lies in the fact that both "word" (understood as a natural phenomenon) and "entity" are elements of finite reality which, however, have the natural power to become the bearers of meaning and the capacity to point beyond themselves to the

---

[83]Tillich, "Nature and Sacrament," *The Protestant Era*, pp. 94-112.

[84]Bernard Martin, *The Existential Theology of Paul Tillich* (New York: Bookman Association, 1963.)

[85]Ibid., p. 178.

[86]Tillich, *The Protestant Era*, pp. 98-99.

Ultimate Reality. On this level, "word" and "entity" are equal in power and in religious utility. However, the word-symbol is more flexible and also deeply influential upon man because language is the realm in which man develops his capacities and his culture—of which man's theology is a part. The word-symbol, then, which functions as a "first order" symbol in its own right, i.e., bears the power of meaning, also becomes in time, a second-order" symbol. The "second-order" symbol describes the "entity-symbol" (i.e., Jesus) which is more subject to the ravages of time than the "word-symbol" which is cast into myth-sequences and/or formed into sacred Scriptures and continues to exercise its power through milleniums of human history. Thus, it is the "word-symbol" and its patterns of organization, the myths, that the modern theologian must deal with in his attempt to deliteralize man's relationship to the holy.

Tillich's conception of man's knowledge of God and the quality of religious language naturally demands that Christian theology undertake a continuous critique of its mythological and symbolic elements. Not to be continually critical of the mythological heritage of Christian faith is to be always in danger of idolatry because of the danger of an easy acceptance of a crude literalism. Thus something like a program of "demythologization" is inherent in the systematic theological task, and is vital to the hermeneutical efforts of theologians and Christian preachers. In this inner critique of myth, Tillich warns the theologian against the false idea that all myth can be removed, for such a situation is not possible, as modern men can only speak of God symbolically in the same way that the Biblical writers employed symbols and myths to record their messages. What Tillich calls for in this situation is a program of "deliteralization" in which Christian believers are led to see that the myths of the Bible are precisely that, myths. Once the believer has been brought to this level, then the myth is "broken" for him and the truth of that myth may still be retained in a symbolic form. Of course, Tillich does not leave the "broken myth" simply as myth. For Tillich, the truth of the myth resides in its ontological affirmation. Tillich takes up the"broken-myth" and attempts to indicate its ontological aspects and develops a modern application of the myth through the use of existentialist terms. We shall discuss Tillich's "reinterpretation" of the "broken myths" later in this chapter.

It is not possible to substitute some other form of language for the symbol in the language of faith. Nor is it possible to avoid the task of deliteralization, for if we try to avoid it, we very likely will fall into idolatry, which Tillich defines as absolutizing, that is, taking literally, symbols of the Holy. Thus it is both as a protest against religious idolatry as well as a protest against literalistic obscurantism, that Tillich undertakes the hermeneutic task of deliteralizing the myths and symbols of the Scriptures and of the Christian tradition.

The Problem of the Relationship of the Historical Events Underlying the Biblical Narratives to the Christian "Eternal Message" which Elicits a Faith-Response

One example of the problem of the relationship between the historical events recorded in the Bible, and the Christian message to which we are asked to respond in faith, is the problem of the relationship of "the Historical Jesus" and "the Kerygmatic Christ." This is the problem to be discussed here. In this discussion, the term "the Historical Jesus" will refer to the man named who was born in Palestine at the beginning of the present era, and who taught various things about the Kingdom of God and man's relationship to God. The term "the Kerygmatic Christ" used in this study refers to the message about Jesus which was proclaimed by the Apostles and recorded by the New Testament writers and which has continued to be proclaimed in various ways by the Church throughout the centuries. "The Kerygmatic Christ" emerges from the process of theological reflection and out of the religious beliefs of Christians, on the basis of their study of the New Testament text. The New Testament certainly presents the "Kergymatic Christ," because the Jesus who is presented in the Synoptic Gospels, and especially in the Fourth Gospel, is a picture of Jesus plus the response of faith of the one making the record. Thus "The Kerygmatic Christ" is the "figure" who arises from the New Testament text and in the context of a proclamation that says, in effect, "This man Jesus is the Christ of God" — whether or not this statement is actually made explicit or not.

What is the relationship between the "Historical Jesus," i.e., the man Jesus of Nazareth who lived about 4 B.C. – 29 A.D., and his words and works and "the Kerygmatic Christ" (of faith) who is proclaimed by the Apostles and the Christian Church down through the centuries, for Paul Tillich? Tillich accepts the value of and the need for historical criticism of the Biblical text,[87] therefore, the question arises, what happens to

---

[87]Tillich, *Systematic Theology*, II, p. 107.

faith when historical research reveals that "there is no picture (of Jesus) behind the Biblical one which could be made scientifically probable?"[88]

Tillich is clear in his answer to this question: We do not hold as the object of faith "the historical Jesus," but the "Kerygamatic Christ"-- the proclaimed Christ of faith—the same answer given by his teacher, Martin Kähler.[89]

As Tillich remarked:

> There are two things which have made Kähler important to a host of pupils, including myself. One was his profound insight into the problem of the historical Jesus in the light of the scholarly research into the sources. . . .
>
> I do not believe that Kähler's answer to the question of the historical Jesus is sufficient for our situation today, especially in view of the problem of demythologization and the ensuing discussions. But I do believe that one emphasis in Kähler's answer is decisive for our present situation namely, the necessity to make the certainty of faith independent of the unavoidable incertitudes of historical research.[90]

It is not only a religious interest that motivates Tillich "to make the certainty of faith independent of the ... incertitudes of historical research," but a systematic interest as well. For while religious devotion ("ultimate concern") must have a stable object of faith,[91] it is equally true that one cannot construct a systematic theology of the Christian message if he doesn't have the center pier of his construction securely "fastened down." If the criterion of every revelation is itself unclear, then we have no operative criterion at all. A Christian theology without a firm and clear position on Christ is impossible. Tillich believed that he must free his central affirmation about Jesus as the Christ as the Bearer of the New Being from the relativities of historical research. As he wrote in *Systematic Theology*, Volume II, concerning the possibility of a "Life of Jesus":

---

[88]Ibid., p. 101ff.

[89]Ibid., p. 101. See Martin Kähler, *The So-Called Historical Jesus and the Historic Biblical Christ*, trans. Carl E. Braaten (Philadelphia: Fortress Press, 1964).

[90]Ibid., pp. xi-xii.

[91]Tillich, *Systematic Theology*, II, p. 107. See also p. 100.

... none can claim to be a probable picture which is the result of the tremendous toil dedicated to this task for two hundred years. At best, they are more or less probable results, able to be the basis neither of an acceptance nor of a rejection of the Christian faith.[92]

However, Tillich also writes:

The term "historical Jesus" is also used to mean that the event "Jesus as the Christ" has a factual element. The term in this sense raises the question of faith and not the question of historical research. If the factual element in the Christian event were denied, the foundation of Christianity would be denied. Methodological skepticism about the work of historical research does not deny this element. Faith cannot even guarantee the name "Jesus" in respect to him who was the Christ.[93] It must leave that to the incertitudes of our historical knowledge. But faith does guarantee the factual transformation of reality in that personal life which the New Testament expresses in its picture of Jesus as the Christ.[94]

This brings us squarely before the question as to how Tillich interprets two of the great "myths" of the Bible, the Creation-Fall story and the accounts of Jesus the Christ which appear in the New Testament. What does Tillich mean by a "factual transformation of reality in a personal life?" Is this an ontological "explanation" of Christ? Or is it a "remythologization"? Or both?

An Analysis of Tillich's Hermeneutic

Principles of Tillich's Interpretation of the Myth of Creation-Fall

In the beginning God created the heavens and the earth (Genesis 1:1).
So when the woman saw that the tree was good for food, and a delight to the eyes, and that the tree was to be desired to

---

[92]Ibid., pp. 102-103.
[93]Ibid., p. 107.
[94]Ibid.

make one wise, she took of the fruit and ate; and she also gave some to her husband, and he ate. Then the eyes of both were opened ... (Genesis 3:6-7a).

In *Symbol and Wirklichkeit*, Tillich discusses his view of the relationship of "Existential Analysis and Religious Symbols,"[95] which is operative in his treatment of the myth of the Creation-Fall.[96] "Nothing finite, nothing partial—that is only a part of the whole of finite relations—can be meant by the religious symbol, and therefore it cannot be established through the empirical-inductive method."[97]

This is pre-eminently true of the symbol "creation"! And yet, Tillich, like Heidegger,[98] begins his existential analysis with an analysis of man. Tillich does so because he feels that "every thought, even the most abstract, must have a basis in our real existence."[99] Moreover, "because the analysis of the existential structures is an analysis of the human situation, then the distinction between existential and essential analysis is clearest with regard to teaching about man ..." But one might ask, "What is the 'Being' of man? ... What makes him into that which he is, which in any form deserves the name, 'man'? ..." Existential philosophy poses the question about the specific difference between mankind and non-human nature. If it answers this question by saying that man is a rational animal, it could be said that this definition is not specific enough or that the essence of rationality is not sufficiently defined. However, the method in itself is correct and unequivocally existentialistic. In opposition to the attitude of essentialistic philosophy, existentialistic analysis has pointed out the concrete situation of man, and its starting point is the immediate consciousness of man of his situation. Therefore existential analysis speaks of finitude, which can be grasped only in direct awareness within the situation itself.[100]

Here we have the clue to how Tillich interprets the myth of the Creation-Fall. Tillich quite simply says that the story of the Creation is a

---

[95]Tillich, *Symbol and Wirklichkeit*, pp. 7ff. What follows in the text is the author's "translation" of Tillich's German work. Tillich discusses "God as Creating" in *Systematic Theology*, I, pp. 252-270.

[96]We use the expression "Creation-Fall," since the two "events" coincide in Tillich's system (*ibid.*, II, p. 44).

[97]Tillich, *Symbol and Wirklichkeit*, p. 7. This author's translation.

[98]Heidegger, p. 67. Heidegger analyzes "Dasein"—the being of human being.

[99]Paul Tillich, *On the Boundary* (New York: Chas. Scribner's Sons, 1966), inside front cover.

[100]Tillich, *Symbol and Wirklichkeit*, p. 16.

myth and must be accepted as such. Then it is "broken" as far as it can ever be—for how would we reinterpret it? The only way Tillich believes it possible to "reinterpret" the Creation-myth, is to describe it in ontological categories (and the fall of man—Dasein—in "existential Existentialia").[101] Tillich might well have had "Creation" in mind when he wrote that "Religious symbols have no basis either in the empirical order or in the cultural order of meaning. Strictly speaking they have no basis at all. In the language of religion, they are an object of faith."[102]

Truly, the "thing" referred to in the mythical symbol of "creation" is the activity of the unconditioned transcendent—the Ground of Being—the source of both existence and meaning, which transcends being-in-itself as well as being-for-us,[103] and yet is "known" to man through its activity in making it possible for creatures to become actualized. Man is able to pose a question about the activity of the unconditioned which is "answered" by the Creation/Fall according to Tillich, because there is a unity of thought and being. Man is "being come to consciousness of itself"—a creature come to "self-consciousness"—which is aware of the conditions that structure its life. Tillich apparently means that to hold a belief in the Creation-myth is to have a particular world-view and personal commitment. Thus in this basic myth, as in all others, Tillich can say: "in every myth a view of God and a view of the world are bound together."[104] We must seek in Tillich's interpretation of the Creation-myth his own view of God and of the world. We shall find it to be an ontological view (and thus, an ontological hermeneutic).

Tillich considers the philosophical category of "existence, " rather than the Biblical symbol of "creation," first in his theology. For Tillich, to exist means to "stand out," to have being, to "stand out of nothingness."[105] But everything that exists "stands in" non-being as well as "out" of it, so that things are both "in" and "out" of the state of non-being. This is existence. Anything which exists has left the state of mere potentiality (the power of being-not-yet realized) and has become actual. Existence is therefore finitude, the unity of being and non-being.

---

[101]Heidegger, *Being and Time*, p. 33.

[102]Paul Tillich, "The Religious Symbol," *The Journal of Liberal Religion*, II, No. 1 (Summer, 1940), p. 15.

[103]Ibid., p. 26

[104]Paul Tillich, "Myth and Mythology," trans. J. C. Cooper, *Die Religion in Geschichte und Gegenwart: Handworterbuch für Theologie und Religionswissenschaft* (2nd. Ed.; Tubingen: Mohn, 1930), IV, 363-370, esp. 360.

[105]Tillich, *Systematic Theology*, II, 20.

Existence, therefore, implies a split in reality between potentiality and actuality—and by reason of this split, "man's existence is judged as a fall from what he essentially is."[106]

This is a thorough-going "ontologizing" of the Creation-myth. Tillich has interpreted Genesis 1-3 in terms of philosophy's identification of the basic structures of Being, i.e., these structural elements which must be present in every experience as the necessary precondition of any experience. For Tillich, God is the "abyss of being" or Being-Itself (Greek: το ον). God is Being which eternally resists non-being (Greek: μη ον), limited non-being (not ουκ ον absolute nothingness). As such, God, who is also called "the power of being to resist non-being," (in reference to Plato in the Sophist, 247), is the answer to the problem which man experiences as his anxiety over the threat of non-being. As Being-Itself is basically what God is, He can only be spoken of symbolically. Man's creation, then, lies in the transition of man from essence (potentiality) to existence (actuality) which causes man to "stand out" of being, so that man "exists." However, this standing out from the essential realm (in which man still stands—in virtue of his remembrance of it)[107] is concomitently a fall, for by becoming actual (existing) man "falls away" from what he essentially is.[108] Thus Creation and Fall occur simultaneously; "the Fall" being a mythological symbol for the human situation universally.[109] Tillich speaks of this phrase "transition from essence to existence" as "a half-way demythologization" of the fall-myth.[110] It is still somewhat mythological because the word "transition" contains a temporal element, and speaking of the divine in temporal terms is still mythological. Tillich defends his half-way demythologization by saying, "Complete demythologization is not possible when speaking about the divine."[111]

Tillich partly-demythologizes the myth in Genesis 1-3, developing his interpretation in four parts, under the title, "Finite Freedom as the Possibility of the Transition from Essence to Existence."[112] He tells us that, in his view, Genesis 1-3, is "the profoundest expression of man's

---

106Ibid., p. 22.
107Ibid., note the correlation of this "remembrance" with the Socratic epistemology in the Meno. (*Great Dialogues of Plato*, trans. W.H.D. Rouse [New York: Mentor Books, 1956], p. 50, para. 85C.)
108Tillich, *Systematic Theology*, II, 22.
109Ibid., p. 29.
110Ibid.
111Ibid.
112Ibid., pp. 31-44.

awareness of his existential estrangement."[113] Let us see what principles Tillich uses in his "half-way demythologization" of the Fall myth.

The Possibility of the Fall

In Tillich's view, the Fall is possible because man has freedom, yet, man is at the same time, finite. Man's freedom points him towards the infinite (God), but his finitude, represented in Tillich's ontological analysis by the polar element, destiny, holds him in bondage to the concrete situation. In Tillich's terms "our destiny is that out of which our decisions arise," which includes the concreteness of our being, our psychic strivings, spiritual character, our community and environment, and all our past decisions. "It is my self as given, formed by nature, history, and myself."[114] Man's freedom is a finite freedom according to Tillich because he has freedom only in polar interdependence with his destiny. Man experiences himself as free only within the larger structures, such as the world, his environment and the several communities to which he belongs. The term "destiny," as used by Tillich, points to this human situation of finite freedom, in which man finds himself standing over against the world to which at the same time he belongs. The world, however, is not the Infinite, nor is it "God." Thus the Infinite transcends the polar-tension of self and world.

One of Tillich's most difficult expressions is the sentence that reads "... man is finite, excluded from the infinity to which he belongs."[115] In this expression Tillich implies that man is at the same time related to the Infinite or the unconditioned and yet is separated from it. How is this possible? It is possible because man, though free, has only finite freedom, that is, freedom within the scope of the larger elements that make up his destiny, perhaps symbolized in the fact of his individuality which is his concreteness, and which illustrates his singularity and limitations. But God, the Infinite, has infinite freedom. God is not limited by concretion. God's freedom is his destiny, whereas man has freedom only in polar interdependence with destiny. God is beyond all polar tensions, transcending every polarity, as the depths which lie behind every finite relation, including the world itself.

Man's freedom is seen in his language. He is able to participate in the philosophic "universals" that lie behind the categories of human speech and reason, and to ask questions about the world he encounters,

---

[113]Ibid., p. 31.
[114]Ibid., I, 184-185.
[115]Ibid., II, 31.

and to penetrate deeper and deeper into reality. Man is free because he can deliberate and decide. Man is so free that he can even contradict his freedom and surrender his humanity. This contradiction of man's freedom is precisely what is involved in the Fall. And yet, man has a destiny which limits his freedom—thus his freedom is finite.

Tillich denies that man's freedom "to fall away from God" by self-contradiction is a weakness or a questionable divine gift. He declares that "the freedom of turning away from God is a quality of the structure of freedom as such. The possibility of the Fall is dependent on all the qualities of human freedom taken in their unity.... Only he who is the image of God has the power of separating himself from God."[116]

Tillich observes that the freedom to fall away from God consists in man's total structure as an individual person, and he identifies this structure as the traditional "image of God." Man's greatness is thus also his weakness. The freedom to fall is necessary if man is to be man, for if man lacked this freedom he would only be a thing unable to respond affirmatively or negatively to God.

The Motives of the Fall:
Dreaming Innocence and Temptation

Tillich declares that the essential stage ("before the Fall") is not an actual stage of human development although it is present, in existential distortion, in all stages of human development.[117] Tillich "deliteralizes" this "before the Fall," calling it the state of "dreaming-innocence." It is a state of potentiality, not actuality. It has no place and no time. It is suprahistorical.[118] Man was "then" innocent because of his non-actualized potentiality, in that he lacked experience, lacked personal responsibility and lacked moral guilt.[119] Tillich is careful to state that both terms, "innocent" and "responsible," are used here analogically.[120] This state is not perfection, and therefore temptation is unavoidable. If one asks what drives him on to actuality, the answer is anxiety. In man, freedom is united with anxiety, in that man is aware of his finitude, aware that nonbeing is mixed with his being. This anxiety drives man on to realization. The myth of the Fall includes the Divine prohibition not to eat the fruit of a tree. This is the most important point

---

[116]Ibid., pp. 32-33.
[117]Ibid.
[118]Ibid.
[119]Ibid., pp. 33-34.
[120]Ibid.

in interpreting the Fall because it discloses a split between the Creator and the created.[121] "Sin," or the state of man's actualization, is thus the consciousness of the estrangement, the alienation of man from God, and of man from man. "Adam" or "man" used his finite freedom to contradict his essential being and so "disobeyed God." The "command to obey God" (the "moral imperative") is the power of man's own being, the demand to essentialize what he potentially is.[122] The moral act called for here is not an act in obedience to an external law but the inner law of our own being. When man "received this command" his freedom was "aroused."[123] A tension occurred in the moment when finite-freedom became conscious of itself. And man in his freedom decided for actualization. This ended man's dreaming innocence.[124] Certainly, we must observe that Tillich's analysis of "what is going on" in the myth of the Fall is just as symbolic as the original story. Tillich has, at best, only "half-way" demythologized the "pre-Fall" state of man.

The difficulties which Tillich's "half-way" demythologization[125] of the Fall brings up cannot be overlooked. On a common sense basis, it appears that man must already exist to hear a command and to make a moral choice on the basis of the freedom "aroused" by that command. Therefore, it follows — on this basis — that the reception of the command to obey God which results in "The Fall" cannot be identical with man's appearance as an existing entity.

A reading of Tillich's discussion of "The Transition from Essence to Existence and the Symbol of the 'Fall'"[126] does not reveal any clear-cut answer to the problem raised here on the basis of common sense. However, Tillich appears to have guarded his interpretation against problems of this nature, by clearly calling "The Fall" "a symbol for the human situation universally."[127] Probably most to the point of this problem, Tillich says (in agreement with Plato) that "existence is not a

---

121Ibid., p. 35.

122Tillich, *Morality and Beyond*, p. 20. "... a moral act is not an act of obedience to an external law, human or divine. It is the inner law of our true being, of our essential or created nature, which demands that we actualize what follows from it. And an antimoral act is not the transgression of one or several precisely circumscribed commands, but an act that contradicts the self-realization of the person and drives toward disintegration."

123Tillich, *Systematic Theology*, II, 35.

124Ibid., p. 36.

125Ibid., p. 29,

126Ibid.

127Ibid.

matter of essential necessity but is a fact,"[128]and declares that existence is not a logical implication of essence. Therefore, we might conclude that Tillich escapes the logical absurdity that would result from a "common sense" understanding of his interpretation; because he makes no claim to have offered anything but a half-mythical description of the human condition. The story of the Fall, whether told by Tillich or by the writer of Genesis 3, remains a myth and is not properly the object of "common sense" questions that *assume that the story of the Fall is in some sense literal enough to bear such questions as the above* which suggest a "Pre-Fall type of existence." Admittedly, such common sense questions often incorporate philosophically important points, and the fact that this question is not answered is a limitation of Tillich's system. Tillich's basic answer to the question raised above is not a "common sense" answer, but refers to man's "pre-Fall" state as one of "dreaming innocence."[129] In Tillich's ontological view, "The transition from essence to existence is not an event in time and space but the transhistorical quality of all events in time and space." To raise "common-sense" questions about "the sequence of events" in such a transition is to miss the meaning of Tillich's interpretation.

A final insight into this problem is available by way of an appreciation of the influence of Heidegger's thought on Tillich's theology. For Heidegger man is his freedom, so there is little point in discussing man apart from the exercise of his freedom. Tillich apparently is following this line of reasoning in reference to the Creation-Fall. Tillich, however, is speaking of man ontologically, essentially, and not of man ontically or existentially. For Tillich the problem of how man's ontic existence arises out of a transition from essence to existence is solved in the doctrine of the multidimensionality of all life. Only where the psychological dimension has appeared within the organic dimension (itself dependent upon the inorganic dimension) is the appearance of spirit and of freedom possible. It is therefore pointless to speak of "man" before he "bears the spirit" or exercises freedom. Only the creature who bears the spirit and exercises freedom is a man.

The Event Itself

The transition from essence to existence is the original fact. It is not the first fact in the temporal sense or a fact beside or before others, but it

---

[128]Ibid.
[129]Ibid., pp. 33ff.

is that which gives validity to every fact. It is the actual in every fact. We do exist and our world with us. This is the original fact.[130]

Tillich thus describes "the Creation-Fall" in Volume II. In Volume I. he expresses the "original fact" in this way:

> Man does exist, and his existence is different from his essence. Man and the rest of reality are not only "inside" of the divine life but also outside" it. Man has left the ground in order to "stand upon" himself, to be actually what he essentially is, in order to be finite-freedom. This is the point at which the doctrine of the creation and fall join.... Fully developed creatureliness is fallen creatureliness. The creature has actualized its freedom insofar as it is outside the creative ground of the divine life....

> "Inside" and "outside" are spatial symbols, but what they say is not spatial.... To be outside the divine life means to stand in actualized freedom in an existence which is no longer united with essence. Seen from the one side this is the end of creation. Seen from the other side this is the beginning of the fall.[131]

Thus creation and fall are the "original fact" that is "actual" in every fact that occurs in the world. This "fact" ontologically precedes everything that happens in time and space.[132] According to Tillich, the transition of essence to existence takes place in all three modes of time: past, present and future.[133]

In Tillich's view, Genesis 3, although derived from the special cultural and social situation of the Hebrews, has a claim to universal validity.[134] Tillich declares that this universal claim is not based on any psychological or ethical grounds, but on a "cosmic myth" which can be discerned behind the text.[135] Just what Tillich means by a "cosmic myth" is unclear, although he seems to think of it as a kind of "archetype," like those archetypical images of the "race consciousness" spoken of by the psychiatrist, Jung.

---

[130]Ibid., p. 36.

[131]Ibid., I, 255ff. It is interesting to note that Reinhold Niebuhr quotes this passage in order to try to refute it in his essay "Biblical Thought and Ontological Speculation," *The Theology of Paul Tillich*, p. 219.

[132]Tillich, *Systematic Theology*, II, 36.

[133]Ibid., p. 37.

[134]Ibid.

[135]Ibid.

The serpent represents the dynamic trends of nature; there is the magical character of the two trees, the rise of sexual consciousness, the curse over the heredity of Adam, the body of woman, the animals and the land.

The cosmic myth reappears in the Bible in the form of the struggle of the divine with the demonic powers and the powers of chaos and darkness.[136]

This cosmic myth underscores the cosmic character of the fall. In Tillich's view, however, it is Plato's myth of the transcendent fall of the souls that is the most consistent description of the Fall's cosmic quality. Such a cosmic view recognizes that *existence cannot be derived from within existence* — existence has a universal dimension.[137] Though Plato's myth of the transcendent fall is not in the Bible, Tillich declares it does not contradict the Bible. Tillich does not elaborate on the principles of Hermeneutics by which he compared Plato's myth and the myths of the Bible. He simply pronounces the two sources "compatible."

As to the "doctrine of original sin," which is based on the cosmic myth in Genesis, Tillich holds that theology must join humanism in rejecting the negative, pessimistic attitude toward man that a literalistic view of this "original sin" may inspire. Theology must protect man's created goodness, while re-interpreting the doctrine of original sin by showing man's existential self-estrangement and by using the existentialist analysis of the human predicament. Original sin must be replaced by a realistic "description of the interpenetration of the moral and the tragic elements in the human situation."[138] Tillich holds that Christianity must "simultaneously acknowledge the tragic universality of estrangement and man's personal responsibility for it."[139]

Tillich does offer some idea as to the basis on which he deliteralizes the myth of Creation-Fall. He identifies this basis as the existential analysis[140] of modern philosophy, and the empirical[141] observations of analytic psychology and analytic sociology.[142]

---

[136]Ibid.
[137]Ibid.
[138]Ibid., pp. 38-39.
[139]Ibid., p. 39.
[140]Ibid.
[141]Ibid.
[142]Ibid.

The Consequences of the Fall

All forms of the Fall-myth hold that man himself makes the decision which earns the divine curse. Tillich argues from this evidence that "Only through man can transition from essence to existence occur."[143] "Man is responsible for the transition from essence to existence because he has finite freedom and because all dimensions of reality are united in him."[144] Here Tillich is invoking the doctrine of the multidimensionality of all life—which meets in man—who includes within himself the dimensions of the inorganic, the organic, the psychological and the spiritual.[145] And yet, for Tillich, the universe is included in man's fallenness chiefly because of the tragic element in life, which grows out of the fact that man's freedom is imbedded in universal destiny.[146] Tillich thus decides to adopt the concept of a "fallen world," later explaining this concept by appeals to the unconscious (to man's psychological powers) as well as to biological and sociological powers at work in man as part of nature. "The universe works through us as part of the universe."[147] ". . . nature participates in every act of human freedom (through man's drives and influences). It represents the side of destiny in the act of freedom."[148]

Finally, Tillich faces the question, "Is sin made ontologically necessary instead of a matter of personal responsibility and guilt, by this process of 'deliteralization and ontologizing?'" (Indeed, Reinhold Niebuhr does accuse Tillich of having made sin ontologically necessary.)[149] Tillich attempts to answer this problem by declaring that:

> ... There is a point where creation and fall coincide, [150]in spite of their logical difference.... Creation and Fall coincide in so far as there is no point in time or space in which created goodness was actualized and had existence.... Actualized creation and estranged existence are identical.... Creation is good in its

---

[143]Ibid.

[144]Ibid., p. 40.

[145]Ibid., III, 17-21.

[146]Ibid., II, 40-41.

[147]Ibid., p. 42.

[148]Ibid., p. 43. It is of note to me -- with my interest in Saint Paul—that Tillich refers to Paul in Romans 8 to underscore his belief that nature participates in "the Fall."

[149]Kegley and Bretall, *The Theology of Paul Tillich*, pp. 220-224.

[150]Tillich, *Systematic Theology*, II, 44.

essential character. If actualized, it falls into universal estrangement through freedom and destiny.

However, sin is not a rational necessity, the original fact of the transition from essence to existence has the character of a leap, and not of structural (ontological) necessity. "Existence cannot be derived from essence."[151]

Summary

Our discussion of Tillich's interpretation of the myth of Creation-Fall has illustrated his hermeneutical approach to the Bible in showing that Tillich begins his interpretation by giving an existential analysis of man and the conditions under which man lives. Additionally, we have seen Tillich's application of his views concerning the mythological character of much of the Biblical literature to the myth of Creation-Fall. Tillich declares that the Fall took place in no period of history or "prehistory," but refers to an essential stage of human development which is present in a distorted way in all the actual or existential stages of human experience. In other words, the Fall refers to the actual state present in man at every actual moment of time.[152] The myth of Creation-Fall took place in no separate space or time, but takes place within every moment of space and time in developing human beings.

The combination of Tillich's existential analysis of man, joined with his discussion of the relationship of man to the unconditioned creative ground out of which man lives, and his program of deliteralization of the Scriptural myths, produces a philosophical interpretation of the Fall. Tillich asks, under the control of these basic presuppositions, "What drives man on to actuality?" and answers this question with the typical existentialist answer, "anxiety." For Tillich, man has freedom united with anxiety, and Tillich sees man's efforts to rid himself of this anxiety as being the motivations and actions that culminate in man's state of fallenness.

The above description of Tillich's method of Scriptural interpretation points up one of the most unique and interesting features of Tillich's treatment of the myth of Creation-Fall. For Tillich, Creation and Fall are aspects *of one thing*, which did not take place at some "moment" before history, but which are the "one original fact" which symbolizes man's actuality. Thus Creation and Fall as the original fact of man's actuality

---

[151]The preceding direct quotes from ibid., p. 44.
[152]Ibid., pp. 40-41.

are present in every fact and event that takes place on the existential level of human life. As Tillich would say, "The transition from essence to existence takes place in all three modes of time: past, present and future." Man is continually being "created" and is constantly "falling" at every moment of space-time.

In conclusion, Tillich's interpretation of the myth of Creation-Fall has sought to make the Biblical myth understandable to modern, educated individuals, to bring out its rather sophisticated psychological insights, and at the same time, acknowledge the universality of human estrangement on the one hand., and man's personal responsibility for it on the other. In this deliteralization and interpretation, Tillich has used the existential analysis of modern philosophy, and made use of the detailed information which modern man has gained from psychology and the other behavioral sciences.

Jesus as the Christ: Tillich's Interpretation of Christology[153]

In Tillich's apologetic theology, with its use of the method of correlation of the questions raised by philosophy on the basis of human experience, and of answers drawn from the eternal message of Christianity,[154] Jesus as the Christ, the Bearer of the New Being, is the answer to the questions and problems raised by existence, estrangement, alienation, and sin.[155]

Existence and the Christ

Tillich's hermeneutical approach is given by his discussion of an incisive insight into Christ within the section of Part III of the *Systematic Theology* that deals with existence. Clearly, Tillich is going to give an

---

[153]Paul says in Romans 4:22-25; 5:1-2, 6: "... that is why his faith was 'reckoned to him as righteousness.' ...;" "It will be reckoned to us (also) who believe in him that raised from the dead Jesus our Lord, who was put to death for our trespasses and raised for our justification;" and "Therefore, since we are justified by faith, we have peace with God through our Lord Jesus Christ. Through him we have obtained access to this grace in which we stand .... While we were yet helpless, at the right time Christ died for the ungodly ...."

[154]Tillich, *Systematic Theology*, I, 64ff.

[155]Ibid., II, 98ff.

ontological interpretation of the meaning of the Christ.[156] He discusses the meaning of Christ as the Bearer of the New Being in his relationship to God, man and the universe. He specifically states that his assessment is "the result of an existential interpretation of both pre-Christian ideas and their criticism and fulfillment in Jesus as the Christ."[157]

Tillich first develops his view of Christ under the rubric of Mediator. "Mediating" means "Bridging the infinite gap between the infinite and the finite, the unconditional and the conditioned."[158] Christ is to represent God to man (not *vice versa)* and show man what God wants man to be. The Christ shows what man essentially is; thus the Christ is essential God-manhood. However, Tillich says specifically that to designate the divine presence in essential manhood is redundant. For this reason Tillich prefers the phrase, "essential manhood" to refer to Christ.[159] Tillich is very precise in saying that the Christ is not a third ontological reality beside God and man. Rather the Christ represents the original image of God embodied in man, under the conditions of existence,i.e., estrangement.[160]

Incarnation Understood as Paradox

Under the rubric of "paradox," Tillich discusses the term "incarnation." Incarnation, such a favorite term with Catholic and orthodox Protestants and with neo-Orthodox theologians, is not one of Tillich's favorite words. He feels that it must be closely guarded if used in religious and theological language. Tillich states that if we say "God has become man," we are not speaking paradoxically, but nonsensically. "God" points to Ultimate Reality, and the one thing "God" cannot do is to cease being "God." Therefore, Tillich maintains,"it is preferable to speak of a divine being which has become man and to refer to the terms 'Son of God' or the 'Spiritual Man' or the 'Man from Above,' as they are used in Biblical language."[161] Even these Biblical designations are dangerous because of the polytheistic background of the ideas of "divine beings," and, indeed, of Incarnation itself. Such ideas are characteristic of paganism, not of Christianity.

156Ibid., pp. 93ff. All of Tillich's discussion of Christ is in connection with Tillich's teaching on Paradox.

157Ibid., p. 93.

158Ibid.

159Ibid., p. 34.

160Ibid.

161Ibid.

Tillich offers a "modifying interpretation" of "Incarnation" in the use of the Johannine "Logos."[162] Tillich will accept the phrase the "Logos became flesh," interpreting it to mean that the Logos is the principle of the divine self-manifestation in God as well as in the universe, in nature as well as in history. "Flesh," for him, does not mean a material substance but stands for historical existence. *"'Became' points to the paradox of God participating in that which did not receive him and in that which is estranged from him."*[163] Tillich claims that this is not a myth of "transmutation" but the assertion that "God is manifest in a personal life-process as a saving participant in the human predicament."[164] According to Tillich, the term "Incarnation" can be used to express the Christian paradox only if qualified in this way. But even this qualified use of the term is so subject to superstitious misunderstanding that it is unwise to employ it at all.[165]

Tillich goes on to observe that because of modern man's understanding of the immensity of the universe, which knowledge is superimposed upon the Biblical claim of the cosmic dimensions of the Messiah, it is necessary to understand the bearer of the New Being as one who is to save not only individual men, but to transform man's historical existence and to renew the universe. Therefore, the only answer to problems like these is to state the meaning of the Christian belief in terms of *"the concept of essential man, appearing in a personal life under the conditions of existential estrangement."*[166] This restricts the expectation of the Christ to historical mankind.[167] The Christ is to be seen as the central event of human history, creating the meaning of history, as he is the manifestation of the eternal relation of God to man.[168]

162Ibid., p. 95.
163Ibid. (My italics.)
164Ibid.
165Ibid.
166Ibid. (My italics.) Note the answer Tillich gives here to the "cosmic" dimensions of the Christ, i.e., Christ is limited to "historical mankind," in contrast to Teilhard de Chardin in *The Future of Man* (New York: Harper & Row, 1964).
167Tillich, *Systematic Theology*, II, 95.
168Ibid., p. 96. Note that this is an ontological interpretation of the Christ not an "incarnational" interpretation. Christ is the "manifestation of the eternal relation between God and man," and not "God become man."

Jesus as the Christ[169]

In Tillich's interpretation, Christianity is based on two sides to one event; the fact which is called "Jesus of Nazareth" and the reception of this fact by those who received him as the Christ.[170] "Christianity was born, not with the birth of the man who is called 'Jesus,' but in the moment in which one of his followers was driven to say, 'Thou art the Christ.'"[171] And yet, "the moment of the disciples' acceptance of Jesus as the Christ is also the moment of his rejection by the powers of history. This gives the story its tremendous symbolic power. He who is the Christ, has to die for his acceptance of the title Christ.'"[172]

For Tillich, this is the simplest report or representation of the Gospel, the statement that the man Jesus is the Christ. This "Jesus as the Christ" is both a historical fact and a subject of believing reception.[173] The "fact" asserts that Essential God-Manhood (Tillich uses capital letters) has appeared within existence and subjected itself to the conditions of existence without being conquered by them.

If there were no personal life in which existential estrangement has been overcome, the New Being would have remained a quest and an expectation, and would not be a reality in time and space. Only if existence is conquered in one point—a personal life, representing existence as a whole—is it conquered in principle, which means "in beginning and in power."[174]

On the other hand, the believing reception of Jesus as the Christ, calls for equal emphasis.Without this reception the Christ would not have been the Christ, namely, the manifestation of the New Being in time and space. If Jesus had not impressed himself as the Christ on his disciples and through them upon all following generations, the man who is called Jesus of Nazareth would perhaps be remembered as a historically and religiously important person ... but not the final manifestation of the New Being itself.[175]

---

[169]The following description is based on ibid., II, 97-180 and ibid., III, 114-149, where Tillich discusses "Spirit-Christology."

[170]Ibid., II, 97.

[171]Ibid.

[172]Ibid.

[173]Ibid., p. 98.

[174]Ibid. Thus the "historical Jesus" or at least the "historical bearer of the New Being," is foundational for Christianity.

[175]Ibid., p. 99.

What of the significance of Jesus in terms of temporal extension? Christ is "God for us," Tillich says,[176] but God is not only for us, but for the entire universe. Jesus as the Christ is related to man's historical development of which he is the center. Such "history" begins the moment human beings start realizing their existential estrangement and raise the question of the New Being. This beginning is not determined by historical research, but is told in "legendary and mythical terms."[177] Consequently, the end of this history (and of Jesus' temporal significance) is the moment when the continuity of that history with Jesus as its center is broken.[178]

Myths and Symbols Used to Describe the Event "Jesus as the Christ"

Tillich writes that one favorable result in "the life of Jesus" research (the old "Quest for the Historical Jesus") is that theology has learned to distinguish between the empirically historical, the legendary, and the mythological elements in the Biblical stories of both Testaments. This distinction into three semantic forms has important consequences for the theologian.[179]

If we inquire as to the distinction between the three elements, which in Tillich's view, make up the Biblical narratives, we find it rather difficult to establish the precise limits of each element. The first element mentioned by Tillich is the empirically historical, which Tillich has already declared to mean that the event "Jesus as the Christ" has a factual element.[180] As Tillich points out, the facts which are established as the result of the historical research of the scholars can be no more than "probable." We may say that the fact that there was a man who lived in Palestine at the beginning of our era who affected the New Testament writers in various ways has a very high degree of probability. But when we have said this we must also say that it is not certain, and that we know little about this figure that is more than moderately probable. Under the assumptions and methods of *Formgeschichte*, it is almost impossible to speak confidently of a genuine separation of the historical and legendary elements in the Gospel records. Thus a life of Jesus that is historically accurate is out of the

---

[176]Ibid., p. 100.
[177]Ibid.
[178]Ibid.
[179]Ibid., p. 108.
[180]Ibid., p. 107.

question, a conclusion which Tillich fully accepts. However, this does not mean we need to be extremely skeptical about the basic outline of the life represented in the Gospel records, for the "facts" which are found in the Gospel enjoy about the same historical probability as do the events recorded in the ancient secular writings, generally. For Tillich's purposes it is enough that what he calls "the power of the New Being" has had historical exemplification in a human being, even though we may not be certain that this historical figure bore the name "Jesus."

The legendary elements which Tillich refers to in the Gospel records include those exaggerated reports of the personal power and influence of Jesus, which developed in the Gospels in ways that are parallel to the development of legendary reports about significant historical figures such as Alexander the Great, or George Washington, in secular history. The legendary material in the New Testament accounts of Jesus include those stories which picture Jesus as possessing miraculous powers. Specifically, we may identify the story of Jesus walking on the water, changing water into wine, healing lepers and predicting the details of His own death, as legendary accretions to the simpler historical events which are reported about Him. The simpler events reported about Jesus such as his baptism by John (Mark 1:9), and his call of the disciples (Mark 1:16-17) are probably far more trustworthy than any supposed historical nucleus contained in the legendary reports.

The mythological elements in the Biblical stories are easier to identify. Bultmann has given a classic definition of myth which states that a myth is a story of the Divine having relationships within this world. The myth speaks of the "other side" in terms of "this side." Bultmann tells us that "the real purpose of myth is not to present an objective picture of the world as it is, but to express man's understanding of himself in the world in which he lives. Myth should be interpreted not cosmologically, but anthropologically, or better still, existentially.[181] The myth speaks of the "other world" (of the divine) in terms of this world, and of the gods in terms derived from human life. It is an expression of man's conviction that the origin and purpose of the world in which man lives are to be sought not within the world but beyond it. Myth expresses man's awareness then that he is not the lord of his own being.[182] The transfiguration account in the Gospels is a good example of this mythological side of Biblical thought.

---

[181]Bultmann, "New Testament and Mythology," p. 19.
[182]Ibid., pp. 10-11.

This analysis of the various elements in the Gospels gives the systematic theologian a tool for dealing with the Christological symbols of the Bible. Some of these Christological symbols are: Son of David, Son of Man, Heavenly Man, Messiah, Son of God, Kyrios, and Logos.[183] These symbols developed in four steps according to Tillich:

(1) The symbols, Son of Man, Son of David, etc., have arisen and grown in their own religious culture and language.

(2) The symbols, Son of Man, Son of David, etc., were used by people to whom they were alive as expressions of their own self-interpretation, and as answers to the questions implied in their existential predicament.

(3) The symbols, Son of Man, Son of David, etc., were transformed when they were used to interpret the Christ-event.

(4) The symbols, Son of Man, Son of David, etc., were later distorted by popular superstition, supported by theological literalism and supranaturalism.[184]

Tillich discusses the symbol, "Son of Man," first, as it is used most frequently by Jesus to refer to himself in all four Gospels. Tillich says this symbol designates an original unity between God and man.[185] (An example of Tillich's ontological interpretation). Tillich interprets this symbol according to his four steps in this way:

—He accepts the existence of a connection between the Persian symbol of the original man and the Paulinian idea of the Spiritual man.

—The "man from above" of this ancient myth is contrasted with man's situation of existential estrangement from God, his world, and himself, then.

—This contrast includes the expectation that the Son of Man will conquer the forces of estrangement and re-establish the unity between God and man.[186]

—The symbol "Son of Man" is attributed to Jesus in the trial scene before the High Priest recorded in Luke 22:69, and occurs elsewhere in Saint Luke and in other Gospels as a term of personal reference used by Jesus. In the trial scene the original function of the symbol is transformed—for Jesus is said to be the Son of Man who will appear as the judge of this age on the clouds of heaven.

---

[183]Ibid.

[184]Tillich, *Systematic Theology*, II, 109.

[185]Ibid., It is of interest to note that Norman Perrin was convinced that none of "the Son of man" sayings are historically genuine as words of Jesus. (Seminar, University of Chicago, March 15, 1965.)

[186]Tillich, *Systematic Theology*, II, 109.

Tillich declares that literalism takes this progression a fourth step "by imagining a transcendent being who, once upon a time, was sent down from his heavenly place and transmuted into man. In this way a true and powerful symbol becomes an absurd story, and the Christ becomes a half-god, a particular being between God and man."[187]

But the chief emphasis of Tillich's avowed course of "deliteralization" does not lie upon the "redefinition" (in order to "revivify") of individual "Symbol-elements" in the "myth-sequence"[188] about the Christ. Tillich's approach to the deliteralization of the symbols of the Christ consists first of all, in a general identification of the entire contents of the Gospel records about "the event Jesus the Christ" as a religious myth. Tillich means that a religious myth is the epic account of the saving facts and deeds that underlie a particular religious tradition. Thus the events concerning Jesus recorded in the Gospels form the epic religious facts and saving deeds that underlie the religious tradition of Christianity. For this reason, Tillich's redefinition of "Son of God"[189] and "Messiah"[190] are interesting as illustrations of the details of his hermeneutical operation, but are not the chief features of his program of deliteralization. In his interpretation, Tillich actually identifies the entire Christ-story as myth, and explains it in coherence with other parts of his system in terms of the ontological structures he identifies in "Being and God" (Part II, Systematic Theology, Volume I) and "Existence and the Christ" (Part III, Systematic Theology, Volume II).

Tillich's explanation of the symbol, Logos,[191] is another matter, however. This symbol is basic to his "ontologization" of the Christ-myth. He calls "Logos" a conceptual symbol because the reality to which the symbol "Logos" points unites rational structure and creative power. He also notes the use of the symbol "Logos" by Philo of Alexandria and the author of the Fourth Gospel (John 1:1-3). These "theologians" used "Logos" in its religious and symbolic sense, while not losing its rational element. For Tillich, as for Alexandrian theology generally (and for Idealistic philosophy), the Logos mediates the rational structure of the universe.[192] It is akin to the Old Testament

---

187Ibid.
188These terms are my neologisms.
189Ibid., pp. 109-110.
190Ibid., pp. 110-111.
191Ibid.,pp. 111-113.
192Ibid., p. 111.

emphasis on the Divine Wisdom in this regard.[193] Tillich refers to the presocratic philosopher, Heraclitus, to show the existential background of Logos, as the principle of order and law in the universe. Philo, later, gave Logos the sense of a mediating principle between God and man, while the Stoics spoke of the wise man who participates in the Logos and of his separation from the foolish mass of men. According to Tillich, Christianity took over both Stoic and "Philonian" elements when it began to use the symbol, "Logos": "The Logos reveals the mystery and reunites the estranged by appearing as a historical reality in a personal life. The universal principle of divine self-manifestation is, in its essential character, qualitatively present in an individual human being. He subjects himself to the conditions of existence and conquers existential estrangement within estranged existence."[194]

Tillich declares that, in the fourth step, Christianity remythologized the symbol "Logos" into the story of the metamorphosis of a divine being into the man Jesus of Nazareth. This is how the term "Incarnation" is sometimes understood. Tillich declares that such an understanding is wrong, and should be rejected.[195]

We have already discussed Tillich's attitude toward the problem of "the Jesus of History and the Christ of Faith," showing that he is clear in holding (with Søren Kierkegaard, Martin Kähler, and Rudolf Bultmann) that the object of faith can never be established by historical critical research. Rather it is:

> ... participation, not historical argument, (that) guarantees the reality of the event upon which Christianity is based. It guarantees a personal life in which the New Being has conquered the old being. But it does not guarantee his name to be Jesus of Nazareth.[196]

However, without the concreteness of the New Being, its newness would be empty.[197] There was such a person, "and it was, and still is,

---

[193]Proverbs 8:1-9:6, e.g., "The Lord created me [wisdom, 8:1] at the beginning of his work, the first of his acts of old" (8:22).

[194]Tillich, *Systematic Theology*, II, 112.

[195]Ibid. This is one of the strongest elements in Tillich's deliteralization of the Christ-myth.

[196]Ibid., p. 114.

[197]Ibid.

the picture (mediated to us by the Gospels), which mediates the transforming power of the New Being."[198]

One can compare the *analogia imaginis* suggested here—not as a method of knowing God, but as a way (actually the only way) of speaking of God. In both cases it is impossible to push behind the analogy and to state directly what can be stated only indirectly, that is, symbolically in the knowledge of God and mediated through faith in the knowledge of Jesus. But this indirect, symbolic, and mediated character of our knowledge does not diminish its truth—value.[199]

Tillich describes "how we know Jesus" in terms of "expressionist" art, in which the painter tries to enter into the deepest levels of the person with whom he deals, by participating in the reality and meaning of his subject. This kind of portrait expresses what the painter has experienced through his participation in the being of his subject. This is what the records of Jesus as the Christ in the Gospels are. In a real sense, we know no one else as well as we know Jesus, for we participate in him in the realm of his own participation in God, which is a universality open to everyone, rather than participating in a contingent human individuality.[200]

Tillich concludes this prolegomenon with the declaration that we must take our Biblical picture of the Christ from the whole New Testament, and not just the Synoptic Gospels. He remarks: "This picture (the Synoptics), and Paul's message of the Christ do not contradict each other. The New Testament witness is unambiguous in its witness to Jesus as the Christ."[201]

What Tillich Means by Ontologizing the Christ-Event

---

[198]Ibid., p. 115. Tillich once remarked: "The name of the Christ might have been Mark. Why not? It is the picture that matters." (February 17, 1964, Seminar, University of Chicago. Repeated at the 1965 Seminar—April 26, 1965—with the remark that such a statement is absurd, but it does show the truth that faith is not dependent upon historic research.)

[199]Tillich, *Systematic Theology*, II, p. 115.

[200]Ibid., p. 116. This assessment reminds one of Herrmann, *Kyrios und Pneuma*. It also reveals the deep influence which Saint Paul's teachings of the "being in the Spirit" and "in Christ" and the background of the two ideas, "the Body of Christ," has had on Tillich. (See Schweitzer, *The Mysticism of Paul the Apostle.*)

[201]Tillich, *Systematic Theology*, II, 118.

In chapter two, Tillich's theological method and the structure of his ontological theology was discussed. The structure of Tillich's ontological theology hinges on his vision of the eternal tension between Being and non-being. We also discussed in the same place Tillich's view of the nature of religious language and his identification of God as the Unconditioned, the Ground of Being Itself. This identification means that Tillich has ontologically described God and that every symbol that Tillich uses to refer to the Divine is a symbol of that depth that lies below every finite thing and every finite relation, being the depth of both sides of Tillich's fundamental ontological polarity, the polarity of self and the world. God is the depth that underlies the self and the world, that is, God is not to be identified with one factor within the world or the totality of Process as in the natural theology of Whitehead. Tillich describes man's state of existence as a mixture of being and non-being, and thus interprets the "Fall" of man as a movement from potentiality of being to actuality, as we have seen in the discussion in an earlier section of this chapter. Because of this approach, Tillich is also committed to an ontological interpretation of the Christ-event. Tillich's over-all solution to the place of Christ in his theological system is, of course, derived from his method of correlation, in which Christ is said to be the theological answer to the questions raised for man by the problems of human existence. The task which Tillich actually has to perform, because of his over-all ontological disposition on the one hand, and because of his use of Existentialist philosophy on the other hand, is to connect the Christ-event with the conditions of human existence on one side, and connect the Christ-event with the Unconditioned or the Divine Ground on the other side.

Tillich's Basic Approach

Like Bultmann, Tillich also claims the theological method of the New Testament writers themselves as an authority for his own method of theological interpretation.[202] Tillich declares that the Biblical reports about Christ do not attempt to psychologize Jesus, but attempt to ontologize him.[203] As is well-known, Bultmann has claimed that the Evangelists themselves, particularly the Fourth Evangelist, attempt to demythologize the Christ-event.[204] Bultmann, then goes on to complete the task of demythologizing the reports about the Christ-event

---

[202]Ibid., p. 124.
[203]Ibid.
[204]Bultmann, "New Testament and Mythology," pp. 11-12.

contained in the New Testament. It is Bultmann's belief that it is possible almost completely to demythologize the reports about Christ and understand him in terms of the demand for an existential self-understanding that sees man as free from his own past and open to the future offered to man in the Word about Christ.[205] Tillich's program is similar and yet has significant differences. In an earlier section of chapter three, we attempted to describe the similarities and differences between Bultmann and Tillich by using the terms, "demythologization" for Bultmann's program, and "deliteralization" for Tillich's program. The essential distinction between Bultmann and Tillich was seen to be Tillich's insistence that it is impossible to do without myth in religious language. For Tillich, every religious assertion must be made in symbolic speech, and a myth is simply an ordered sequence of religious symbols. What Tillich demands in his program of deliteralization is that every myth be "broken" and ontologized which means that every myth is understood to be precisely a myth or indirect mode of speech about the Unconditioned Ground of existence and not as a literal report about some supranatural order that parallels the world.

One of the most interesting discussions in modern theology is the controversy between Bultmann who holds that the authentic existence that enables man to be free from the past and open to the future is possible only because of a particular historical event, Jesus of Nazareth, and Fritz Buri and Karl Jaspers, who say that this authentic existence is possible as a universal possibility entirely apart from the Christ-event.[206] The Radical theologian, Paul van Buren has clearly outlined this controversy in the attempts of the left-wing Hartshornian theologian, Shubert M. Ogden, to find a mediating solution to the problem in his *The Secular Meaning of the Gospel*.[207] We might observe that this controversy underlines the serious theological difficulties that can arise when one attempts to describe the Christ-event in philosophical terms. Our reason for alluding to this problem at this point in our discussion lies in the fact that Tillich has been subjected to a similar kind of criticism by right-wing theologians, such as Kenneth Hamilton, in *The System and the Gospel*.[208] We are concerned to turn the thrust of this criticism at the very outset of our discussion of Tillich's

---

[205]Ibid., "Demythologizing in Outline," pp. 22-43.
[206]E.L. Mascall, *The Secularization of Christianity* (New York: Holt, Rinehart & Winston, 1966), pp. 45-47, 54-61.
[207]Van Buren, *The Secular Meaning of the Gospel*.
[208]Kenneth Hamilton, *The System and the Gospel, A Critique of Paul Tillich* (New York: Macmillan, 1963).

ontological treatment of the Christ-event; because for Tillich, no less than for Bultmann, the Christ-event is the one absolutely unique feature of Christianity, and it is not to be dissolved away by any method of interpretation. In the Introduction to *Systematic Theology*, Volume III, Tillich clearly states that "Certainly, these three books would not have been written if I had not been convinced that the event in which Christianity was born has central significance for all mankind, both before and after the event."[209]

We would misunderstand Tillich's whole theological outlook if we were to believe that the Christ-event was optional in the establishment of a theological system. For Tillich's whole system revolves around his conception of the meaning of the Pauline phrase, "If anyone is in Christ he is a new creation." Tillich's ontologization of the Christ-event is simply his way of developing the doctrine of the New Being which has been historically exemplified in Jesus the Christ.

In this section we will describe Tillich's ontologization of the Christ-event and Tillich's interpretation of Christ as the Bearer of the New Being. Before we turn to this description, let us first investigate Tillich's claim that the New Testament itself attempts to ontologize Jesus the Christ.

When we approach the question of what Tillich means by ontologization there is an important methological step that must be taken first. This step consists of distinguishing between various meanings of the word "ontology." A study of Tillich's theological system reveals at least three different senses in which ontology is used in his theological interpretation.

First, there is ontology as the uncovering of the framework or structure of finite existence; a task carried out by man's natural reason. This procedure establishes the self-world polarity and moves from that basis to establish the other principles reason discerns to be necessary for there to be any kind of experience at all. It is such a process of thought that produces philosophy, and that drives finite man on to ask the questions about the ultimate, which Tillich declares to be the precondition for the reception of revelation. It is in this sense that the term ontology is used in this study. We might call it primordial ontology or ontology A.

But secondly, in Tillich, there is another use of the term ontology—to refer to the concepts of the structures of being that are contained by implication in the Biblical documents. Tillich has written[210] that there is

---

[209]Tillich, *Systematic Theology*, Introduction, III, 4.
[210]Tillich, *BRSUR*, pp. 63-64. See chaps vii-viii *in toto*.

both an implicit and explicit ontology in the Scriptures. As this "ontology" forms part of the "answer" to philosophy's questions, drawn from the Christian tradition, it is not referred to herein, unless specifically designated as "answer," or ontology B.

And thirdly, we must identify a third sense in which the adjective "ontological" might be used, with reference to Tillich's theology as a whole. Tillich's theology is an "ontological theology" because it is the result of the questions brought to bear upon the Christian message by the instrument of ontological reflection (ontology A) and of the answers supplied by the Christian message which in itself contains implicitly an ontology (ontology B). This synthesis or resultant system might be called ontology C.

Tillich's claim that the New Testament writers themselves at least attempt to ontologize the Christ-event in an interesting one which turns out to be a theological truism when we reflect upon the procedure of the Fourth Evangelist and of the Ephesian and Colossian epistles. In the Fourth Gospel the Christ-event is interpreted as an expression of the power and activity of the universal Logos. The identification of the eternal Word and the man, Christ Jesus, is obviously an ontologization. The universal Logos, as it was understood in the Hellenistic philosophy of the first and second centuries, A.D., was understood as an element in the Divine Ground of Being, the principle of self-manifestation of the Divine. Tillich further illustrates the ontologizing process in the Gospels by identifying the Biblical stories that speak of Jesus' life-long possession of the Spirit and of his unity with God the Father. As Tillich says the Gospel stories "show the presence of the New Being in him under the conditions of existence."[211]

In chapter two, we discussed the use of the originally Stoic metaphor of the *Soma*, the Body and its several members, observing that there is an ultimate ontological reference in the term *soma*. In chapter one, the important position of the *soma* idea in Paul's Epistles was clearly described.[212] This important Pauline concept was originally devised by the Stoic philosophers to describe the construction of the universe and its binding structures. The use of the *soma* metaphor by Saint Paul certainly introduced the ontological dimension into New Testament Christology.

The clearest example of a New Testament ontological Christology, however, is the teaching of the Colossian and Ephesian letters. In those epistles Christ is called the head of the body and the agent of creation in

---

[211]Tillich, *Systematic Theology*, II, 134.
[212]See chap I, p. 40.

whom all things in the universe hang together and in whom all things are to be summed up at the consummation of the world process. Certainly Tillich has a clear warrant to ontologize the Christ-event and claim the New Testament itself as a source of inspiration for his method.

It is not necessary to prolong this assestment of Tillich's claim. We can quote the Johannine saying, "I am the Way, the Truth and the Life" (John 14:6), which could hardly be understood in anything but an ontological sense. The early history of theology also understood Christ in an ontological way as can be seen in the theology of Irenaeus who constructed the Recapitulation theory of the Atonement, and in the creedal formulations of Nicea and Chalcedon and the so-called Athanasian Creed. It would seem that Tillich is in good company in his procedure of ontologizing the Christ-event.

Tillich's ontologization of the "Christ-event" may be expressed briefly in this way: The New Being (which is equivalent to a manifestation of the Spirit, as we shall see) grasps us and brings us into a position of having an ultimate concern which takes Jesus to be the Christ (due to the Restitution of "the Resurrection") and which frees us from a life of autonomy (individualism) and/or heteronomy (legalism) for a life of theonomy (participation in the Ground of Being) in love to "God, " to our fellowmen and acceptance of ourselves (a union of eros and agape).

This New Being meets us in the Biblical picture of Jesus as the Christ (or in its proclamation by the church), and this picture is thus the creative authority of the Bible. This "picture of Jesus as the Christ" is mediated to us through myth and symbol (indeed it cannot be mediated otherwise), so, to make it available to ourselves today, we must so handle the Bible, not merely according to rules, either ecclesiastic or scientific, but by participation *(verstehen)* in that self-same New Being which has grasped us and made itself our ultimate concern. This participation ushers in an understanding of the Bible which then enables us to draw out the implicit (as well as explicit) ontology in the Biblical record.[213] Although the Biblical message that the divine Word was "incarnate" in the personal life of Jesus is the epitome of what Tillich calls "Biblical personalism," this event nevertheless is basically to be understood ontologically, as

[Jesus'] words are expressions of his being, and they are this in unity with his deeds and sufferings. Together they all point to a personal center which is completely determined by the divine

---

[213]Tillich, *BRSUR*, chap v, pp. 35ff.

presence, by the "Spirit without limit." This makes him Jesus the Christ. The word [Logos] appears as a person and only secondarily in the words of a person. The word [Logos], the principle of the divine self-manifestation, appearing as a person, is the fulfilment of biblical personalism . . . [But] the Logos, who for biblical religion can reveal the heart of divinity only in a concrete personal life, is, for ontology, present in everything. Ontology generalizes, while biblical religion individualizes.[214]

This "generalizing" is what Tillich does, although it is done not only out of a rational, intellectual interest, but it grows out of our life which is constantly being "renewed," and "deepened" by the New Reality that partially and fragmentarily overcomes our estrangement from God, nature, ourselves and our fellowmen. Thus we are moved to ontologize the "fact of Christ" from within the 'theological circle," even as the fourth Evangelist was so moved to have his "picture" of Christ say, "I am the Way, the Truth and the Life."

Tillich's Description of Christ, Ontologically Understood as the Bearer of the New Being

Tillich's major symbol for the contemporary interpretation of the Christ-event is his description of the Christ as the Bearer of the New Being. Tillich clearly bases his conception of the New Being on the Pauline idea of the New Creation which is at work in those persons who are "in Christ."[215] As we established in chapter one, the Pauline conception of being "in Christ" is equivalent to being "in the Spirit." Tillich speaks explicitly of the New Being as being the condition of participating in the creativity of the Divine Spirit.[216] Of course, the term New Being also rests upon Tillich's ontological reinterpretation of Christian theology. For Tillich, the New Being is essential being under the conditions of existence which conquers the gap between essence amd existence. "The term 'New Being,' ... points directly to the cleavage between essential and existential being — and is the restorative principle of the whole of ... (Tillich's) ... theological system."[217] Tillich

---

214Ibid., pp. 38-39.
215See chapter I. Also see Tillich, *Systematic Theology*, II, 119.
216Ibid.
217Ibid.

also connects the term New Being with Christ in another Pauline way, saying that this term expresses the fact that Christ is the end of the law, that is, the conquest of man's situation under judgment and condemnation.

Jesus as the Christ is the bearer of the New Being,[218] in the totality of his being. It is his being that makes him the Christ. It is basically what Christ is, not what he does that is "salvatory." In him his being is beyond the split of essential and existential being. Jesus' being is expressed, however, through his Words, his deeds, and his suffering.[219] It is this third expression of the New Being that Tillich sees as important for interpreting the Christ-myth." Jesus is the Word (Logos), for "being precedes speaking,[220] and yet "only by taking suffering and death upon himself could Jesus be the Christ, because only in this way could he participate completely in existence and conquer every force of estrangement which tried to dissolve his unity with God."[221] Again, "without the continuous sacrifice of himself as a particular individual under the conditions of existence to himself as the bearer of the New Being, he could not have been the Christ.... He proves and confirms his character as the Christ in the sacrifice of himself as Jesus to himself as the Christ." [222]

The New Being in Jesus as the Christ as the Conquest of Estrangement

Here is the heart of Tillich's ontological reinterpretation of the Christ-event. He holds that the "concrete" details of the Biblical picture of Jesus as the Christ confirm his character as the bearer of the New Being (itself a symbol) which is interpreted to mean "the one in whom the conflict between the essential unity of God and man and man's existential estrangement is overcome."[223] In fact, the picture of Christ point by point contradicts the marks of human estrangement which Tillich elaborated in the first section of Part III ("Existence"). There are no traces of estrangement between the Christ and God. "The paradoxical character of his being consists in the fact that, although he has only finite freedom under the conditions of time and space, he is not

---

[218]Ibid., p. 121.
[219]Ibid., pp. 121-123.
[220]Ibid., p. 122.
[221]Ibid., p. 123.
[222]Ibid.
[223]Ibid., p. 125.

estranged from the ground of his being."[224] Jesus as the Christ shows no unbelief, no *hubris* (although he was aware of his messianic vocation), which Tillich says is stressed by Paul in Philippians.[225]

But Tillich's favorite Biblical quotation is from the Fourth Gospel, which he applies to Jesus as the Christ as the distinguishing mark of the "Christ-hood" of Jesus. "He who believes in me does not believe in me, but in Him who has sent me.[226]

The New Being in the Christ as
the Power of Salvation

The significance of the Christ-event can also be stated in the mytho-symbolic term "Salvation." Under this mythological approach, Jesus is called "Savior," "Mediator," or "Redeemer." Salvation can have two connotations: the first, salvation from ultimate negativity (called condemnation or eternal death) which involves the loss of the inner telos of one's being, and—in a more limited sense—death and error. Secondly, salvation may also be interpreted in terms of "being saved" from guilt, hell, the law (and a bad conscience), special sins, and the state of godlessness.

Tillich interprets "Salvation" to mean "healing." It means the reuniting of that which is estranged, giving a center to what is split, overcoming the split between God and man, man and the world, and man and himself.[227] Tillich says it is out of this kind of interpretation that he has developed the concept of the New Being. Here, we may note that Tillich makes use both of his ontology and of the insights of modern psychology in the hermeneutical appropriation of this Biblical symbol. This salvation has made its appearance in Jesus as the Christ and it must not be separated from him. There is a history of revelation, of which Jesus as the Christ is the center. *And wherever there is revelation, there is salvation.*[228] Revelation must be redefined also, as it is not the receiving of information about divine things, but the ecstatic manifestation of the Ground of Being in event, persons, and things. And such manifestations have healing (reuniting) power.[229] On Tillich's view his salvation is either total or non-existent. For only if salvation is

---

[224]Ibid., p. 126.
[225]Ibid.
[226]Ibid., See John 12:44.
[227]Tillich, *Systematic Theology*, II, 165-169.
[228]Ibid., p. 166.
[229]Ibid., p. 167.

understood as healing (reuniting) universally, in all history, through the power of the New Being, do we escape the demonic distortion that says only a few men will be "saved" and the rest "lost." As Tillich says: "In some degree all men participate in the healing power of the New Being. Otherwise, they would have no being."[230] This means that we must not say that "apart from Jesus as the Christ there is no salvation," but rather that "Jesus as the Christ is the ultimate criterion of every healing and saving process." According to Tillich, wherever saving power appears in history, it must be judged by the saving power in Jesus as the Christ.

The Universal Significance of the Event, Jesus as the Christ

Because Tillich ontologizes the Biblical picture of Jesus as the Christ (beyond the point where the New Testament itself has ontologized the event), this section was predictable and is easy to assess. The universal meaning of the event of Jesus as the Christ is expressed through myths and symbols, and it becomes Christology, a function of soteriology.[231] These Christological symbols (Jesus is the "Savior," the "Light of the World," etc.) are the ways in which Jesus has been received by those who accept him as the Christ.[232] They must be seen as symbols and not taken literally. Tillich again declares that he does not want to "demythologize" but to "deliteralize." He wants to accept these symbols as symbols and to affirm them.[233] Tillich singles out two central symbols of the Christ, one of which ("the cross of the Christ"), shows Christ's subjection to existential estrangement, and the other ("the Resurrection of the Christ") which shows Christ's conquest of this estrangement.[234]

The Christological Symbols:
Cross and Resurrection

The two symbols, Cross and Resurrection, cannot be separated without loss of their meaning. The cross is the cross of the one who conquered the death of existential estrangement; otherwise it would

---

[230]Ibid.
[231]Ibid., pp. 150-151.
[232]Ibid., p. 152.
[233]Ibid.
[234]Ibid., pp. 152-153.

only be one more tragic event. The Resurrection is the resurrection of the one who, as the Christ, subjected himself to that death of estrangement; otherwise it would only be one more questionable miracle story.[235] And both of these "events" are both reality and symbol, for in both cases something happened within existence. Otherwise, Christ would not have entered — and conquered — existence. However, there is a difference between the two, the cross being public, and the Resurrection, a private experience of a few. Thus, in the New Testament, the cross is both event and symbol, and the Resurrection both symbol and an event. And yet both " events" are part of the myth of the bearer of the New Eon.[236]

Tillich declares that the Resurrection is perhaps best explained by the activity of the early disciples. When the certainty of some kind of real experience of Jesus grasped the demoralized disciples, the church was born, and since the Christ is not the Christ without the church which receives him, Jesus became the Christ through this transaction. The disciples' assertion that the symbol, Resurrection, became an event was dependent on their certainty (as well as upon our "certainty of faith") that the one who had brought in the new age could not finally have been conquered by the powers of the old age; therefore, historical research can never affect Christian faith in the Resurrection positively or negatively.[237]

Faith can give certainty only to the victory of the Christ over the ultimate consequences of the existential estrangement to which he subjected himself. And faith can give this certainty because it is itself based on it. Faith is based on the experience of being grasped by the power of the New Being through which the destructive consequences of estrangement are conquered.[238]

Here, ontological, psychological, Pauline and Lutheran elements combine in Tillich's assessment of the meaning and place of the Resurrection in the Christian faith. Tillich himself interprets the Resurrection symbol as the overcoming of a negativity in early Christian experience. That is, it overcomes the negativity of the disappearance of "Him whose being was the New Being "[239] Jesus as the Christ could not be overcome by transitoriness, or else he would not

---

[235]Ibid., p. 153. Tillich adds: "Which it (the Resurrection) is in the records."

[236]Ibid., pp. 153-154. Tillich accepts the category, "Historical Myths." See Tillich, *Dynamics of Faith*, chapter three, p. 54.

[237]Tillich, *Systematic Theology*, II, 155.

[238]Ibid.

[239]Ibid., p. 156.

have been the bearer of the New Being, and his power had impressed the disciples as the power of the New Being, so, "in an ecstatic experience the concrete picture of Jesus of Nazareth became indissolubly united with the reality of the New Being!"[240] Now, Jesus is present wherever the New Being is present, but He is present not as a revived body or as an individual soul, but as Spiritual Presence. He "is the Spirit" and we "know him now" only because he is the Spirit.[241] John Knox, in *The Church and the Reality of Christ*,[242] expressed a similar interpretation of the Resurrection, saying: "The Church affirms the Resurrection because its own existence as the community of memory and the Spirit is the essential and continuing meaning of the Resurrection."[243] The Spiritual Jesus is present wherever the New Being is present, and as the New Being has a continual impact upon believers. Because of this impact, the result of Divine power, the concrete life of the man, Jesus of Nazareth, is raised above the transitoriness of historical existence and is elevated into the eternal presence of God. The disciples' experience of the Spirit is not to be understood as effecting the union of Jesus and the New Being, but rather as effecting the disciples' affirmation of the eternal New Being that is present in Him. Because of the kind of receptivity given to Jesus as the Christ by the disciples and the Church, it is now possible to speak of "the risen Christ" as Spirit.[244]

In Tillich's view this same "event" happens to all those people in every age who experience his living presence here and now.[245] Tillich hopes to dismiss both physical and spiritualistic literalism by this "theory"[246] and follows Paul (1 Corinthians 15) here rather than the Gospel accounts. Tillich calls this interpretation the "restitution theory." That is, "the Resurrection is the restitution of Jesus as the Christ, a restitution which is rooted in the personal unity between Jesus and God, and in the impact of this unity on the minds of the apostles:"[247] Tillich insists that this is only a theory and does not have the certainty of faith,

---

[240]Ibid., p. 157.

[241]Ibid. Note Tillich's dependence upon 2 Cor. 3:17-18.

[242]John Knox, *The Church and the Reality of Christ* (New York: Harper & Row, 1962).

[243]Ibid., pp. 77ff.

[244]Tillich, *Systematic Theology*, II, 157.

[245]Ibid., Cf. Ibid., III, 111ff.

[246]Ibid., II, 157.

[247]Ibid.

although he claims that the "non-literalistic apostle Paul justifies" his theory.[248]

"The Cross of the Christ" expresses the subjection of him who is the Christ to the ultimate negativities of existence, without, however, being separated from his unity with God. Tillich sees this well-expressed by Paul in the mythical terms of Philippians 2. This myth, with its emphasis on pre-existence, is not to be taken literally, for it only serves to corroborate the symbol of the cross.[249] This utilization of myths and legends to corroborate the symbolic meaning of the cross is also true of the birth legends: the manger, the flight to Egypt, Herod's attempt to slay Jesus, etc. In all of these, the picture attempts to present the "tension between his messianic dignity and the low conditions of his existence."[250]

All of this comes to a climax at Gethsemane, at the trial, the crucifixion and burial. They are all expressions of the meaning of the symbol of the cross. "They are symbols of the divine paradox of the appearance of the God-man unity within existential estrangement."[251]

Later in this chapter we will specify the distinct hermeneutical principles which Tillich utilizes in his interpretation of the Scriptural text. Therefore, we will not identify just what principles Tillich has used in dealing with the Christ-event in this section.

Other Christological Symbols:
Birth, Transfiguration, Miracles

While Jesus' birth story is a symbol corroborating the cross, the virgin-birth symbol is one that corroborates the Resurrection. Tillich makes this distinction between the birth story and the virgin-birth symbol because he sees in the virgin birth a reference to the connection of the Divine Spirit and the man Jesus. For Tillich, the virgin-birth symbol is an expression of the apostles' conviction that the Spirit who had made the man Jesus into the Messiah had already created him as the vessel or bearer of the Spirit so that the appearance of the New Being in Jesus Christ is independent of historical contingencies and dependent upon God alone.[252]

---

[248]Ibid., p. 180.
[249]Ibid., p. 158.
[250]Ibid.
[251]Ibid., pp. 158-159.
[252]Ibid., p. 160.

Tillich also sees the symbol of Jesus' transfiguration as a symbol belonging to the Resurrection. The transfiguration anticipates Jesus' resurrection mode of being in that in the myth-sequence called "the transfiguration," Jesus is spoken to by the ancient prophets, Moses and Elijah, and God declares Jesus' Divine Sonship to the awe-struck disciples.

Both the virgin birth and transfiguration symbols are anticipations of Jesus' resurrected mode of being and are inserted in the Gospel record as disclosures of what is in store for the one who bears the New Being under the conditions of existence.

The Biblical records are also full of miracle-stories. Some are indicators of the presence of the New Being. "In all the miracles performed by Jesus, some of the evils of existential self-destruction are conquered."[253] Tillich declares that in the miracle-stories the evils of existential self-destruction are not fully conquered, but in Jesus' miraculous action there is seen a representation of the anticipated victory of the New Being over all existential self-destruction.[254] In these miracles, God's power is to be seen, not as supranatural interference in history, but in the power of the New Being to overcome the self-destructive consequences of existential estrangement. In this sense, the miracles of the Christ are symbols of victory and corroborate the Resurrection.[255]

The Symbols of the Pre- and
Post-Existence of the Christ

Tillich next deals with the mythological symbols of pre- and post-existence, which he says are to be understood as expressing the eternal root of the New Being as it is historically present in the event Jesus the Christ. They are also indicative of the Logos doctrine, pointing to the presence of the eternal principle of the divine self-manifestation in Jesus of Nazareth.[256]

Neither pre- nor post-existence are to be taken literally, including the symbol of Ascension (which reduplicates the Resurrection) and "sitting at the right hand of God" (which is absurd, if taken literally). Tillich accepts Luther's deliteralization of this last symbol, i.e., that it is God's omnipotence that is referred to here. Tillich discusses the symbol

---

[253]Ibid.
[254]Ibid.
[255]Ibid., p. 161.
[256]Ibid.

of Jesus' rule over the church, answering that this is through the Spirit,[257] and of Jesus' rule over history. Tillich interprets this rule over history in ontological terms, which go far towards making an almost literal "bringing over" of the New Testament symbol possible.

> He who is the Christ and has brought the new eon is the ruler of the new eon. History is the creation of the new in every moment. But the ultimately new toward which history moves is the New Being; it is the end of history, namely, the end of the preparatory period of history and its aim.... The symbol of the Christ as the Lord of history means neither external interference by a heavenly being nor fulfillment of the New Being in history or its transformation into the Kingdom of God; but it does mean the certainty that nothing can happen in history which would make the work of the New Being impossible.[258]

Summary of Tillich's Treatment of the Myths of Creation-Fall and the Christ-Event

In the last two sections of this chapter, we have discussed Tillich's procedure in dealing with the myth of Creation-Fall and the myth of the Christ-Event, stressing the manner in which he organizes the traditional content of these myth-sequences, and noting the ontologization and psychologization of the traditional events that form his program of deliteralization. Now we shall investigate the principles established as part of Tillich's hermeneutic by our investigation of what he has actually done.

The first impression that we receive of Tillich's treatment of the Biblical myths is that in his interpretation we are in a world characterized by an unusual (for the twentieth century) philosophical Realism, which nevertheless retains some Idealistic assumptions.

Tillich's philosophical-theological interpretation of the Biblical myths begins with the assumption that existence proceeds from essence by estrangement, which is not an Idealistic assumption. Moreover, existence is not a matter of essential necessity, but must simply be accepted as a fact. However, Tillich does view the logos principle or essence as being the coherent manifestation of the most basic reality which he terms the abyss of Being. Here we see Tillich's rather complex

---

[257]"The Spirit" as a symbol, conveys the same meaning and power as the "New Being" in Tillich's theology.

[258]Ibid., II, 162.

relationship to Idealistic thought: The logos principle or reason is a principle of reality, but it is not the most basic reality. The most basic reality, the ultimate ground which is God, is an abyss of Being and meaning which includes rational as well as irrational elements. Tillich discusses this abyssmal quality of the Divine under the rubric "'God as living,"[259] where he states that "Life as spirit is the inclusive symbol for the divine life. It contains all the ontological elements." Tillich goes on to declare that God is as close to the creative darkness of the unconscious as he is to cognitive reason. In other places Tillich declares that there is an element of negativity in God out of which flows the continuing struggle within the Divine life between Being and non-being, in which Being continually triumphs over non-being. This is certainly not Idealism in the usual sense, for it is quite clear that, for Tillich, the most basic ontological reality is beyond the separation into reason and non-reason, beyond the separation of mind and matter. Moreover, man's relationship to the Divine, as we have frequently noted in this study, is by way of ecstasy or through the grasp of the Spirit and not by the normal processes of thought. Thus, Tillich must be considered not as an Idealist, but as the representative of a philosophical position whose aim is to incorporate those aspects of Idealism that are useful and to correct those aspects of Idealism that obscure the true nature of the Divine and man's relationship to it.[260] Tillich's clearest word on this importent point is: "Nothing divine is irrational — if irrational means contradicting reason — for reason is the finite manifestation of the divine Logos. Only the transition from essence to existence, the act of self-estrangement, is irrational."

James Luther Adams in his definitive study of Tillich's thought,[261] has analyzed Tillich's attempt to transcend Idealism in the direction of a renewal of moderate Realism.[262] Adams observes that Tillich has maintained a yes and no relationship to the Idealistic philosophy of the nineteenth century, which was in the ascendency during his youth, similar to the dialectical relationship Tillich has maintained towards other elements of the Western intellectual tradition. The objective Idealism of Hegel and other nineteenth century thinkers was not the extreme subjectivism that interpreted all reality in terms of mind. Rather the objective Idealists regarded the organization and form of the

---

[259]Ibid., I, 241-252.
[260]Ibid., III, 283-294.
[261]Adams, *Theology of Paul Tillich*, pp. 35f. , 130ff., 137, 189, 191, 196f., 209ff., 227, 231ff., 250f., 252.
[262]Ibid., pp. 91f., 116ff., 130f.

world as determined by the nature of the world itself. The mind, therefore, discovers what is in the order of the world. The Idealistic assumption was the interpretation of the universe as an intelligible order. The systematic structure of the universe, as it was discussed by Hegel, and by Kant (a phenomenalist, but close to the objective Idealism under discussion) expressed a rational order.[263] Tillich affirms the rational order of the universe, naming it the Logos principle, but goes beyond objective Idealism in stressing the fact that ultimate reality includes both the Divine Logos and the abyss which is the ultimate ground of God.

Therefore Tillich can begin his interpretation of the Biblical symbols with the assumption that the world is rational because thought (Logos) is a key part of the structure of reality. However, Tillich's "Belief-ful Realism" holds that the Ground or Depths of Reality is prior to thought and so Tillich escapes the unfortunate tendency of Idealism that sees reality as proceeding from thought. Adams describes Tillich's transcending of Idealism in terms of Tillich's criticism of that philosophy. He notes that Tillich rejects the claim of Idealism that its system of categories portrays reality as a whole, holding that Idealistic categories express only a limited relation to reality.[264] Specifically, Adams notes that Tillich rejects the rationalism inherent in Idealism and its philosophy of identity. Here Tillich follows Schelling, observing that "reality is not only the appearance of essence, but also the contradiction of it, and that, above all, human existence is the expression of the contradiction of its essence."[265] This expresses Tillich's foundational belief that both the mind and the world are related to the Ground and abyss of the Divine through the dimension of depth.

By way of summary, we observe that Tillich consistently denies that he can be understood as an Idealist, although as Adams also observes, Tillich retains some Idealistic presuppositions.[266] In many respects, Tillich shared Idealistic notions, for example, the unity of all being, the identity of reality and thought and the rationality of being. Adams has remarked that Tillich retained the view that there is a certain identity between knower and known. Thus "in the religious act the cleavage between subject ond object is in principle overcome and a new community (of meaning-fulfillment) between knower and known is

---

[263]Harold H. Titus, *Living Issues in Philosophy* (3rd ed.; New York: American Book Co., 1959), pp. 226-233.

[264]Adams, *The Theology of Paul Tillich*, p. 130.

[265]Ibid., pp. 130-131, quoted from Tillich, *The Interpretation of History*, p. 61.

[266]Adams, *The Theology of Paul Tillich*, p. 252.

established." Adams also observes that Tillich here is close to Hegel's view of the unity of the consciousness of God and the reality of God.[267] On the other hand, Tillich criticized Idealism frequently and denied that he was an Idealist but spoke of himself as a moderate Realist. Tillich identified his moderate realism as a belief "in the inner telos (*entelecheia*) of life-processes which directs them in all particulars in a definite direction ."[268]

Tillich's transcending of Idealism includes three major elements, some of which we have discussed above. Briefly, Tillich's thought includes these correctives to objective Idealism: Reality is clearly shown not to proceed from thought, but rather is declared to transcend thought in the abyss of the Unconditioned which is the Ground of the Divine life, and existence is declared to be in contradiction to thought. On the basis of these major disagreements with the Idealistic tradition, Tillich separated himself from it. An additional influence on Tillich's critique of Idealism is the major effect of existentialism upon his system. In Tillich's basic conception of the Unconditioned, in his affinity for existentialism and in his acceptance of psychoanalysis (all of which elements are seen in his interpretation of the Biblical myths), Tillich transcended Idealism.

Turning to Tillich's treatment of the myth of the Fall, we see that in his interpretation the "time" before the Fall was really a stage of dreaming innocence. This stage is not an actual stage in human development, that is, it does not conceive of the "time" in which man lives under the power of sin in a straight-forward, horizontal Hegelian manner that sees history as unfolding the development of spirituality, but it is seen in a uniquely vertical way as being present in every stage of human development. Tillich feels that he has "deliteralized" the myth of the Fall when he calls it "suprahistorical." In a sense, Tillich has also psychologized the myth of the Fall by his reliance upon these philosophical categories, for he has internalized the story of man's alienation and removed it from serious consideration as a factor in human "history," considered as an actual event.

Tillich makes special reference to the Platonic myth of the Fall of the soul. For Tillich, Plato's story is an example of the cosmic myth of the eternal struggle between Being and Non-Being, between the struggle of the Divine principle of order and the demonic powers of chaos and darkness. Such a cosmic background is necessary in Tillich's view, because it points beyond the world and its structure to the universal

---

[267]Ibid.

[268]Sydney Rome and Beatrice Rome (eds.), *Philosophical Interrogations* (New York: Holt, Rinehart and Winston, 1964), p. 389.

ground of the Unconditioned, the abyss of meaning and being on which the world and all that exists rests. For Tillich this is necessary not only as a principle of his philosophy, but also to meet the Biblical teaching that existence cannot be derived from itself but is rather "created." In this regard, Tillich follows Plotinus and rejects Aristotle's notion that the universe is eternal. This consideration also delineates Tillich's cosmological thought from that of Whitehead in *Process and Reality*.[269]

Tillich's claim is that he is deliteralizing the myth of Creation-Fall on the basis of the analysis provided by modern existentialist philosophy and with the aid of the insights of modern psychological theory and sociological interpretation. It is clear that Tillich does rely upon existentialist philosophy for one side of his approach to the deliteralization of the Biblical myth, in that he uses again and again the insights of existentialist psychology that stress man's sense of alienation from himself, from his fellowmen and from nature.

When we investigate the question, "Does Tillich ontologize the myth of Creation-Fall?" we find several diverse answers. In the first place, like many philosophical-theologians, Tillich does interpret the Biblical myth of the Fall in ontological terms. Tillich does make basic in his system the interpretation of man's wrong choice as the human decision which brings about the transition from essence to existence. Tillich's ontologization of the Christ-event leads us to ask the following question: "Does not the Bible itself ontologize the Fall when it explicitly states that the relationship between man and God (the Ground of Being) is changed by the Fall?" In the Genesis story, even the earth itself undergoes a transition in that the ground is to be cursed because of Adam's sin and is to yield its fruit only at the expense of hard labor. Moreover, the Biblical narrative explicitly states that mankind is subject to death because of the Fall, an assertion which Tillich—along with most modern commentators—is disposed to deny. It is also clear on the basis of the Biblical myth itself that the inner structure of man's consciousness is changed by the event of the Fall in that man now knows good and evil—something he apparently was not supposed to know before succumbing to temptation.

The above considerations would make it justifiable to say that Tillich shares the general metaphysical tendency that detaches an idea from the accidents of the time and place under which it becomes known and presents it as a general principle. In other words, Tillich is inclined to

---

[269]Alfred North Whitehead, *Process and Reality* (Harper Torchbooks; New York: Harper & Bros., 1960); cf. Pp. 519ff., esp. Pp. 528-529.

psychologize material which is presented in the concrete manner of Biblical myths, and to call this intellectualization a "deliteralization." This is no accident of this one section of Tillich's work. The drive towards such an intellectualization of the Christian tradition underlies Tillich's whole system and in the chief effect of his handling of the Biblical material. Tillich's conception of God as the Ground of Being is certainly a creative advance over literalistic personalism on the one side, and the Idealistic conception of God as the Absolute on the other. Tillich speaks of God as imminent in the world process, always and everywhere present to everyone and with every particle of matter. Tillich, of course, shares this emphasis with other philosophical writers, such as Hegel and Bradley, among the Idealists, and with Whitehead among the Naturalists. Tillich does not speak of Divine interventions, however, a fact which is made very clear by his treatment of the Christ-myth, as we shall see below. And yet, God is not merely imminent, He is not merely a finite factor in the world process, as Process theology, following Whitehead,[270] would say, but God is also transcendent over the universe—being the divine creative depths which lies beneath and beyond every event and experience rather than being in the concretion of those events themselves. Here Tillich shows the influence of traditional Christian theology and escapes the strictures of Absolute Idealism, on the one hand and the naturalism of Process theology on the other.

Because Tillich escapes the errors of Absolute Idealism he is able to attribute reality to individual human personalities and to teach the Idealistically influenced doctrine of the unity of mankind and of the imminence of the Divine Spirit in men, and in the material world of nature, without reducing man or nature to mere "masks" of the single reality, God. However, Tillich retains modified Idealistic elements, as can be seen in the starting point of his deliteralization of the myth of Creation-Fall and of the Christ. Stated simply, Tillich sees the relationship of the universal spirit to the material world, and to mankind which forms part of that world, as being a relationship of unity in which the "dimension of Spirit" is primary. Therefore, since Tillich assumes the basic underlying unity of God, man, and nature, he is able to use as his starting point the knowledge we have of ourselves, that is, our experience of ourselves as subjects standing over against the world as object, which he asserts is ultimately united in the principle of unity, God, or the Ground of Being Itself. It appears that Tillich, like all thinkers influenced by Idealistic elements (here, the unity of all being)

---

[270]Ibid.

comes close to pantheism, but escapes it in the same manner as the neo-Hegelians such as Edward Caird[271] did by stressing God's transcendence over the world process at the same time.

In summary, Tillich's approach to the myth of Creation-Fall is an ontological or metaphysical one, that is, it is a universalization of the original Biblical myth which in its own primitive way also tried to universalize the story of human failure to resist temptation. The temptation itself is seen by Tillich as being a movement on the ontological level in that it is the original fact upon which all the facts of human history rely, that is, the act of giving in to temptation is the transition from essence to existence, that which makes existence possible, and that which is included in every moment of existence as the continuous possibility which is becoming actual in every human act. For Tillich, Creation and Fall are thus one and the same thing, the original fact that we do exist and that the world exists. This "original fact" has taken place at no "time" in pre -history or history, but has taken place, is now taking place, and will continue to take place as long as man exists.

An Evaluation of Tillich's Interpretation of the Christ

The moderate Realism (with Idealistic elements) which we identified in Tillich's interpretation of the myth of Creation-Fall is also apparent in his ontologization of the Christ-Event. Essentially, Tillich gives us a Spirit-Christology in which Tillich speaks of Jesus as the Christ in the sense that he is the bearer of the New Being, who makes available the Divine power that is able to answer the problems that have arisen in existence, which Tillich identifies as estrangement, alienation and sin. The Christ is the mediator, who bridges the infinite gap between the unconditioned and the conditioned. And yet the Christ in not some strange figure on the order of one of the mythological gods but is essentially what man ought to be. The Christ manifests the Logos in history, showing the paradox of the Incarnation in that in him the Divine participates in the world which is estranged from him. The Christ is to be understood as the transformer of man's historical existence, whose appearance has made available the powers that make possible the renewal of the universe. The New Being present in Jesus as

---

[271]John Macquarrie, *Twentieth Century Religious Thought* (New York: Harper & Row, 1963), pp. 25ff.

the Christ, although discussed by Tillich under the theme of the self-negation of Jesus, is a powerful positive principle that offers the possibility of the healing of man's estrangement from God and the further possibility of communal, historical and organic creativity. The reception of the New Being by men results in an affirmation of one's self-hood, along with the reception of courage, serenity, meaning and love for the living of finite life.

Since Tillich's system is a definitely Christian one, it must be very clearly grounded upon the central importance of the Christ. Both man's religious life (his ultimate concern) and the systematic interest of the theologian demand that the central symbol of Christianity be clearly and firmly grounded. Therefore Tillich has made clear that he must establish the certainty of the appearance of the New Being in history, apart from the relativities of critical scholarship. Tillich consequently affirms that the event we know as Jesus the Christ definitely has a factual element. This factual element, the fact that the New Being was manifested in a personal life under the conditions of human existence, is the foundation of Christianity, and is guaranteed for the man of faith by the transformation of reality he sees in the Biblical picture of Jesus as the Christ and experiences in the Spiritual community.

As we have discussed at length in chapter two in reference to Tillich's doctrine of the Spiritual Presence, and in chapter three above in reference to his interpretation of the Christ-event, Tillich has developed a Spirit-Christology based on the theology of Saint Paul. The Christ can be spoken of as the bearer of the New Being and as the manifestation of the Spirit in its fullness, for both expressions convey the same meaning. The New Being and the Spiritual Presence both symbolize the presence of the creative Ground of Being in human life, which heals and renews all those who are open to its influence. Tillich identifies the saving element in the life and death of Jesus the Christ as the New Being, which, of course, has its foundation in Saint Paul's teaching about the New Creation which takes place through Christ. However, Tillich goes on to develop his conception of the New Being, equating it with a manifestation of the Divine Spirit. The New Being, in the last analysis, is the manifestation of God in a human life which manifestation was made transparently clear by the kenosis or self-emptying of the man Jesus who negated everything that was particular and personal about himself in order to point beyond himself to the Divine Ground. "Looking through" the self-negating figure of the Christ, mankind is enabled to glimpse, in an indirect way, the creative Ground on which everything rests and from which we have come. This manifestation of the Unconditioned under the conditions of space and time in the death of Jesus on the Cross, exercises a fascinating power on the human mind, so that man is "grasped" by the power of the New Being and re-oriented towards the Unconditioned, taking "God" as the object of his ultimate concern. This new form of existence now looks upon Jesus as the Christ or the Savior, and enables the believer to escape from the follies of individualistic existence (autonomy), on the one hand, and from the burdens of legalism (heteronomy) on the other. Life in Christ, that is, life lived with God as man's true ultimate concern, then becomes a life of theonomy, that is, a life in which God is the central fact of one's existence and one lives out of the powers that come from participation in the ground of one's being, powers that enable one to live in love.

It is clear that Tillich does ontologize the Christ-figure. However, it is equally clear that Tillich is not the first to so ontologize Christ. Within the Gospels themselves, especially in the Fourth Gospel, Jesus has been ontologized in language that refers to him as an ultimate structure of existence. In the Epistles of Saint Paul, and especially in those Epistles that are often attributed to Paul, Colossians and Ephesians, the ontologization of the Christ is carried out to the point where the Christ is identified as the agent through which creation takes place. The new element in Tillich's ontologization of the Christ-event is his introduction of the New Testament's "high Christology," into the framework of a Spirit-Christology, with a strongly kenotic emphasis. In the New Testament, there is no clear teaching of the essential unity of man and God, and in those portions of the New Testament where Christ is ontologized to the greatest extent there is no indication that he is thought of as being an ordinary human being. In actual fact, the portions of the New Testament that ontologize Christ do come dangerously close to Monophysitism, the theological heresy that attributes only one nature to Christ, a Divine one. In Tillich's interpretation, however, the emphasis is upon Christ as a human being. Jesus becomes the Christ in his very being, just because he becomes more and more throughout life, and fully so at his death, the bearer of the New Being. It is not that God has somehow become incarnate in a human being, or that Jesus is some *Tertium Quid*, or third kind of being between God and man, but rather that Jesus is a genuine human being. In Tillich's view, Jesus is perhaps the only fully developed human being, in that in him by reason of the continuous action of his self-negation, the unconditioned Ground of Being is allowed to become "visible" through him. In Jesus the Christ there is thus a perfect unity between man and the Divine. In Christ, as the result of his ultimate concern and obedience, there is an expression of the eternal unity of

God and man. This expression, "the eternal unity of God and man," is Tillich's own,[272] and it clearly reveals the residual Idealistic elements in his approach. Moreover, it is an interpretation that denies the possiblity of the Divine's becoming incarnate in an historical individual, as Tillich holds that the divine nature cannot be attributed to Christ in a meaningful way. Tillich declares that if Christ were of a divine nature he would have to be beyond essence and existence and, therefore, Christ could not then have had a personal life under the conditions of finitude.[273] It is on this basis that Tillich offers his conception of the nature of Christ. Tillich believes that Christ is the historical bearer of the New Being in whom the New Being becomes actual (it is always potential in every time and space, according to Tillich) and which Tillich designates by the phrase "eternal-God-man-unity" or "Eternal-God-Manhood."

In Tillich's description of Christ as the one in whom Eternal-God-Manhood has become actual under the conditions of existence, the emphasis remains upon the eternal unity of God and man within the Divine life. The term "eternal" is Tillich's reminder of this essential unity of mankind and the Divine Ground. Not only does this factor in his Christology illustrate Tillich's adherence to the concept of the paradoxical unity of man and God, but it also demonstrates his belief in the paradoxical unity of man and nature. The unity between God and man, and between man and nature is paradoxical because man participates in the Divine Ground at the same time as he is separated (alienated) from it. Similarly, man is also alienated from nature and from other men. For Tillich, the New Being manifested in Christ has salvatory effect upon the creation itself, as Tillich has beautifully expressed this thought in his sermon, "Nature, also, Mourns for a Lost Good," in his volume, *The Shaking of the Foundations.*[274] However, Tillich carefully avoids making the Idealistic assumption that views man's existence as an unfolding of the Divine essence. For Tillich man is both related to the Divine Ground and separated from it.[275]

A Synthesis of the Hermeneutic
Principles of Paul Tillich

---

[272]Tillich, *Systematic Theology,* II, 148.

[273]Paul Tillich, *The Shaking of the Foundations* (New York: Chas. Scribner's Sons, 1948), pp. 76-86.

[274]Paul Tillich, *The Shaking of the Foundations,* pp. 76-86.

[275]Adams, *The Theology of Paul Tillich,* p. 216.

In this chapter we have moved a great distance through the theological literature of the decades during which Tillich produced the *Systematic Theology*, beginning with a discussion of the revival of interest in the problem of hermeneutic and its immediate background in the older controversy between Bultmann, Tillich, and Barth over the nature of theological language. Passing through the various roads followed by the participants in these controversies, we have illustrated the various options selected by the New Hermeneutic theologians, Fuchs and Ebeling, the astringent conclusions of the Radical theologians of the Death-of-God school, and the continuing positions of Bultmann and Tillich.

In turning our full attention to the hermeneutic position of Paul Tillich, we identified his position as one which claims that an ontological dimension is necessary for the proper fulfillment of the hermeneutic task. Its elements in Tillich's ontology, and Tillich's actual usage of these elements in his interpretation of the myths of Creation-Fall and the Christ-event were fully presented. From time to time we have paused to summarize how far we have come, and have criticized and explained just what seems to be going on in Tillich's theological work. Now we have come to the end of our theological journey and it is time to precisely name and identify the hermeneutical principles which seem to lie beneath the surface of Tillich's *Systematic Theology*.

The hermeneutical principles which we shall name and describe here are not to be thought of as canons by which the Scriptural documents are translated from their historical and philosophical settings into some timeless and changeless ontological philosophy that holds good for all periods of man's history. Tillich is clear in saying that his Systematic Theology is but one possible means of understanding the human condition and the resources of grace available in the Christian tradition. Moreover, Tillich's hermeneutical principles are not canons of interpretation that are rigidly applied to the Scriptural text in the manner of the older hermeneutic. In Tillich's usage, hermeneutic is similar to the understanding of the art of interpretation which we described as the "New Hermeneutic" approach of Ebeling, Fuchs, and Ott. Tillich's hermeneutic might be summed up in the obvious phrase, "The method of correlation." However, there is more to Tillich's hermeneutical approach than the use of a theological method no matter how fundamental and helpful that method may be.

Tillich's hermeneutic grows directly out of his insistence upon the necessity of an explicit ontological grounding of any theology. This is the second element which is discernible in Tillich's hermeneutical work, exemplified by his treatment of the doctrine of the Holy Spirit which we treated in chapter two, and by his handling of the myths of Creation-Fall and of the Christ-event, which we discussed earlier in chapter three.

We observe that Tillich's hermeneutic has two sides, the side that is founded in an existentialist philosophical analysis of the human condition, which results in his view of hermeneutic as being the investigation of man's own self-understanding, and the other side which rests in his belief in the divine which he understands to be the very Ground and source of all Being, which results in his demand that all theological teachings be grounded in an ontological awareness that connects them with the Divine Abyss of meaning and being.

On the basis of these insights into the character of Tillich's hermeneutical approach, we offer the following *operational concept* as a symbol of the kind of hermeneutical task performed by Tillich in his Systematic Theology.

Tillich seems to operate on the following assumption: The meaning of a Biblical symbol (or myth) is interpreted for our age when it is transposed into an ontological statement, and transposed into an existentialist statement in terms of man's present situation. One might see the above operational concept as another example of Tillich's well-known proclivity for identifying polar elements in his philosophical analysis. However, a further consideration shows us that this operational concept is not a polarity, for the identification of a polarity implies that both polar elements are equally fundamental in ontological status, having the power to balance each other for both are mutually dependent. Looked at in this light it becomes clear that Tillich's operational concept is not a polarity, for the ontological side of his interpretation refers, even though only symbolically, to the unconditioned, Divine depths, while the existentialist side of Tillich's interpretation refers to existence which is a mixture of being and non-being. For Tillich existence is wholly dependent upon the divine ground which is the depths of all polar elements including the basic polarity of self and world on which Tillich erects his philosophical theology. For Tillich the infinite or the divine is not a boundary between two possibilities or balanced polar elements, but is a limit set on everything finite and is the divine depths of both the world and self. We must recognize the fact that Tillich emphasizes the transcendence of God, indeed his selection of the concept of the Ground of Being as the one statement that approaches an univocal "name" for God, expresses Tillich's belief that God is more than the world and is not just another being, no matter how powerful, alongside other existing beings.

These same considerations, which preclude our seeing Tillich's hermeneutical concepts as a polarity, also make it necessary that Tillich cast his systematic theology in the form of symbols. Tillich's method of deliteralization does not remove myth and symbol from theology, as one sometimes suspects Bultmann would like to do. Rather, Tillich's method of deliteralization consists chiefly in identifying the Biblical myths as myths which produces a "broken" myth which Tillich believes is therefore free from the temptation to be literalized into an idolatrous doctrine. In Tillich's hermeneutical approach, the deliteratized symbol is still a symbol for it can only point beyond itself to the infinite. No symbol, "broken" or "unbroken, " can ever encompass its full meaning. Therefore, the two-fold operational concept in Tillich's hermeneutic remains symbolic and mythological at least on the side that points to the infinite. It would apparently follow that the several hermeneutical principles which we are now to identify are themselves symbols, symbols that point in two directions, on the one side is man's own self-understanding and his apprehensions of the problems of human life and on the other hand which point beyond themselves to the divine depth of meaning and being, out of which flows the restorative power that answers human questions.

Tillich once said: "There is nothing in heaven and earth, or beyond them, to which the philosopher must subject himself except the universal logos of being as it gives itself to him in being."[276] This declaration, and every sentence of this study, drives home with an inescapable inner logic the insight that Tillich's basic hermeneutical consideration is the necessity of a philosophical analysis in the construction of a systematic theology. Tillich's basic theological method, that of correlation, is based upon his belief that a suitable philosophical analysis can delineate man's existential situation and give voice to the questions that are implied in the problems of human life. A second hermeneutical consideration in Tillich's approach clearly emerges from our prior discussion of Tillich's approach to religious language. This consideration is one which Tillich shares with most modern theologians, the necessity for the critical study of the Scriptures. Tillich's devising of the method of deliteralization and of the method of correlation are decisions for intellectual integrity in religious thinking. Tillich's critical approach and his hermeneutical principles have wider application than the Bible alone, but form a universal hermeneutic which he applies to every religious tradition, both Christian and non-Christian, and to

---

[276]Paul Tillich, cited in David E. Trueblood, *Philosophy of Religion* (New York: Harper & Row, 1957), p. 3.

every philosophy, as well as to political, literary and scientific concepts. The universality of Tillich's hermeneutical approach grows out of his search for intellectual integrity, in that he seeks equality of treatment for religious and secular materials. Tillich exemplifies, in his hermeneutical approach, a dependence upon theonomous reason which he understands as the depth of reason that lies in the divine ground, below both secular and sacred attempts to insure that the questions of existential philosophy are not derived from the answers that lie in the Christian tradition, and that the answers of Christianity are not derived from the questions of philosophy. It is not always clear how successful he is in this attempt to preserve the independence of both sides of his operational concept, but the effort to give equality of treatment to both sides is always made.

Another hermeneutical consideration that grows out of Tillich's operational concept, and indeed is necessary if the concept is to have any validity at all, is the necessity of continual self-criticism. Tillich has identified this principle of self-criticism as the "Protestant principle."[277] This principle protests "against the identification of our ultimate concern with any creation of the Church, including the Biblical writings in so far as their witness to what is really ultimate concern is also a conditioned expression of their own spirituality."[278] Tillich's application of this "Protestant principle" to his own task is seen in his insistence that any system of theology is provisional and incomplete and must be done again and again to meet the changing conditions of every age.

A final hermeneutic consideration which we must discuss before "naming" Tillich's hermeneutical principles is Tillich's assumption that there is a connection between the kind of answers given to human questions in the Bible and the other resources of the Christian tradition on the one hand, and the human being who asks questions about his existential situation in the very different historical setting of the twentieth century, on the other. This situation differs radically in its self-understanding and outlook on the world from the era in which the biblical books were written. We might designate this hermeneutical consideration Tillich's concept of *Verstehen* or understanding by participation. In this basic assumption Tillich sees the Biblical texts as answering human questions and attributes to the texts adequacy in answering those questions. Here Tillich's relationship to the "New Hermeneutic" movement—a connection which undoubtedly grows out of the importance of Heidegger for Tillich, Bultmann, Ebeling and

---

[277]Tillich, *Systematic Theology*, I, 37.
[278]Ibid.

Fuchs—becomes clear. Tillich understands hermeneutic as an investigation of and recognition of man's own self-understanding. Tillich believes that in analyzing the structures of human thought the philosophical theologian is driven to recognize that these structures are the categories of a finite being, which point beyond themselves to an unconditioned ground that lies behind human thought and the objects which are the content of that thought. Tillich's relationship with Heidegger and the other contemporary existentialist philosopher, Jaspers, has been discussod above in chapter two.

Let it suffice here to remind ourselves of the influence of Heidegger's concept of "Dasein" and say that in his hermeneutical approach, Tillich assumes that a universally valid interpretation of theological material can be derived from an understanding of human understanding as participation—in a fragmentary and distorted way to be sure—in the divine depths of being and meaning. In this hermeneutical consideration Tillich sees the individuality of the auditor of the Scriptural text and that of the author of the text, as not standing over against each other, but rather as both "standing in" the ground of being. Tillich sees the eternal message (the *Kerygma*) and the human situation as held together through their mutual dependence upon the infinite in such a way that the message can be presented to the modern mind through the method of correlation without the message losing its uniqueness. In *The Protestant Era*, Tillich said: "The criterion of all theology is its ability to prescribe the absolute tension between the conditional and the unconditional."[279] This describes the operational concept that we identified above quite well.

Hermeneutical Principles Derived from Tillich's Operational Concept

As we noted above the following principles are symbols which serve as indicators of the kind of two-directional interpretation that Tillich performs in his Systematic Theology. These principles are not canons or touchstones by which Tillich interprets any one Biblical myth or symbol, but are indications of the kind of self-understanding he has (and attributes to modern men), and of the kind of self-understanding he sees presented in the Christian message itself.

The first hermeneutical principle is "Ultimate Concern." This first principle must be carefully explained as it is a psychological category rather than an ontological element. Man's Ultimate Concern is his

---

[279]Tillich, *The Protestant Era*, p. 79.

response to the unconditioned which lies behind every finite reality as the depth of meaning and being. The most striking element in Tillich's system is his uncovering of the universality of an ultimate concern among human beings, and his demonstration that this ultimate concern in always motivated by the unconditioned ground of our being and is a response to it even when man does not recognize the unconditioned's grasp upon his life and substitutes an idol for the divine Ground. As Tillich describes the Christian message's answer to the questions raised by human beings about that which concerns them ultimately, he clearly points out that only the Ground of Being Itself is worthy to be man's ultimate concern and identifies the unconditioned depths of meaning and being with the New Being historically manifested in Jesus as the Christ.[280] Thus, the material norm of Tillich's systematic theology is "The New Being in Jesus as the Christ as our Ultimate Concern."[281] Ultimate Concern clearly functions as a hermeneutical principle in Tillich's writings. [282]It is related there to Tillich's doctrine of *eros*,[283] which he takes as a driving force within every thing that exists—the drive for the reunion of the separated. Anders Nygren[284] has written that Augustine joined eros to agape into a new piety; and surely this is true of Tillich—that he has so redefined "faith" that faith and love are aspects of the one impulse—the Ultimate Concern that drives everything that exists toward reunion with the Divine Ground from which it is separated.

The second hermeneutical principle is "justification by Faith," which Tillich has modified to mean justification of the sinner in his doubt, as we have noted previously. Tillich's view that faith includes doubt within it[285] is a priceless hermeneutical tool for it enables him to meet the situation of modern men who are moved by their own self-understanding to doubt the traditional symbols of the Christian tradition. Moreover, this principle enables Tillich to relate faith to ontology, for in his view, Faith includes the ontological question, whether the question is asked explicitly or not."[286] Thus, Tillich's

---

[280]I owe this insight to George H. Tavard, *Paul Tillich and the Christian Message* (New York: Chas. Scribner's Sons, 1962), p. 22.

[281]Tillich, *Systematic Theology*, I, 50.

[282]See Tillich, *BRSUR*.

[283]See Tillich, *Love, Power and Justice*, pp. 18-34.

[284]Anders Nygren, *Agape and Eros* (Philadelphia: Westminster Press, 1953), trans. Philip Watson.

[285]Tillich, *Dynamics of Faith*, pp. 16-22.

[286]Tillich, *BRSUR*, p. 59.

understanding of justification by faith is an existential one which recognizes the "tension within itself and the doubt within itself"[287] that makes manifest an immediate awareness of something unconditional (the depths of being itself). The awareness of the unconditional which lies behind every finite reality gives man the courage to take the risk of uncertainty upon himself and enables man to live without despair.

The third hermeneutical principle which we may identify as an interpretative symbol in Tillich's thought is a genuine polarity between the mutually dependent and complementary elements of Catholic Substance and Protestant Principle. This principle sums up Tillich's dual attitude towards the Christian faith. On the one hand, he is deeply committed to the ancient Christian symbols, and on the other, he stands as a self-conscious modern man, critical of the distortions and misunderstandings of these symbols that have so often characterized the history of the Church. By the Catholic Substance of theology, Tillich means the great fund of wisdom and insight and the history of the manifestation of the New Being in an individual human life that is common to all truly Christian traditions. And Tillich also means by Catholic Substance the sacramental reality around which Catholic piety is built. By the Protestant Principle, Tillich means that glory of Protestantism, the ability to view all things critically including itself. The Protestant Principle for Tillich is not a principle of autonomy but of theonomy, which makes "protest against any finite authority which takes upon itself an infinite claim."[288] In all parts of Tillich's theological system we find this dual approach to the interpretation of religious symbols, on the one side, an appreciation of the depth of meaning and insight in the symbol, and on the other, a positive criticism of every distortion of the symbol that keeps it from pointing beyond itself to the divine.

The fourth hermeneutical principle which we can identify in Tillich's hermeneutic task may be symbolized by the expression "the Word of God and the Word of Man."[289] Tillich has written that every theologian must be Biblical for the Bible represents the basic document of the Christian faith which contains the clearest answers that the theologian must give to the questions raised by the problems man encounters in human life. The Biblical documents must be subjected to historical criticism, of course, so that the deepest meanings of the religious symbols used by the Biblical writers might become clear to the

---

[287]Ibid., p. 60.
[288]Tillich, *Systematic Theology*, I, 37.
[289]Ibid., pp. 34-68. Cf. Ebeling, *Word and Faith*, chap xi, pp. 305ff.

theologian.[290] Tillich has specified a three-fold procedure by which the systematic theologian may criticize the Bible:

> *Firstly*, systematic theology must accept and define the method, though not any special results, of historical criticism as an expression of the full humanity of the revelation;
>
> *Secondly*, systematic theology must decide about the degree and the way in which the symbolic, legendary, and mythical material of the Biblical literature can be used and reinterpreted in present-day terms;
>
> *Thirdly*, systematic theology must, in the power of the Biblical standard which it applies, subject all Biblical writings to the test of their adequacy or inadequacy to this standard.[291]

The standard by which all Biblical writings are to be tested is, of course, the material norm of systematic theology, the New Being in Jesus as the Christ.[292] Jesus as the Christ is the criterion of every revelation, both before the appearance of the New Being in its most perfect expression, in the life of Jesus Christ, and in every revelatory experience that has taken place in history, and that will take place in the future after the Christ-event. Thus, for Tillich, the New Being is the test by which both the original Biblical document and the theological interpretation of that document must be judged.

The New Being which functions as the norm and criterion for Tillich's system, and indeed, for every Christian theological system, is described by Tillich as a manifestation of the Spirit, which Tillich further describes as a situation in which finite persons and objects become transparent to the Divine depths of being and meaning. Thus, there is connection between this hermeneutical principle or symbol and the remaining two, the necessity of the appearance of the New Being occurring in an "absolutely universal and absolutely concrete" situation, and the "New Being" itself—viewed as a hermeneutical principle. Perhaps it would be equally valid to call this principle "the Logos principle" for what we are really trying to express here is that for Tillich any word can become the Word of God if it opens the way to the Ground of Being by pointing beyond itself, which is brought about by

---

[290]Paul Tillich, unpublished "Personal Introduction" for *Systematic Theology*. On file at Meadville Theological Seminary, Chicago, see pp. 9ff.

[291]Tillich, Address delivered in Washington, D.C. The manuscript of this address was kindly furnished to the author by Dr. A. T. Mollegen.

[292]Tillich, *Sysyematic Theology*, I, 50.

negating its own particular concrete characteristics. On the other hand, even the words of the Bible are not to be considered the Words of God as they do not lead to such a transparency to the divine depths. As Tillich says, "The Word of God is not limited to the words of a book and the act of revelation is not the inspiring of a book of revelations, even if the book is a document of the final Word of God, the fulfillment and criterion of all revelation."[293]

The point of this hermeneutical principle is that in the Christian tradition the belief in the incarnation of the Logos includes the paradox that the Word of God has become an object of vision and touch.[294] This means that the Word of God always is communicated through the Word of man or through finite concrete objects. The Word of God in the Bible is written in human words and in symbols that arise out of the concrete realities of human life. As we described Tillich's Christological position in the section above dealing with his interpretation of the Christ-event, we saw that the manifestation of the New Being means, for Tillich, that the Logos became a being in history under the conditions of existence.[295] This consideration, the necessity of the historical exemplification of the New Being under the conditions of space and time, leads us to the fifth hermeneutical principle which functions as an interpretative symbol in Tillich's theology, which we designate "the Absolutely Universal amd Absolutely Concrete" nature of the norm and criterion of Christian theology.

Tillich's hermeneutical principle, the necessity that the appearance of the New Being be Absolutely Universal and Absolutely Concrete, stands as a guard against any interpretation of Tillich's theology that would attempt to see authentic existence as being possible on the basis of some other disclosure of authentic existence apart from the Christ-event. For Tillich, the New Being is not only a possibility that is universally available, but is a divine act (in symbolic language) that expresses the basic Christian belief in the centrality and necessity of Christ for man's salvation. The New Being is historically factual and actual, something that really took place in a human life under the conditions of space and time at the beginning of the Christian era. The actuality of the exemplification of the New Being in Christ also underscores Tillich's belief that "in relation to God everything is by God."[296] The absolute concretization of the New Being is attested by the

---

293Ibid., p. 35.
294Ibid., p. 123; cf. Pp. 157ff.
295Ibid., pp. 137ff.
296Ibid., III, 43. See ibid., II, 16ff., especially p. 173.

proclamation of the earliest disciples and by the New Testament record which they produced. On the other hand the New Being exemplified in the Christ-event is not limited to the Christ-event, but had partial expression throughout the history of religion, especially in the prophets of the Old Testament, and has fragmentary expression in every experience where man comes to awareness of the divine and finds healing for the estrangement that characterizes human existence apart from awareness of God. This means that the New Being is universal as well as concrete.

The last hermeneutical principle which we may identify in Tillich's Systematic Theology bears close relationship to the first. Thus, we end our discussion of Tillich's hermeneutical principles in a circular demonstration.

The sixth symbol which Tillich uses in his interpretative work is "the New Being" which is the material norm of his Systematic Theology,[297] and the criterion of every religious revelation. The New Being is not identical with man's Ultimate Concern (Principle One), for as we noted above, Ultimate Concern is a psychological category, a response to the New Being which lies in the Divine depths of Being itself. The New Being is the ontological reality which gives us an awareness of the divine depths of life to which our Ultimate Concern is the proper response. As Tillich has written:

> When man is ultimately concerned, when he has reached the bottom of his being and has given himself to it, even though in doubt and with hesitancy ... then he is indeed justified by faith. Whether he knows it or not, whether he has heard of Christ or not, he is then grasped by the New Being.[298]

It is to help humans understand their life situation and the "bottom of [their] being" so that they may become open to the possibility of a New Being which is proclaimed by the Christian tradition, that Tillich has elected as his theological task. In a real sense, the New Being is not only one hermeneutical principle or interpretative symbol among others in Tillich's system, but is the only hermeneutical principle just as it is Tillich's material norm. The apologetical theologian thus ends by showing himself to be also a kerygmatic proclaimer of the reality of the New Being and its availability to those who will accept the acceptance of God, which is its inner meaning. Tillich, in the last analysis, approved

---

[297]Ibid., I, 50.
[298]Travard, *Paul Tillich and the Christian Message*, p. 22.

of the modern attempts to relate the myths and symbols of the Biblical message to man's existential situation, but believed that the hermeneutic task was only half done, leaving theology open to the inevitable erosion of religious language without a complementary translation into ontological terms. Thus he maintained that ontology is necessary to the proper carrying out of the hermeneutic task today, as always. In this regard Tillich's writings suggest that no adequate interpretation of the Christian message has been achieved until the Biblical myths and symbols are transposed, on the one hand, into ontological statements, and on the other hand, are transposed into existentialist statements that take account of man's present situation, with its hopes, fears and needs. Among those hopes Tillich gives prominence to that passionate concern for the ultimate and transcending which lies in the depths of the flux and struggle of the processes of life.

4

CONCLUSION

Saint Paul's Significance
for Paul Tillich's
Doctrine of the
Spiritual Presence

Paul Tillich demonstrates a high regard for the Pauline doctrine of the Spirit in his *Systematic Theology* (vol. III), as we have had occasion to discover in our investigation of Tillich's Doctrine of the Spiritual Presence in chapter three. In Volume III, Tillich writes:

> The unity of ecstasy and structure is classically expressed in Paul's doctrine of the Spirit. Paul is primarily the theologian of the Spirit. Paul strongly emphasizes the ecstatic element in the experience of the Spiritual Presence.... The formula—being in Christ—which Paul often uses, does not suggest a psychological empathy with Jesus Christ; rather it involves an ecstatic participation in the Christ who is the Spirit whereby one lives in the sphere of his Spiritual power ....[1]

In developing this insight, Tillich asserts that the doctrine of the Spirit is the center of everything Saint Paul says. In this doctrine, Tillich declares that Paul has intentionally united the rational element, understood as ontological reason, and the ecstatic element, understood

---

[1]Tillich, *Systematic Theology*, III, pp. 116-117.

as the sense of being driven by the Spirit, to express all the functions of the human spirit under the grasp of the Spirit.[2] Tillich sees this intentional union of these elements in Paul's famous description of the gifts of the Spirit in 1 Corinthians 12-13.

We might offer many other statements of Tillich that would underscore his dependence upon Saint Paul's teaching concerning the Spirit for the development of his doctrine of the Spiritual Presence. But as we have made this point quite clear in chapter three,[3] we forego repetition here,

A rather remarkable phenomena occurs in Tillich's discussion of the Spirit. This phenomena is Tillich's lavish (for him) references to the Biblical basis of his thought whenever he is dealing with the Spirit. The fact that Tillich does not, in other parts of his *Systematic Theology*, give frequent reference to the Scripture passages he may have in mind,[4] but does so refer to Paul in regard to the Spirit, would lead us to suspect the importance of Paul for this aspect of the system.[5]

Moreover, aside from such considerations of style, there is a readily discernable Pauline influence on Tillich's development of a Spirit-Christology in his doctrine of the Spiritual Presence. The fact that Tillich feels it necessary to write about Spirit-Christology in the midst of a system in which the *Logos* concept is a decisive principle, makes an awareness of the almost exclusively Pauline character of Tillich's doctrine of the Spirit necessary if one is to understand Tillich's theology.

It will be the purpose of this chapter to draw together the structure of the Pauline Spirit-Christology, studied in chapter two, and the structure of the Tillichian doctrine of the Spiritual Presence, discussed in chapter three, by recourse to the application of the hermeneutical principles by which Tillich develops his theology (delineated in chapter three), in order to assess the actual significance of Saint Paul for Tillich's doctrine of the Spiritual Presence.

In carrying through this assessment of Tillich's Spirit-doctrine, the following influences of Saint Paul on Tillich's thought are investigated. First, the Pauline conception of the Spirit as the Spiritual Presence of the Risen Christ is important. In chapter two, we noted the significance of the Pauline phrase, "the Lord is the Spirit" (2 Corinthians 3:17a), which reveals the identification of the Risen Christ as the Spiritual Presence in

---

[2]*Ibid.*, p. 116.

[3]See chap three.

[4]See Tillich, *Systematic Theology*, Introduction, III, 4, for Tillich's reply to criticism of his deviation from the use of Biblical language in *Systematic Theology*, Vol. I-III.

[5]There are no less than forty references to Saint Paul by name in Volume III.

Paul's thought. Tillich utilizes this insight in *Systematic Theology,*
Volume III, where he writes: "In the divine economy, the Spirit follows
the Son, but in essence, the Son is the Spirit. The Spirit does not himself
originate what he reveals."[6]

The thrust of this part of the inquiry is to demonstrate that the
Pauline idea of the identity of the Spiritual Presence with the Risen
Christ is determinative for the Tillichian development of the doctrine of
Spiritual Presence.

Secondly, we shall investigate the influence of Paul's belief that the
reception of the Spirit is the result of Divine grace upon Tillich's
thought. Tillich reveals the Pauline conception of man's dependence
upon divine grace in his development of the Spirit-doctrine. From
many other statements of Tillich, we call attention to the following:

> Man in his self-transcendence can reach for it, but man cannot
> grasp it, unless he is first grasped by it ....[7] the human spirit is
> unable to compel the Divine Spirit to enter the human spirit ...
> [8][and] In relation to God everything is done by God.[9]

A third Pauline influence on Tillich's thought that shall engage our
attention is Tillich's revival in Protestant theology of the Pauline
metaphor of the "outpouring" of the Spirit. Tillich believes that this
metaphor is useful, and feels that theology needs to speak of the Spirit's
infusion as well as of the Spirit's inspiration.[10]

A fourth Pauline influence on Tillich is his interpretation of 1
Corinthians 12-14. As we noted above, Tillich believes that Paul teaches
the unity of Spiritual ecstasy and rational structure in the human spirit
in his Corinthian Epistle. Tillich interprets Paul as teaching that the
presence of the Spirit does not distort or disrupt man's mental processes
but heals them.[11]

Paul's teaching concerning the activity of the Divine Spirit in a
genuine prayer forms the fifth Pauline influence on Tillich's thought
that we shall investigate. Tillich makes frequent reference to Romans 8
in *Systematic Theology,* Volume III, stating in one place: "We can only
pray to the God who prays to himself through us.[12]

---

[6]Ibid., III, p. 148.
[7]Ibid., p. 112.
[8]Ibid.
[9]Ibid., p. 133.
[10]Ibid., p. 116.
[11]Ibid., pp. 116-117.
[12]Ibid., p. 120.

Finally, we shall discuss the sixth important Pauline Influence on Tillich's thought, the conception of Jesus as the Bearer of the New Being, the one who manifested the Spirit without distortion.[13] Paul, of course, identified the Risen Lord as the Spiritual-Presence (2 Corinthians 3:17a) and spoke of the "New Creation" in Christ (2 Corinthians 5:17). Paul also wrote:

> ...the gospel concerning his Son, who was descended from David according to the flesh and designated Son of God in power according to the Spirit of holiness by his resurrection from the dead, Jesus Christ our Lord [Romans 1:3-4].

We shall investigate Paul's influence on Tillich's "Spirit-Christology," which is his designation for the doctrine of the Spiritual Presence in Jesus as the Christ.[14]

The Pauline Basis of Tillich's Doctrine of the Spiritual Presence

The Pauline materials concerning the Christian's "being in Christ" and "being in the Spirit" in chapter two made it clear that "the heart of Paul's religion is union with Christ."[15] In that same investigation, we discussed the modern recognition of the centrality of union with Christ in Paul's thought, which is best seen in the works of Adolf Deissmann[16] and Albert Schweitzer.[17] The studies of these two German theologians appeared, or were in the making, at the same period in which Tillich was undergoing his theological development. It would therefore appear that the general interest in Saint Paul shown by Tillich is not unusual, considering the background of his thought. If one wished to answer the question as to why the Pauline Christ-mysticism is influential on Tillich's thought, he need not give too much weight to Tillich's Lutheran background, but merely point to the prevailing tendencies in the theological scholarship of his homeland in the first two decades of this century.[18]

---

[13]Ibid., pp. 144ff.

[14]Ibid.

[15]Stewart, *A Man in Christ*, p. 147.

[16]Adolf Deissmann, *Die Neutestamentliche formel "in Christo Jesu"* (Marburg: N.G. Elevert, 1892); and *Paul – A Study in Social and Religious History*.

[17]A. Schweitzer, *Paul and His Interpreters* and *The Mysticism of Paul the Apostle*.

[18]See Tillich's autobiographical essay in *The Interpretation of History*.

As has been demonstrated in the study of Paul's references to the Spirit in chapter two, Paul's whole theology grows out of his experience with the kerygmatic Christ—the Risen, Spirit-Christ of faith.[19] The Pauline key is the phrase, "if anyone is in Christ he is a new creation." (2 Corinthians 5:17).[20] Paul Tillich has explicitly declared that his conception of the New Being is based on this strand of Paul's thought.[21]

It is the contention of this writer that just as the Pauline idea of the "New Creation" is the root of Tillich's concept of the "New Being,"[22] so also the Pauline conception of "being in Christ" is the root of Tillich's conception of "being grasped by the Spiritual Presence."[23] Tillich has expressed this conception in *Systematic Theology*, Volume III: "The general assertion ... (is) that the Spiritual Presence in history is essentially the same as the Spiritual Presence in Jesus as the Christ."[24]

Paul most clearly expresses this participation in the Spiritual Christ in the passage in Romans 8, where he speaks of the Christian's participation in the mystical body of Christ:

> ... you are not in the flesh, you are in the Spirit, if the Spirit of God really dwells in you. Anyone who does not have the Spirit of Christ does not belong to him. But if Christ is in you, although your bodies are dead because of sin, your spirits are alive because of righteousness [8:9-10].

This is Paul's attempted explanation of the meaning of Christ for the Christian in terms of the operative power and presence of the Spirit-Christ, and it is obviously related to those "confessions" of Paul's inner life, i.e., of his Christ-mysticism, such as Galatians 2:15-21:

> I have been crucified with Christ; it is no longer I who live, but Christ who lives in me; and the life I now live in the flesh I live by faith in the Son of God, who loved me and gave himself for me.

---

[19]See chap.two.

[20]Cf. Galatians 6:15.

[21]Tillich, *Systematic Theology*, III, pp. 116-117.

[22]Ibid., II, pp. 118-119. Tillich equates the terms, "New Being," "New Creature" (2 Corinthians 5:17; Galatians 6:15) and "in Christ." Deissmann made this same observation in *Paul—A Study in Social and Religious History*, pp. 139 and 178.

[23]Tillich, *Systematic Theology*, III, p. 117.

[24]Ibid., p. 147; cf. p. 148.

As was discussed in chapter two, the historical Jesus is of little importance to Paul, so much so that we might conclude that the life of Christ was but the necessary pre-condition for the appearance of the Christ–Spirit, i.e., that the historical Jesus fulfilled his function by his death.[25] Wherever we look in the New Testament we see the vestiges of the primitive Christology, either in the Synoptics where the Spirit is said to have grasped Jesus at his conception (Luke 1:35), or at his Baptism (Luke 3:21-22); or at the moment of his passage from flesh through death to life as a Spirit (Luke 23:46), or in Paul where we read "the gospel concerning his Son ... designated Son of God in power according to the Spirit ... by his resurrection from the dead ...."[26]

Thus we may conclude that Jesus was a man completely grasped by the Spirit and that his existence and his resurrection were accomplished by the Divine Spirit. It is not surprising that Eduard Schweizer could state:

> It is clearly stated, then, that the Spirit is the ascended Christ, and that turning unto him is union with the realm of the Spirit. Whoever approaches him enters the realm of the Spirit.[27]

Tillich's Ontologization of the Pauline Material

In chapter two Tillich's doctrine of the Spiritual Presence with particular emphasis on the influence on Paul's teachings concerning Christ and the Spirit on Tillich was discussed. In that discussion, as well as in the discussion of Tillich's hermeneutical procedure in chapter three, we again and again made reference to the ontological basis of Tillich's thought. Although we have given several explanations of what we mean by Tillich's ontologization of philosophical and theological concepts, stressing that this mode of thinking pursues its analysis until some basic structure of existence is uncovered, we will make clear at this point how Tillich ontologizes the material drawn from Saint Paul.[28]

The most general statement about the nature of existence, that is, about the essential basis of existence, or of Being itself, in Tillich's thought, is the assertion that God is *Esse Ipsum Subsistens* or Being Itself. Tillich's theology goes on to assert that Being Itself is the power of being which eternally resists non-being. Spirit in Tillich's thought is the manifestation of the creativity of being, a manifestation which becomes

---

[25]See chap. two.

[26]Romans 1:3-4.

[27]E. Schweizer, *Paul and His Interpreters*, p. 60.

[28]See chap. three.

known in the dimension of consciousness, which dimension characterizes the human race. Man, therefore, exists in a dimension of spirit, and man can be spoken of as the bearer of the Spirit. The Spirit is the imminence of the Divine in the world, which unites the power of being and the meaning of being. The possibility of the actualization of the unity of power and value exists only in historical mankind. Now, superimposed upon the ontological basis of all things, that is, God as Being–Itself, and the Spirit as the indwelling of the Divine in the world and in man, which "created order" is utterly dependent upon God, Tillich proposes the ontological doctrine of the multi-dimensionality of all life. This doctrine asserts that in mankind all the various realms of the created order meet. The inorganic realm of substances, the organic realm of all the species of creatures, and the psychic realm of consciousness which characterizes mankind, all meet and are unified in man. Therefore, whatever dealings man has in the dimension of Spirit affect all the other dimensions of life—through man. The ontologization of the Christ-event was discussed in chapter three; hence we will simply connect Tillich's treatment of the Christ to his basic ontologizing scheme. Basically, Jesus was a man, completely grasped by the Spirit. Jesus, whom Tillich calls the Bearer of the New Being in its fullness, was an individual through whom the realm of the Spirit came to fullest expression. In Tillich's theology, the appearance of the New Being is the same as a perfect manifestation of the Spirit. He is the center of history and the criterion by which all other Spiritual manifestations are to be judged. The Christ, then, in Tillich's view, is the place of transcendence in the life of historical mankind, who reveals the inner nature of Ultimate Reality. While the New Being or Spiritual manifestation did take place in the life of a historical individual, that individual became the Christ only insofar as he negated his own particularity and allowed himself to become transparent to the manifestation of the Spirit. It is this kind of theological understanding of God, Christ and the Spirit that we call Tillich's ontologization of the Biblical symbols. With Tillich's program in mind,, we turn now to his use of the Pauline material.

Tillich's ontologization of the Pauline teaching concerning the relationship of Christ and the Spirit may be expressed in these terms: The New Being, which is equivalent to a manifestation of the Spiritual Presence, is present without distortion in Jesus as the Christ; thus he is pre-eminently the Bearer of the Spirit. The relationship to the Christian is as follows: The New Being or the Spirit grasps a man in the experience of insight into the unity of things and in the feeling of dependence upon the source of life, the Ground of Being itself, and this takes him into a state of having an ultimate concern of which Jesus as the Christ is both subject and object. The state of being grasped by the

Spirit may also be described as "being in Christ" since it always brings Jesus the Christ to mind. Tillich attributes this Christ-character of the Spiritual Presence to the Resurrection. The Resurrection, according to Tillich, is that experience of the early disciples which Tillich calls "restitution." By "restitution" Tillich means that the Church's historical experience compensates the individual, Jesus, by associating Jesus with every experience of Spiritual manifestation. This experience of believers takes place because the most perfect experience of being united to the Divine ground was seen in Jesus. Henceforth every experience of being so grasped and taken into a state of transcendent unity of unambiguous life is experienced with overtones of the life of the historical man who was the Bearer of the Spirit in its fullness.[29]

That Tillich attempts to be faithful to the Pauline documents is clear from Tillich's own references to the Pauline doctrine of "being in Christ" which he himself equates with "being in the Spirit,"[30] or with being elevated towards the eternal in a transcendent union of unambiguous life. This spiritual participation is experienced only fragmentarily, or momentarily, however, in man's state of existence under the conditions of space and time. Tillich's identification of the Spiritual Presence and the Risen Christ is manifestly the Pauline teaching, for Paul definitely speaks interchangeably of "being in Christ" and of "being in the Spirit."[31] Paul had a very mystical view of the relationship to the Risen Jesus who is proclaimed as the Christ by the Church. Paul says "the Lord is the Spirit" and speaks of "the Lord who in the Spirit," and says plainly, "If there is any encouragement in Christ, any incentive of love, any participation in the Spirit..." (2 Corinthians 3:17, 18; Romans 8:2, 9-10; Philippians 2:1). On the basis of statements such as these, we may gather that "Lord" and "Spirit" are clearly equivalent terms in Paul's thought. As we demonstrated in chapter two, Paul does speak of the Spirit as being equivalent to the Presence of the Living Christ, although he is imprecise and at times speaks of the Spirit as the extension of God's personality into the world, and in a few cases, speaks as if the Spirit is a separate hypostasis of the Godhead.[32] We concluded from the investigation of the passages concerning the Spirit in the Pauline espistles that Paul did not have any clear conception of an hypostasis of the Spirit. Paul made no attempt to draw what would be, of necessity, a rather artificial distinction between

---

[29]Tillich, *Systematic Theology*, II, pp. 157-158. Tillich calls the concept of restitution "a theory" and says "it remains in the realm of probablity," p. 158.

[30]Ibid., p. 119; and ibid., III, p. 117.

[31]See chap ii.

[32]Ibid., pp. 50-51.

the indwelling of the Holy Spirit (a separate "element" in the Godhead) and the indwelling of the Risen Christ who had become, in Paul's own words, after the Resurrection experience, "A life-giving Spirit" (1 Corinthians 15:45). Thus Tillich is on Pauline ground when he speaks of the Spirit and the Son as being One in the Divine economy.[33]

Tillich's conception of the multi-dimensional unity of life in mankind is an explicit development of what is evidently an unexpressed position of Saint Paul. Paul speaks of the unity of the human race and of organic and inorganic natures. "For the Creation waits with eager longing for the revealing of the sons of God; for the Creation was subjected to futility..." (Romans 8:19-23). It is Paul who teaches that the inorganic and organic realms of the creation itself share together with the psychic and spiritual realms in the condition of estrangement and alienation from the Divine Ground of Being.[34] Paul says "the creation groans," waiting for the redemption which is now coming to fragmentary and anticipatory realization among the Sons of God, i.e., among those men who have been grasped by the Spirit and are being transformed by the renewal of their minds to conform to the image of essential humanity, made manifest in the Christ.[35]

Participation is as basic to Paul as it is to Tillich, and the emphasis on the mystical element is as basic to Paul as it is to a theological rendering of Tillich's system. Of course, Tillich's system is designed to be susceptible to a philosophical rendering also, whereas Paul's teaching is not. Again, neither Paul nor Tillich are exclusively mystical and both contain rational, ontological and moral elments in a harmonious balance in their approach to the discussion of what it means to believe in God, and in the central importance of the historical event, Jesus as the Christ. Participation, for Tillich, is rooted in his epistemology. Understanding, for Tillich, is *Verstehen*.[36] That is, in line with his position of moderate Realism, knowing is an act which participates in being; it is actually an ontic relation. Thus knowing anything or experiencing anything (or being grasped by anything) means actually to become in part one with that thing.[37] This is what Tillich calls ontological reason.[38]

It is at this point of participation that Tillich uniquely combines the doctrine of the universal *Logos* with his development of a Spirit-Christology or of a Christ-Pneumatology. Here Tillich combines what he

---

[33]Tillich, *Systematic Theology*, III, p. 148.

[34]Romans 8:20-22.

[35]Romans 12:2 and Ephesians 4:23.

[36]Tillich, *Das System der Wissenschaften nach Gegenstanden und Methoden*, 6.

[37]Tillich, *Systematic Theology*, I, p. 19.

[38]Ibid., pp. 72-73, 75 and 77.

calls the classical tradition in philosophy with the Biblical tradition in theology.[39] The universal *Logos* is an element in the Divine Ground of Being, the principle of self-manifestation of the Divine. It is analagous to Reason which is the structure of the human mind, and which includes emotional and rational elements. The *Logos* is not only the Wisdom of God and the universal rational structure of things, but it is also the love of God, the driving force in all life that drives man and nature towards the reunion of every separated existing thing with the Ground of Being itself. On this basis Tillich can speak of the unity of thought and being, saying that thought is itself being, the seat of the spirit.[40]

Participation, on the level of the reception of the New Being made manifest in Christ, comes about in this way: The New Being meets us, i.e., the Spirit grasps us, in the Biblical picture of Jesus as the Christ or in its proclamation by the Church. This picture of the Christ is mediated to us through myth and symbol, for it could not be mediated in any other way without being distorted. By participation in this picture of the Christ, we are grasped, or as Tillich has said in one of his sermons, we are "arrested" by God[41] and brought to participation in that self-same New Being which from then on becomes our ultimate concern. This new life then is constantly renewed and deepened by the New Reality that partially and fragmentarily brings us to a transcendent unity which points beyond itself to the eternal, and which overcomes our estrangement from nature, our fellowmen, and ourselves. This is the case because the experience of the New Being has overcome, if only momentarily, our estrangment from God.

Thus Tillich ontologizes the Christ-event and relates it to the multidimensional unity of all life, which unity comes to a nexus in man himself, who is at once a total-person consisting of inorganic, organic, psychic and spiritual dimensions. Tillich is right in saying that the Biblical stories about Jesus themselves so ontologize Jesus when they speak of his life-long possession of the Spirit and of his unity with the Father.[42] Certainly, the high Christology of the Pauline letters, of the undoubtedly genuine Pauline letters, like 1 Corinthians (chap. 12) and Romans (chap. 4:14-16) — and of the letters which are at least from the hand of the disciples of Paul, if not from Paul himself — Colossians and

---

[39]Ibid., p. 72, and Tillich, *BRSUR*, pp. 14, 85. (Cf. Tillich, *Systematic Theology*, I, p. 163.)

[40]Tillich, *Das System der Wissenschaften nach Gegenstanden und Methoden*, 6.

[41]Paul Tillich, "God's Pursuit of Man," *The Eternal Now* (New York: Charles Scribners' Sons, 1963), pp. 108-111.

[42]Tillich, *Systematic Theology*, II, p. 124.

Ephesians—also ontologize Christ.[43] These New Testament documents "ontologize" Christ in the same sense that they define and identify the Christ-event as a structure of being itself, and as an agent in the creation of the universe. When Christ is called the Head of the Body and the agent of creation in whom all things in the universe hang together and in whom all things are to be summed up, we are in the presence of an ontologization of the Spiritual or Risen-Christ. Thus, it is not necessary to derive Tillich's basic approach towards some ontologization of the Christian message, at this point of the description of Christ and the Spirit, from the philosophical background of Realism and German Idealism, for it is present already in Paul's own letters at least implicitly, and it is explicit in Colossians and Ephesians. No proper exegesis of such Biblical documents can avoid dealing with the ontological implications of the event, Jesus as the Christ, and with the ontological dimensions of the experience of the Spiritual Presence. Therefore, Tillich's theology, despite its studied avoidance of traditional Biblical terms, and its unusual structure, as compared to more conservative Biblical theologies, is actually more faithful to the full implications of the Pauline teaching than the traditional approach. It seems clear here, as in other cases, that the hermeneutic task demands an ontological approach if the full range of the Bible's teaching is to be made understandable to any generation of people.

In Paul, participation is chiefly seen as the mystical experience of fellowship with the Risen Lord who is spoken of as "the Spirit," or as "Christ Jesus," or as "Jesus Christ," or as "the Son of God," with no apparent distinction intended, when Paul is speaking of the experience of being a Christian and a member of the Church. Paul implicitly ontologizes this experience of "being in Christ" or "in the Spirit" when he refers to Christ as being the head of the mystical body which is the church. Paul, or one of his disciples, explicitly ontologizes this experience when he speaks of Christ as the agent of creation and the bond of unity which holds all things together, as well as being the inner *telos* towards which all things in the universe are driven for their consummation. The Paulinist says:

> For he has made known to us in all wisdom and insight the mystery of his will, according to his purpose which he set forth

---

[43]Colossians 1:13-20; 2:19-20. Ephesians 1:3-23; 2:4-22; 3:7-12, 14-21; 4:4-16. Cf. Philippians 2:5-11 (certainly from Paul's own hand). It is the conclusion of this writer that Paul himself explicitly "ontologizes" the Risen or Spiritual-Christ.

in Christ as a plan for the fullness of time, to unite all things in him, things in heaven and things on earth [Ephesians 1:9-10].

This passage, and others like it, certainly present Christ as an ontological structure, indeed, as the plan or model on which the Divine has brought the world into existence, and in which all the discrete elements of the universe will be united again in the consummation of the universe.

Usually in Paul's generally accepted letters, such as Romans and the Corinthian epistles, the participation "in Christ" or "in the Spirit" is spoken of in a metaphorical sense that refers to the underlying ontological reality that has been made manifest in the Christ-event. In these metaphorical passages that point towards underlying ontological structures, we find such phrases as "being dead to sin and alive to God in Christ"(Romans 6:11), and "a participation in the body (and blood) of Christ" (1 Corinthians 10:16). The chief passage in this line of thought is Galatians 2:20, which declares that Paul has actually been crucified with Christ, and it is no longer himself who lives, but it is the Christ, i.e., the Spirit-Christ, who is living in him.

Paul's Ontologization of the Body of Christ Metaphor

In his significant study of Pauline theology, J. A. T. Robinson[44] discusses the concept of the Body of Christ in relation to Paul's total theological view. Robinson stresses, correctly I believe, the centrality of the Body of Christ concept for Paul's thought. He calls it the keystone of Paul's theology, the key not only to its unity but the most striking mark of its distinctiveness.[45] Robinson says, "For no other New Testament writer has the word σῶμα any doctrinal significance."[46]

However, Robinson develops Paul's doctrine of the *soma* on the basis of what he calls Paul's view of the socialization of man. While it is true that Paul's thought on the *soma* grows out of his view that man is bound up in a solidarity of historical existence, both that which denies him freedom—the body of sin and death—and that in which he is saved—the Body of Christ—the fact is that Paul develops the Body of Christ concept as an ontologization of the power he experienced in the Risen Christ, the Spirit.

---

[44]Robinson, *The Body — A Study in Pauline Theology*, pp. 7ff.
[45]Ibid., p. 9.
[46]Ibid.

For Paul, the Body of Christ is the most *real* of the structures in the universe; the Body exists in extensional relations throughout the universe. It includes all those on earth who have been joined to Christ in Baptism, and who have thus been transferred from the structural relation Paul calls "the flesh," which is marked by a lack of hope and spiritual death, and those saints who have passed from earthly life to union with God beyond history and above time. The fact is often overlooked that Paul's terms *sarx* and *soma* are ontological terms. These and other terms in the Pauline vocabulary are often referred to as anthropological terms. Indeed, *sarx* does signify man in his solidarity with creation which is marked by alienation from God, and *soma* stands for man in the solidarity of the New Creation reunited with God.[47] However, these terms, and other terms such as *pneuma*, death and sin, are not only descriptions of man's stance in the corporate body of mankind vis-à-vis God, but are descriptions of man's position in regard to ultimate reality, and hence are ontological terms.

Paul's discussion of the individual Christian as a member or organ in the mystical body of the Church is spelled out in great analogical detail. In one example, Paul asks what the case would be if every member of the body was an eye? If such a situation existed, where would the other functions be carried out?[48] This analogy would make little sense if Paul did not have in mind something more real than a man's feeling of belongingness and of usefulness to a social organization. Actually, the Body of Christ concept is an extended analogy that refers to an ontological reality. We might understand the Body-analogy as a sacramental view of the Christian life, in which view, each member (person) of the Body *is* the Body of Christ, as well as being a participant in the Body, just as the elements of bread and wine are said to *be* the Body of Christ, as well as being participating parts of the whole sacramental action. Each member of the Body, and the totality of all members, share in a structure of reality and constitute an extension of the Christ-event, i.e., they all express the power of the New Creation perfectly exemplified in the Christ. Thus Paul can say that the Christian lives in Christ and Christ lives in the Christian.[49] These aspects of Paul's teaching, therefore, reflect an ontological mysticism, and in order to be correctly interpreted require a theology that can handle both ontology and mysticism—a theology like Tillich's.

---

[47]Ibid., p. 31.

[48]1 Corinthians 12:14-26, especially vs. 17 (also vss. 15-16).

[49]1 Corinthians 6:17 and 2 Corinthians 13:5.

The Universal Lordship of Christ

When we turn to the concept of Christ's Lordship over creation, such as is seen in Colossians and Ephesians, which certainly reflect Paul's theology, even if not being actually written by Paul, we see the far-reaching ontology that is implied and expressed in such passages as Ephesians 3:1-10 and Colossians 1:15-20.

> He is the image of the invisible God, the first-born of all creation; for in him all things were created, in heaven and on earth, visible and invisible, whether thrones or dominions or principalities or authorities—all things were created through him and for him. He is before all things, and in him all things hold together. He is the head of the body, the church; he is the beginning, the first-born from the dead, that in everything he might be pre-eminent. For in him all the fullness of God was pleased to dwell, and through him to reconcile to himself all things, whether on earth or in heaven, making peace by the blood of his cross [Colossians 1:15-20].

As this passage demonstrates, the authors of Ephesians and Colossians speak of Jesus Christ as an ultimate element in reality—they are not speaking of a finite individual or of an historical parsonage but of the Lord who is an ontological structure (the same idea as the *logos* concept in John 1:1ff) in whom we were chosen to *methexis*,[50] i.e., to participate from eternity (Ephesians 1:3-4). In this Lord Jesus Christ, we receive redemption and insight (Ephesians 1:7, 9) into the mystery of the Divine will. The Christ, understood as an ontological structure, the basic manifestation of the Divine Being, is thus our location, our salvation and our *telos* or goal. Thus the author of Ephesians can pass from the ontological concept of "Christ the Lord of Creation" to the most basic ontological concept of "Christ the unity of creation," in whom all things human and natural, from all realms of life, are to be summed up and consummated (vs. 11). Verse 11 cannot possibly be understood without reference to an explicit ontology, as it says that God will unite all things in heaven and earth in Christ in the fullness of time. Certainly in passages like this, Christ is understood as a structure in the ontological sense, and not merely as an individual. Saint Paul, and his

---

[50]This word is from Plato, who used it to express the participation of the individual exemplification in the Universal Idea or Form. See Tillich, *The Courage To Be*, pp. 86-90, esp. p. 88. ("Participation is a partial identity and a partial nonidentity.")

disciples, as we have demonstrated above, have ontologized the conception of Christ, and have identified Christ as an ultimate ontological structure. Saint Paul has also married the *logos* concept (which is expressed by the term "Head of the Body" or "Lord') and the concept of Christ as the Bearer of the Spirit, by his occasional references to the Christ as the Spirit (2 Corinthians 3:17 and parallels). Actually, what is involved here is the identification, at least implicitly, of the *logos* idea which antedates Christianity in both Greek thought and in the Jewish Hellenistic writer, Philo, with the concept of wisdom which is derived from the Jewish wisdom literature such as is seen in Proverbs 8 and 9. Paul has not completely identified the *logos* and the wisdom of God, but the ideas are so closely related in his thinking concerning the Body of Christ, or the Lordship of Christ concept, that we have, implicitly, an enrichment and a development of the relatively colorless concept of the Holy Spirit. The Holy Spirit in the Synoptic Gospels, for instance, or even in Acts, lacks the development we find in Paul. For Paul the Spirit is—at the most basic level—what earlier writers and the Fourth Gospel call the *Logos,* or the Wisdom of God. And this Spirit, i.e., this ontological structure or principle of the Divine self-manifestation, is that which Jesus exemplified in his historical life under the conditions of space and time. For Paul, too, Jesus is the Bearer of the Spirit who perfectly manifested the Spirit, for he is the Christ, and the Christ for Paul is that element of the Divine which pre-existed as the Logos or wisdom, or in his words, as "the Lord," and who exists throughout eternity an the Lord-who-is-the-spirit. Moreover, Paul, also speculated that in the Last Judgment, the Christ would "surrender his power" to God. In 1 Corinthians 15:28, Paul declares "… Then the Son Himself will also be subjected to Him (God) …."[51] Clearly, for Paul, God is made manifest through Christ and through Christ man is reunited to the Divine Ground. As the writer of Ephesians says, "Through him we have access in one spirit to the Father" and "In whom you also are built … for a dwelling place of God in the Spirit" (Ephesians 2:18, 22).

Although we concluded in chapter one that Paul was not clear in his own mind as to the precise status of the Spirit, we saw that in the instances in which he referred to the Spirit in terms of his personal experience, he thought of the Spirit as the structure in which the believer participated in the presence of the Risen Christ. What we have in Paul is an implicit identification of the Son and the Spirit in the divine economy, with a consequent enrichment of the very concept of

---

[51]1 Timothy 6:15 also implies that God is the "only Sovereign" — "The King of Kings and the Lord of Lords."

the Holy Spirit. This identification and enrichment amounts to a creation of a theological basis for describing the mystical participation of the believer in the Divine manifestation. Therefore, Paul's construction is an ontologization—and therefore a vindication—of what the Christian confessed about his experience with the Lord Jesus Christ.

The Significance of Paul's Teaching for Tillich's Doctrine

In a word, Paul Tillich's theology develops in a full-orbed manner what Paul throws out in an off-hand, responsive way, as partial answers to the existential questions put to him by his converts. Tillich makes explicit what Paul leaves implicit. Tillich develops in a systematic manner what is in Paul's letters merely a collection of suitable answers to vital questions which were fired at Paul so quickly that he had no other recourse but to answer in a topical, undeveloped way.

As we see above and as we have seen in chapter three, Tillich takes over the Pauline teachings concerning the Spiritual Presence in their entirety, and follows them faithfully, while developing them in a systematic way that attempts to draw out the meaning of what Paul wrote, both in Paul's words and in words that are understandable to modern men. In this attempt to deal faithfully with Paul, Tillich borrows—does not invent, but borrows and develops—the Pauline near-identification of the Spirit and the Christ, and the Pauline ontologization of the Christ in the concepts of the Body of Christ and the Lordship of Christ, and uses them as a determinative line of development for his own theology. We mean by this that those aspects of Tillich's doctrine of the Spiritual Presence which look most unique and seem most "unbiblical" to many readers, e.g., his Spirit-Christology, his ontologization of Christ and his stress on ecstasy or mystical participation, are actually derived from Paul and are not elements dictated by Tillich's background in the moderate Realistic tradition of philosophy which he adopted. If such ideas are found elsewhere, such as in Paul of Samosata,[52] or in the medieval mystics, the appearance of these ideas there are marks of the influence of Saint Paul. Tillich was certainly influenced by the medieval writers, but in reality, the major elements of the Tillichian doctrines of Christ and the Spirit are found already in the Pauline epsitles, either implicitly or explicitly.

Our investigation of the Pauline material also reveals that the unity of ecstacy and structure which Tillich has declared to be basic to his own

---

[52]See O'Meara and Weisser, *Paul Tillich in Catholic Thought*, pp. 295-296.

thought, is found already in Paul, the theologian of the Spirit. Paul emphasizes the ecstatic element in the experience of the Spiritual Presence, particularly in his references to the believer's participation in the Risen Christ. The element of structure is included in such participation, since the Spirit-Christ is the head of the mystical Body, the Body of Christ, which is an ultimate structure of reality.

The Necessity of Grace in Saint Paul and Tillich

As was seen in chapter two, Tillich has adopted the Pauline view that everything having to do with God is done by God. The human spirit cannot reach self-transcendence alone. The reception of the Spirit is the result of grace. This was expressed by Paul in Galatians 3:2: "Did you receive the Spirit by works of the law, or by hearing with faith?" Tillich is basically Pauline and Lutheran in his emphasis upon faith as a gift of the Spirit which changes our Spiritual, and therefore our ontological, situation in the universe. This change of situation is clearly described by Paul in his discussions of *sarx* and *pneuma*. For Paul, to live in the *sarx*, in the realm of the flesh, is to live in estrangement from God. If one accepts the Christ, however, he receives the Spirit and lives in *pneuma*. Life in *pneuma* is life in communion with God. Insofar as we view God as the Ground of Being Itself, we can understand how life in the *sarx* and in the *pneuma* is actually ontological in its meaning. How we are related to Ultimate Reality *is* an ontological question.

Because Tillich has such a devotion to Paul and has an ontological conception of the Spirit, he is willing to use the concept of infusion as well as of the out-pouring of the Spirit upon the Christian. Tillich can speak of infusion, he declares, because of the modern rediscovery of the unconscious basis of the human mind, and also because of the writings of Jung about the archetypical images that are present in every human unconscious. But it is just as true to say that he is willing to speak of infusion or inspiration because Paul does.[53]

Other determinative ideas on Tillich's doctrine derived from Paul are those ontologically-based-teachings which Paul uses to refer to the Spirit as the presence of the Divine in us that actually prays through us to God (Romans 8:26-27). In the matter of referring to Jesus as the Bearer of the Spirit or of the New Creation, Tillich also has a Pauline parallel, Romans 1:3-4, which comes very close to an Adoptionistic view of Christology. In any event, Paul does speak of Jesus Christ as being "designated Son of God in power according to the Spirit" by his

---

[53]Tillich, *Systematic Theology*, III, pp. 115-116.

Resurrection. This, rather than the usual *logos* Christology, fits better with the Christ mysticism seen in Paul's letters. If one has adopted a Spirit-Christology, as Tillich has done, an Adoptionistic-type of Christological theory seems necessary. Thomas A. O'Meara has criticized Tillich for being an Adoptionist in the line of Paul of Samosata (260 A.D.) and Wellhausen (nineteenth century). O'Meara says: "Tillich has changed the place of Jesus' adoption to Calvary, but the Christology is the same."[54] Tillich's reply to this criticism acknowledged that the charge may be true, on the basis of the "accepted dogma." However, Tillich maintained that theological ideas rejected in the ancient past can contain truths that must be expressed in modern categories. Tillich explicitly claims to have given such an expression in his Spirit-Christology.[55] We may note that Tillich's Christology is not really adoptionistic, as *all* of Jesus' life expressed The New Being. Jesus did not earn The New Being but manifested it.

Tillich's Hermeneutical Principles and the Pauline Doctrine of the Spirit

When we turn to Tillich's utilization of his implicit hermeneutical principles (chapter three) in his interpretation of Paul's teaching concerning the Spirit, we must hold in mind this question: How adequate is Tillich's hermeneutic for dealing with the Pauline material?

In chapter three, we described the basic hermeneutical principles that can be discerned in Paul Tillich's systematic theology, naming them as: (1) Ultimate Concern, which is a blend of what Paul and Augustine would call faith and love understood as an ontological element; (2) Justification by Faith and Doubt—which we saw to be a development of Paul's emphasis on grace, influenced by Tillich's own theological development; (3) Catholic Substance-Protestant Principle, which expresses the Tillichian concept of the tension between the tradition of Christian faith and the need for constant criticism; (4) the Word of God and the word of man, which stresses the manifestation of the Spirit through symbols; (5) the Absolutely Universal-Absolutely Concrete concept, which expresses Tillich's belief in the historicity of the One who was the Bearer of the New Being; and (6) the New Being, that makes Tillich's hermeneutical principles fit into a circle, as the New Being is identified as the object of man's ultimate concern. The New Being is both the material norm of Tillich's systematic theology and the

---

[54]O'Meara and Weisser, *Paul Tillich in Catholic Thought*, p. 296.
[55]Ibid., pp. 309-310.

criterion by which all manifestations of the Spiritual Presence or revelations are to be judged.[56]

How well do these hermeneutical principles draw out the inner meaning of the Pauline theology? The answer we give to this question depends upon our willingness to accept the serious intention of Tillich to be faithful to the Bible, and yet to produce a theology that is expressed in non-Biblical terms. Tillich attempts to write a theology that deals with the problems of our culture and of our century rather than being a systematization of the answers of the Bible to the problems of twenty centuries past, expressed in personalistic and mythological terms. If we are willing to take the "pole called situation" as seriously as Tillich and the exponents of liberal theology in general do (and as seriously as Saint Paul evidently took his existential situation), then we may go on to find that Tillich utilizes his hermeneutic in ways that do draw out the meaning of Saint Paul for our time. As was mentioned in chapter three, Saint Paul presents an existential theology, always holding in mind the message of Christ to be preached, on the one hand; and on the other hand, the situation in which his hearers lived with their problems and needs. Thus on this basis, Tillich's basic approach is similar to that of Paul.

We have had occasion to mention above that Saint Paul's theology was so situation-centered (or existential) that we actually have only bits and pieces of a theological system which Paul threw out to answer the questions asked by his congregations. The recognition of this fact makes it necessary for the systematic theologian to develop the implications of Paul's answers in an extended, explicit system of thought. Tillich has done precisely this, making explicit what Paul left implicit as the background of his thought. Thinking along these lines leads us to see that, in some measure, Tillich's method of correlation is implicitly present in the Pauline Epistles. However, the method is not carefully worked out in Paul, as the questions are derived by Paul, without systematization, from the problems and conflicts which arose in his congregations, Paul's answers are then derived from his knowledge of the Old Testament, of the tradition of the Apostles, and from his own mystical experiences with the Risen, Spiritual-Christ. In regard to questions that apparently had no "answers" in the fund of tradition and revelation available to him, Paul fell back upon his own reason for comon sense answers. As one example of this procedure, Paul gave an answer from Christian common sense in I Corinthians 7:25: "Now concerning the unmarried, I have no command of the Lord, but I give

---

[56]Tillich, *Systematic Theology*, I, 50 and 132ff. The Christ is the final revelation because he has the power of negating himself without losing himself.

my opinion as one who by the Lord's mercy is trustworthy." The Pauline epistles thus give us a clear example of an unsystematic method of correlation of the questions of Pauline converts and the answers Saint Paul was able to put together on the basis of his resources.

Saint Paul demonstrates an implicit ontology in his Epistles. Paul's ontology is seen particularly in his development of the doctrine of Christ, of the structural relationship existing between the Risen Christ and the total body of believers—the Body of Christ concept—and the concepts of the Lordship of Christ and of Christ as the nexus of unity which holds all the creation together and which is its inner *telos*. Thus Tilllch's use of Paul is an example of his drawing out of the implicit ontology of the Bible.[57]

Certainly Tillich's first principle, ultimate concern, which is his way of rendering the Christian stance of faith in Christ, is Pauline. Tillich's development of ultimate concern by ontologization, which shows that a man's ultimate concern is his commitment to Being Itself, or God, cannot be seen as a degradation of the New Testament message. One of the Synoptic Jesus' shortest sentences is "Have faith in God" (Mark 11:22). What is new in Tillich is his association of faith with love, which grows out of his ontological analysis of the *eros* element in love. Tillich defines *eros* as the driving force within all life, which drives all the creation toward reunion of its separated parts in the Divine Ground of Being. This equation is not far from Saint Paul's own statement that love is greater than faith in 1 Corinthians 13. It is also close to the emphasis of Saint Augustine on the restlessness of the soul of man until it finds its rest in God.[58]

There can be no doubt of the Pauline basis of Tillich's principle of justification by faith. For Tillich, as for Paul, Christianity is a religion of grace. No one has written more stirringly than Tillich of the God who pursues man "until man allows himself to be arrested by God.[59] Tillich does, however, ontologize this principle and extend it to cover the situation of modern men. And, it is Tillich's contention, modern men, more often than not, do not find themselves in the situation of legalistically working out their salvation; but do find themselves in doubt about the articles of faith. From Martin Kähler, Tillich learned to extend the Reformation article of "by-faith-alone" to cover even the situation of man in doubt. Tillich therefore teaches that God not only justifies man while he is yet a sinner, but also while he is yet a doubter.

---

[57]Tillich, *BRSUR*, esp. chaps. vi-viii.

[58]Augustine, *Confessions* i.i.

[59]Paul Tillich, *The Eternal Now* (New York: Chas. Scribner's Sons, 1963), pp. 101-111.

Saint Paul, who wrote that "at the right time Christ died for the ungodly," while they were yet in their sin, might have agreed that Christ justifies the doubter, but probably would have held that the justified person would no longer doubt. Tillich has also developed the principle of justification by faith in the direction of an affirmation of life which is "the courage to be." The Apostle who wrote, "Quit you like men, be strong," could not take exception to this development.

The 'Catholic Substance-Protestant principle' is derived more from a reassessment of the Reformation than from Saint Paul. The idea of Catholic substance is the positive value Tillich lays on the orthodox, traditional teachings of the Christian Church. While the Protestant principle in Tillich's thought protests against the union of the divine and the created, a union which may—and often has—become demonic in the history of the Church. The "Catholic substance" element of Tillich's thought retains the historic emphasis on the intervention of the Divine in history. The Catholic substance always stresses the fact that "God must reveal Himself," and that the Spiritual Presence has had concrete embodiment in history, especially in the Christ-event.[60] In replying to his Roman Catholic critics in the volume, *Paul Tillich in Catholic Thought*,[61] Tillich declares that the concept of "participation," so basic to his thought, is actually a part of the "Catholic substance" in that it bears witness to the experience of the Spiritual Presence in the concrete structures of the Church.[62]

The Protestant Principle, on the other hand, Tillich believes is the glory of Protestantism, that will hold true long after the "Protestant Era" has ended. It is "a protest against any finite authority which takes upon itself an infinite claim."[63] The Protestant principle is one of the basic principles of Tillich's hermeneutic, also serving him as an instrumental principle—to be used in specific situations to judge the appropriateness or non-appropriateness of a doctrine or symbol. In a very real sense, Tillich's recovery of the emphasis upon Catholic substance, along with his devotion to the Protestant principle, heralds a new day for theology in which Protestant thought might become fuller, richer and perhaps more faithful to the New Testament message than has hitherto been the case.

The principle 'Word of God and word of man' is not necessarily dependent upon Paul, but upon the history of the development of

---

[60]O'Meara and Weisser, *Paul Tillich in Catholic Thought*, pp. 277-278.

[61]Ibid.

[62]Ibid., p. 303.

[63]Tillich, *The Protestant Era*, pp. 162-163. (All of chap. xi is important on this point.)

Protestant theology. The Word of God and word of man principle grows directly out of Tillich's belief that in relation to God everything is by God, yet the Spirit has manifested itself under the conditions of space and time in human life. The "Word of God," or a manifestation of the Spirit comes into human history through finite persons and objects which become transparent to the Divine depths of being and meaning. This self-manifestation of the Spirit was absolutely complete in Jesus the Christ, the Bearer of the Spirit in its fullness, but other Spiritual manifestations take place, and have taken place, fragmentarily, all through history. The "Word of Man" element in this principle stresses Tillich's belief that any word of man—or anything—can become the Word of God, or a revelatory experience, if it becomes transparent (negates itself) and opens the way to an awareness of the Ground of Being by pointing beyond itself. Tillich has declared that the Word of God is not limited to the words of a book, not even to the Bible, but rather any word may become the Word of God.[64]

The principle 'Absolutely Universal/Absolutely Concrete,' developed by Tillich, definitely shares a Pauline emphasis.[65] The absolute concretization of the New Being is attested to by the proclamation of the earliest disciples, and by the New Testament record; it does not depend upon historical knowledge of Jesus of Nazareth. On the other hand, the exemplification of the New Being must have been under the conditions of existence (estrangement, error), it must have been borne by a human being—one who sacrificed all that was personal (relative) in him to that which was absolute in Him (Jesus as the Christ). Tillich believes that this basic principle must be expressed in every theological interpretation.

The principle 'Absolutely Universal and Absolutely Concrete,' means that systematic theology must be kerygmatic, i.e., it must proclaim the message of the historical foundation of the exemplification of the New Being under the conditions of space and time. Tillich combines a kerygmatic with an apologetic approach to theology. This emphasis he receives from the whole New Testament including Paul. The wisdom of this kerygmatic procedure lies in its inseparable connection of Christ's death and his new mode of life (Spirit, "Risen"), so that the experience of communion with the Spirit was always understood as having connection with the name of and traditions about Jesus. In fact there could be for Paul, no cult (church) or piety that was

---

[64]Tillich, *Systematic Theology*, I, 35.

[65]In order for the New Being to be factual in our experience (ontic), it must be historically actual (unlike a Hartshornian idea that may be either possible or actual, it must be actual, it must have had exemplification).

participant in the New Reality that appeared in Jesus Christ, apart from a living experience of the Spiritual Presence which presence was always judged by the supreme Spiritual manifestation that took place in Jesus' life and death. The Paulinist who produced Colossians particularly stresses that the Christian's life is hid with Christ in God and that Christ is our life (Colossians 3:3-4). If the experience of the Spiritual Presence had not continually been subjected to testing by the primal manifestation of the Spirit in Jesus, Christianity would have developed into a minor sect of Judaism, bound to the law, in which the freedom and joy of Jesus (theonomy) would have degenerated into a new legalism (heteronomy, as in the Ebionite sect), or else it would have cut loose all its moorings in the acts of God in history and become a Palestinian strain of gnosticism, as in Valentinianism. The significance of Paul, and of the struggle reflected in Galatians 2, is that under this rigorous thinker, who was also a reacting mystic,[66] the church was guided away from both of these blind alleys and was enabled to develop in fidelity to its own spirit. Paul's blunt reminder that "the Lord is the Spirit," demonstrated the equal need of the Christian faith for a continuing experience of the Spirit and of a baseline in the primal Spiritual experience in the life and death of Jesus the Christ.

In conclusion, Tillich's principle 'The New Being' is most certainly a Pauline emphasis. Saint Paul is the source of the term, "a new creation" (2 Corinthians 5:17). This is echoed in Galatians 6:15, and certainly is a brief statement of what Paul meant by "being in Christ," and being reconciled to God. The Principle of New Being, or new creation, or new birth (John 3), is the central thread of the New Testament, and it has the merit of being a thread by which one can develop a theology which is at once a theology of the Person of Christ and a functional theology which stresses the work of Christ. Tillich's use of the New Being as the material norm of theology and as the criterion of every revelation, is completely in line with Paul's emphasis on the centrality of Christ, of faith in him, and of participation in his mystical Body, as well as being true to the Apostolic belief that Jesus is the fulfillment of every prophecy spoken by men of the Spirit throughout the history of the people of God (Acts 2:14ff.). The emphasis on the victory over estrangement from God through the power of the New Being, which runs through Tillich's thought, is absolutely true to all the metaphors used by Paul to describe the victory of Christ, including the Christus Victor motif which is so central to Biblical theologians.

In chapter three Paul's teaching concerning the Spirit was compared side by side with Tillich's teaching on the Spirit, under eight major

---

[66]Deissmann, *Paul – A Study in Social and Religious History*, 152.

headings, and we saw that Tillich was in line with each of Paul's major threads of doctrine, with the exception of the Pauline usage of personalistic terms in reference to the Divine Spirit. We concluded that we could not allow this difference to keep us from appreciating the basic faithfulness of Tillich to Paul, because the use of ontological and non-personalistic language by Tillich is part of the price that the theologian must be willing to pay in order systematically to set forth the explicit meanings inherent in the Biblical witness to the manifestation of the Spirit in Christ. Now we may attempt to answer the question with which we began this section: "How adequate is Tillich's hermeneutic in dealing with the Pauline material?"

We conclude, therefore, that Tillich's hermeneutical principles (as well as his development of the doctrine of the Spiritual Presence) are quite adequate to a faithful interpretation of the Pauline material, even more so than traditional approaches that refuse to deal with the ontological elements implicit and explicit in Paul. We further conclude that Tillich's approach to more adequate to the Pauline material than (so-called) historical approaches that tend to develop doctrinal principles and ethical insights found in Paul, and almost certainly fail to deal clearly and constructively with the mystical elements in Paul's religion. Here Tillich's broad definition of religion as ultimate concern helps him towards a broader and fairer reading of Paul. A narrow definition of Christianity that denies the value of religion, condemning it as a human work (as in Barth), is inadequate to deal with the Pauline material which contains so many elements that are understandable only in the light of an appreciation of the phenomenology of the History of Religions. Here Tillich's background in the History of Religions, and the continuing conversations he held with scholars such as Mircea Eliade[67] and representatives of non-Christian religions,[68] aided him in his appreciation of the living record of Paul's Christ-mysticism, which is so different from the rather stereotyped views of what is called "Pauline theology" in conservative or "orthodox" theology.

Tillich's doctrine of the Spiritual Presence, therefore, is an attempt to be faithful both to Paul and to our own historical situation. We conclude that it is more successful in its attempt to be at once Biblical and relevant than Neo-Orthodoxy or Conservatism precisely because it is

---

[67]Tillich held these conversations on the History of Religions in the Seminars held jointly with Professor Eliade at the University of Chicago in 1963 and 1964, which I attended and served as secretary.

[68]On his visits to Japan, Tillich discussed religious problems with the leaders of several Asian religions. See his *Christianity and the Encounter of World Religions*, (Minneapolis: Fortress Press, 1994).

philosophical, and thus can deal with the living religion of the Bible in a fuller, richer way; and because it is based on a latitudinarian (or broad) view of religion and can thus deal with the mystical elements that are the living heart of all religion and especially of Saint Paul's Epistles.

Finally, Tillich's theology better deals with our historical situation because it avoids the traditional language of the Bible and of theology[69] in an attempt to express the old ideas in new, more vital ways. If it is not fully successful in this attempt to reach the mind of modern man (nor can any attempt be fully successful), this is because Tillich's new terminology is itself difficult and strange. Beyond this, Tillich's method of correlation is ultimately revealed as an attempt to use the *Weltgeist* of Existentialism to explain the situation of, and to gain the attention of, modern man, but his own philosophical foundations are those of moderate Realism (or Idealism) and not Existentialism. This means that many of his answers are not really acceptable to modern men any more than the traditionally expressed answers of the Biblical theologians, since that Nominalism we inherit by birth[70] keeps us from easily accepting Realistic answers almost as successfully as it keeps us from accepting answers couched in personalistic or mythological terms. But in the end, it is our contention that Tillich's attempt to be faithful to the Bible and to our time is a move in the right direction and points beyond itself to a restoration[71] of an intelligent, appreciative awareness of the eternal message of Christianity.

---

[69]Tillich, *Systematic Theology*, Preface, II, viii.

[70]See Rome and Rome, *Phiosophical Interrogations*, p. 389; "On Universals." "... I used to tell my American students: 'You are Nominalists by birth.'"

[71]See the assessment of Tillich in D. Mackenzie Brown, *Ultimate Concern* (New York: Harper & Row, 1965), p. xiv.

APPENDIXES

TABLE 1

"IN CHRIST"

SEVENTEEN INSTANCES: ROMANS

Roms. 3:22 — ". . . faith in Jesus Christ for all who . . ." N.A.
Roms. 3:24 — ". . . redemption which is in Christ Jesus . . ." Us. 3-d
Roms. 6:3 — ". . . baptized into Christ Jesus were . . ." Us. 3-a
Roms. 6:11 — ". . . dead to sin and alive to God in Christ Jesus." Us. 3-a
Roms. 6:23 — ". . . eternal life in Christ Jesus our Lord." Us. 3-2
Roms. 8:1 — ". . . for those who are in Christ Jesus." Us. 3-a
Roms. 8:2 — ". . . of life in Christ Jesus has set me . . ." Us. 3-a and d
Roms. 8:10 — "But if Christ is in you, although you . . ." Us. 4
Roms. 8:39 — "love of God in Christ Jesus our Lord." Us. 3-2 and d
Roms. 9:1 — "I am speaking the truth in Christ." Us. 3-b
Roms. 12:5 — "Though many are one body in Christ." (Unity) Us. 3-e
Roms. 15:5 — "another in accord with Christ Jesus." (Unity) Us. 3-e
Roms. 15:17 — "In Christ Jesus, then, I have reason to . . ." Us. 3-c
Roms. 16:3 — "my fellow workers in Christ Jesus." Us. 3-b
Roms. 16:7 — "and they were in Christ before me." Us. 3-b In the church
Roms. 16:9 — "Greet Urbanus, our fellow worker in Christ." Us. 3-b
Roms. 16:10— "Greet Apelles, who is approved in Christ." Us. 3-c

SEVENTEEN INSTANCES: 1 CORINTHIANS

1 Cor. 1:2 — "To those sacrificed in Christ Jesus." Us. 3-a and c
1 Cor. 1:4 — "which was given you in Christ Jesus." (Grace) Us. 3-d
1 Cor. 1:8 — "in the day of our Lord Jesus Christ." N.A.
1 Cor. 1:30 — "source of your life in Christ Jesus." Us. 3-d
1 Cor. 3:1 — "men of the flesh, as babes in Christ." Us. 3-c
1 Cor. 4:10 — "sake, but you are wise in Christ." Us. 3-c
1 Cor. 4:15 — "you have countless guides in Christ." Us. 3-c
1 Cor. 4:15b— "your father in Christ Jesus through." Us. 3-c
1 Cor. 4:17 — "to remind you of my ways in Christ." Us. 3-b
1 Cor. 9:12 — "in the way of the gospel of Christ." Us. 3-b
1 Cor. 10:16 — "a participation in the blood of Christ." (Truly mystical)
　　　　　　　　Us. 3-d

1 Cor. 10:16 — *"a participation in the body of Christ."* Us. 3-d
1 Cor. 15:18 — "fallen asleep in Christ have perished." Us. 3-a (equals "in
      the faith")
1 Cor. 15:19 — "we who are in Christ have perished." Us. 3-a
1 Cor. 15:22 — "so also in Christ shall all be made." Us. 3-a
1 Cor. 15:31 — "which I have in Christ Jesus our Lord." Us. 3-a
1 Cor. 16:24 — "my love be with you all in Christ Jesus." Us. 3-a

TEN INSTANCES: 2 CORINTHIANS

2 Cor. 1:21 — "Who establishes us with you in Christ . . ." Us. 3-e
2 Cor. 2:10 — "your sake in the presence of Christ . . ." Us. 3-a and e
2 Cor. 2:17 — "in the sight of God we speak in Christ." Us. 3-b and e
2 Cor. 4:6 — "the glory of God in the face of Christ." (N.A. Refers to The
      Incarnation of Christ. Perhaps Us. 3-d)
2 Cor. 5:17 — "therefore, if anyone is in Christ." Us. 3-a
2 Cor. 5:19 — "God was in Christ reconciling the world . . ." Us. 3-d See
      below .b
2 Cor. 12:19 — "That we have been speaking in Christ." Us. 3-b, c and e
2 Cor. 12:2 — "I know a man in Christ who fourteen . . ." Us. 3-a (very
      mystical) See below .c
2 Cor. 13:5 — "realize that Jesus Christ is in you?" Us. 4

FIFTEEN INSTANCES: GALATIANS

Gals. 1:6 — "in the grace of Christ and turning to . . ." Us. 3-d
Gals. 2:4 — "freedom which we have in Christ Jesus." Us. 3-a
Gals. 2:16 — "law but through faith in Jesus Christ." Us. 3-d
    — "even we have believed in Christ Jesus." Us. 3-d
    — "to be justified by faith in Christ." Us. 3-d
Gals. 2:17 — "our endeavor to be justified in Christ." Us. 3-d (equals faith)
Gals. 2:20 — "but Christ who lives in me . . ." (and) "the life I now live by
      faith in the Son of God . . ." Us. 4
Gals. 3:14 — "that in Christ Jesus the blessing . . ." Us. 3-d
Gals. 3:22 — "faith in Jesus Christ might be given." Us. 3-d
Gals. 3:36 — "For in Christ Jesus you are all sons . . ." Us. 3-a
Gals. 3:27 — "baptized *into* Christ have *put on* Christ." Us. 3-d and a (Note
      the parallel between into and put on)
Gals. 3:38 — "for you are all one in Christ Jesus." Us. 3-e
Gals. 4:19 — "Travail until Christ be formed in you." Us. 4
Gals. 5:6 — "For in Christ Jesus neither circumcision." Us. 3-a and d
Gals. 6:14 — "in the cross of our Lord Jesus Christ." N.A. perhaps 3-d

SIX INSTANCES: I THESSALONIANS

I Thessa. 1:3 — "hope in our Lord Jesus Christ." Us. 3-d
I Thessa. 2:14 — "The churches of God in Christ Jesus." Us. 3-e
I Thessa. 3:3 — "servant in the gospel of Christ." Us. 3-c
I Thessa. 4:1 — "Exhort you in the Lord Jesus." Us. 3-d
I Thessa. 4:16 — "the dead in Christ." Us. 3-d
I Thessa. 5:9-10 — "Our Lord Jesus Christ who died for us so that whether we wake or sleep we might live with him." (Christ–mysticism) N.A.
I Thessa. 5:18 — "The will of God in Christ Jesus for you." Us. 3-d

ELEVEN INSTANCES: PHILIPPIANS

Phil. 1:1b — "The saints in Christ Jesus who are at Philippi." Us. 3-a
(Phil. 1:8 — "The affection of Christ Jesus . . .") N.A.
(Phil. 1:19 — "of the Spirit of Jesus Christ . . .") N.A.
(Phil. 1:21 — "Christ will be honored in my body ... for me to live is Christ) N.A.
Phil. 1:26 — "To glory in Christ Jesus." Us. 3-d
Phil. 2:1 — "encouragement in Christ . . . participation in the Spirit . . ." Us. 3-d
Phil. 2:5 — "(mind) which you have in Christ Jesus . . ." Us. 3-a and d
Phil. 2:16 — "in the day of Christ." Us. 3-d (Also, 1:6, 10 — Day of Christ — identifiied with Old Testament "Day of the Lord")
Phil. 3:3 — "worship God in spirit, and glory in Christ Jesus . . ." Us. 3-d (Note this whole passage, 3:4-21, as example of mysticism.)
Phil. 3:9 — "faith in Christ." N.A.
(Phil. 3:10 — "becoming like him (Christ) in his death . . ." Note for mysticism. — N.A.)
Phil. 3:14 — "the upward call of God in Christ Jesus . . ." Us. 3-d
Phil. 4:7 — "keep your hearts and your minds in Christ Jesus." Us. 3-a
Phil. 4:19 — "his (God's) riches in glory in Christ Jesus." Us. 3-d
Phil. 4:21 — "Greet every saint in Christ Jesus." Us. 3-e

FOUR INSTANCES: PHILEMON

vs. 6 — "all the good that is ours in Christ." Us. 3-a and d

vs. 8 — "bold enough in Christ." Us 3-d
vs. 20 — "Refresh my heart in Christ." Us. 3-d
vs. 23 — "prisoner in Christ Jesus." Us. 3-a
Legend:

Usage 3: εν used in phrases like εν χριστω

Type a: Designates Christ's connection with Christian congregation.
Type b: Designates an activity or position as characteristically "Christian."
Type c: Designates a value-judgment in the moral sphere.
Type d: Designates the objective foundations of our salvation and the
         kingdom of God
Type e: Designates unity, especially the unity of the church
Type 4: Designates Christ in the believer; the idea of "indwelling."
N.A.: —Not applicable to our study.

Usaage 2: εν used in phrases like εν πνευματι ("In the Spirit")

Type a: Designates the place of the Spirit in humans, localized by εν
         (Internal).
type b: Designates the state of the human's being in the Spirit (External).

Note: The passages in parenthesis are not included in the enumeration of
passages, nor taken into account in the text. They are included here because they
give supporting evidence to the thesis that Paul wrote of his relationship with
Christ in quite mystical terms.

a — Here, I note that these lines express both Christ in the congregation and
the congregation in unity with one another and with Paul. I feel that "in Christ"
here is equivalent to "in the Spirit," i.e., the Spiritual Presence of Christ in the
congregation which conduces to unity among believers. Paul is especially
stressing "Christian unity" in II Corinthians 1-9.

b — 2 Corinthians 11:10—"As the truth of Christ is in me." (Perhaps usage
4.) Included for comparison only—not included in statistics.

c — 2 Corinthians 13:3 — 'Proof that Christ is speaking in me." (Perhaps
usage 4.) This definitely is to be included as a "Christ in me" passage. It is the
eleventh instance.

TABLE 2

"IN THE SPIRIT"

Roms. 7:6 — "code but in the new life of the Spirit." Us. 2-b (b)
Roms. 8:2 — "For the law of the Spirit of life in Christ Jesus ..." N.A. (c)
Roms. 8:9 — "in the flesh, you are in the Spirit, . . ." Us. 2-b
  "If the Spirit of God really dwells in you. . ." Us. 2-a (d)
  "not have the Spirit which dwells in you. . ." Us. 2-b (e)
Roms. 8:11 — "through his Spirit which dwells in you. . ." Us. 2-a (f)
Roms. 9:1 — "bears me witness in the Holy Spirit . . ." Us. 2-b (g)
Roms. 14:17 — "and peace and joy in the Holy Spirit . . ." Us. 2-b.
Roms. 15:13 — ". . . By (εν) the power of the Holy Spirit . . ." Us. 2-a
Roms. 15:16 — "sanctified by (εν) the Holy Spirit." Us. 2-a.
Roms. 15:19 — ". . . by (εν) the power of the Holy Spirit . . ." Us. 2-a (h).

SIXTEEN INSTANCES: 1 CORINTHIANS

1 Cor. 2:4 — "in demonstaration of the Spirit and in power ..." Us. 2-a.
1 Cor. 2:10-16 —*In toto* (No εν, but very important) ("A secret and hidden wisdom of God" — vs. 7) "...God has revealed to us through (δια) the Spirit. For the Spirit searches everything, even the depths of God.... now we have received not the spirit of the world, but the Spirit which is from God, that we might understand the gifts bestowed on us by God. And we impart this in words not taught by human wisdom but taught by the Spirit. The unspiritual (φυχικος) man does not receive the gifts of the Spirit of God, for they are folly to him, and he is not able to understand them because they are spiritually discerned. The spiritual man judges all things, but is himself to be judged by no one. 'For who has known the mind of the Lord so as to instruct him?' But we have the mind of Christ." (Qv. Philip. 2:5ff.) N.A. (I).
1 Cor. 3:16—"Do you not know that you are God's temple and that God's spirit dwells in you." Us. 2-a (j).
1 Cor. 4:21—"Shall I come to you with a rod, or with love in a spirit of gentleness." (RSV —lit. εν αγαπηπνευματι) N.A.
1 Cor. 5:3—"present in the spirit." N.A.
1 Cor. 5:4—"my spirit is present, with the power of our Lord Jesus." N.A. — this is a very strange passage.
1 Cor. 5:5—"...the destruction of the flesh, that his spirit may be saved ..." N.A.

1 Cor. 12:9—"to another faith by the same Spirit, to another gifts of healing by the one Spirit ..." N.A. Us. 2-b.

1 Cor. 12:11—"all these are inspired by one and the same Spirit, who apportions to each one individually as he wills." N.A. Us. 2-b.

1 Cor. 12:13—(2 instances) "For by one Spirit, we were all baptized into one body — Jews or Greeks, slaves or free—and all were made to drink of one Spirit" (Us. 3-e). (l)

1 Cor. 14:2—In R.S.V., out as it actually does not contain εν. "For one who speaks in a tongue speaks not to men but to God; for no one understands him, but he utters mysteries in the Spirit." N.A.

FIVE INSTANCES: 2 CORINTHIANS

2 Cor. 1:5 — "For as we share abundantly in Christ's sufferings, so through Christ we share abundantly in comfort too." (Not εν but τα παθηματα του χριστου εις ημας.) N.A.—but of Us. 3-d.

2 Cor. 3:6—In RSV as "in the Spirit" does not contain εν, but reads: αμα πνευματος, lit. — "but spiritual." N.A.

2 Cor. 3:17 — (No εν but extremely important. ο ζε κυριος το πνευμα εστιν. "The Lord is the Spirit." N.A.—but important for this study.

2 Cor. 3:18—Καθαπερ απο κυριου πνευματος,"come from the Lord (who is the) Spirit." N.A., not εν, but very important for this study.

2 Cor. 6:6—" εν πνευματι αχω,"—"by the Holy Spirit" in R.S.V. Paul's explanation of how he commended himself to the Corinthians as a true Christian minister. Us. 2-b.

(2 Cor. 12:18—Mentioned in R.S.V. as "in the same spirit," does not contain εν, and is N.A.)

TWO INSTANCES: GALATIANS

Gals. 4:6 —"...God has sent the Spirit of his Son into our hearts, crying, 'Abba, Father.'"

(Not εν but extremely important for our study.) Really Us. 2-a.

(Gals. 6:1 —"A spirit of gentleness." N.A.)

Gals. 6:8 —"... but he who sows to the Spirit will from the Spirit reap eternal life." (Not εν , But important.)

FOUR INSTANCES: 1 THESSALONIANS

A. SPIRIT:
1 Thessa. 5:19—"Do not quench the Spirit," (20) "do not despise prophesying." N.A.

B. HOLY SPIRIT:
1 Thessa. 1:5-6—"For our gospel came to you not only

FIVE INSTANCES: PHILIPPIANS

A. SPIRIT:
Phil. 2:1—"So if there is any encouragement in Christ, any incentive of love, any participation in the Spirit, any affection and sympathy...." US. 2-b (and 3-d). (Here "in Christ" is equated with "in the Spirit," and both are equated with love.)

B. SPIRIT OF JESUS CHRIST:
Phil. 1:19—"... for I know that through your prayers and the help of the Spirit of Jesus Christ this will turn out for my deliverance." N.A.

Phil. 1:21—"For me to live is Christ, and to die is gain." N.A. (Christ-mysticism) cf. Gal. 2:20.

C. HUMAN SPIRIT:
Phil. 3:3—"...who worship God *in spirit*, and glory in Christ Jesus ...." Us. 2-b. (Other MSS read: "worship by the Spirit of God." E.g., MSS, versions, etc. θεω is found in "D" on the first hand; ρ, and the Latin and Syriac MS. It is missing from ρ 46.) Arndt and Gingrich, p. 682, 5a. seem to prefer this last reading.

D. SPIRIT (GENERAL USE):
Phil. 1:27 —"...I may hear of you that you stand firm *in* one spirit, with one mind ...." N.A. (equals "in unity").

ONE INSTANCE: PHILEMON

A. HUMAN SPIRIT:
Vs. 25 —"The grace of our Lord Jesus Christ be with your spirit." N.A.

Legend

a   (1) The word πνευμα and its various forms occurs 35 times in Romans; 40 times in 1 Corinthians; 16 times in 2 Corinthians, and 17 times in Galatians. These occurrences have been "sifted through" to give pertinent instances listed here. Information gained from a count of the passages recorded in W. F. Moulton, *A Concordance to the Greek Testament* (New York: Charles Scribner's Sons, 1897), pp. 819-822. Also 4 times in 1 Thessalonians; 5 times in Philippians and 1 time in Philemon.

(2) Captial letter "S" used for "Spirit" wherever R.S.V. uses it.

b   But this translation should be checked by the Greek. εν καινοτητι πνευματος

c   This passage clearly shows the connection of the Spirit and the glorified "Christ Jesus"

d   Note close connection, one cannot be "in the Spirit," without having the Spirit "in him."

e   This verse must be seen in connection with verse 10: "But if Christ is in you…" This shows the almost complete identification of "the Spirit" and "the glorified Christ" in Paul; at least in these major Epistles.

f   Note, here "Spirit" probably refers to "God," in the sense of "God the Father," see v. 11. "The Spirit of him who raised Jesus (note omission of "Christ") from the dead dwells in you …" Here the imprecision of Paul's language is apparent. Thus we conclude (a) he had no precisely fixed concept of the Spirit, and (b) we cannot say that the identification of the Spirit and Christ is complete, although it is almost in the most important passages.

g   Note, "Holy Spirit" here probably refers to the same reference as "in Christ," e.g., "in the church," as well as "in my sense of personal communion with God."

h   Note: Instances 9, 10, and 11 are not to be found by consulting the RSV or its concordance, as εν is rendered as "by" in refernce to "power" by that version.

i   The gifts of the Spirit of God are equated with the mind of the Lord and with the mind of Christ.

j   Rudolf Bultmann's interpretation, *New Testament Theology*, trans. K. Grobel (New York: Charles Scribner's Sons, 1951), I, p. 195.

k   Here is Paul's mysticism (reacting or devotional mysticism) in its clearest expression. We are to become one spirit with the Lord, who is the Spirit.

l   1 Cor 12:13 shows that Paul made little distinction between Christ and Spirit in their "indwellingness" in the believer.

TABLE 3

SEVEN INSTANCES: ROMANS

Rom 16:2—"...receive her in the Lord as fits the saints..." Us. 3-b
Rom 16:8—"Greet Amphilatus, my beloved in the Lord." Us. 3-c
Rom 16:11— "Those in the Lord who belong to..." Us. 3-e (Refers to being in the church; here "in the Lord" equals "in the church.")
Rom 16:12— "Greet thsoe workers in the Lord..." Us. 3b
Rom 16:12— "Who has worked hard in the Lord..." Us. 3-b
Rom 16:13— "Greet Rufus, eminent in the Lord..." Us. 3-c
Rom 16:22— "...we greet you in the Lord..." Us. 3-b

TEN INSTANCES: 1 CORINTHIANS

1 Cor. 4:17— "...faithful child in the Lord" Us. 3-c
1 Cor. 7:22— "For he who was called in the Lord as a slave is a freedman of the Lord." Us. 3-d
1 Cor. 7:39— "To whom she wishes, only in the Lord." Us. 3-c (Refers "to a Chistian.")
1 Cor. 9:1— "...you my workmanship in the Lord." Us. 3-c
1 Cor. 9:2— "The seal of my apostleship in the Lord." Us. 3-c (In context, where Paul appeals to his having seen "Jesus our Lord," these two passages take on a very mystical color, "in the Lord" may thus equal "in communion with our common [universal] Lord.")
1 Cor. 11:11— "...in the Lord woman is not independent..." Us. 3-a and e (refers to status of unity of all in the church).
1 Cor. 15:31— "...I have in Christ Jesus our Lord..." NA
1 Cor. 15:58— "abounding in the work of the Lord..." Us. 3-b
1 Cor. 15:58— "...that in the Lord your labor is not..." Us. 3-a
1 Cor. 16:19— "you hearty greetings in the Lord." Us. 3-b

ONE INSTANCE: 2 CORINTHIANS

2 Cor 2:12— "...a door was opened for me in the Lord..." Us. 3-a (refers to Christ opening the door.)

ONE INSTANCE: GALATIANS

Gal 5:10— "I have confidence in the Lord that you will take no other view than mine..." Us. 3-c

TWO INSTANCES: 1 THESSALONIANS
1 Thess 3:8— "stand fast in the Lord." Us. 3-d
1 Thess 5:12— "over you in the Lord." Us. 3-a

NINE INSTANCES: PHILIPPIANS

Phil. 1:14—"confident in the Lord." Us. 3-d
Phil. 2:19—"hope in the Lord Jesus." Us. 3-d
Phil. 2:24—"trust in the Lord . . ." Us. 3-d
Phil. 2:29—"receive him in the Lord . . ." Us. 3-e
Phil. 3:1—"rejoice in the Lord . . ." Us. 3-d
Phil. 4:1—"stand firm thus in the Lord . . ." Us. 3-d
Phil. 4:2—"to agree in the Lord . . ." Us. 3-e
Phil. 4:4—"Rejoice in the Lord always; . . ." Us. 3-d
Phil. 4:10—"I rejoice in the Lord . . ." Us. 3-d

TWO INSTANCES: PHILEMON

vs. 16— "both in the flesh and in the Lord." Us. 3-a and 3-d (equivalent to "in the Spirit.")
vs. 20— "Some benefit from you in the Lord." Us. 3-e

TABLE 4

THE "BODY OF CHRIST"

A. ROMANS:

1. Roms. 7:4 —   "Likewise, my brethren, you have died to the law through *the body of Christ*, so that you belong to another, to him who has been raised from the dead in order that we may bear fruit for God." (This probably refers to the sacrifice of Christ, his bodily death, on the cross.)

2. Roms. 12:4-5— (4) "For as in *one body* we have many members, and all the members do not have the same function, (5) so we, though many, are *one body in Christ*, and individually members one of another." (This passage undoubtedly uses the term "body" to refer to the Church.)

B. 1 CORINTHIANS:

1. 1 Cors. 10:16-17 — (16) "The cup of blessing which we bless, is it not a participation in *the body of Christ*? (17) Because there is one loaf, we who are many are *one body*, for we all partake of the same loaf." (Here "body" is used in vs. 16 to refer to participation in the effects of the sacrifice of Christ on the cross. Vs 17 uses the phrase "one body" to designate the unity of Christians in the church.)

2. 1 Cors. 11:24 —   The Institution of the Lord's Supper. Here "body" refers to the sacrifice of Christ.

3. 1 Cors. 11:27 —   ". . . profaning the body and blood of the Lord ...." (This refers to the Communion elements, and by extension [analogy] to the sacrifice of Christ.)

4. 1 Cors. 11:29 — Same as No. 3.

5. 1 Cors. 12:12-27 — Paul's Discourse on "The Body":

a. 12:12-13 —   (12) "For just as the body is one and has many members, and all the members of the body, though many, are one body, so it is with Christ. (13) "For by one Spirit we were all baptized into one body—Jews or Greeks, slaves or free—and all were made to drink of one Spirit."

b. 12:14-26 —   The analogy of the physical body and "The Body of Christ" or church.

c. 12:27   —   "Now *you are the body of Christ* and individually members of it."

(I) (1 Cor. 12:13 is very useful for this study, for it unites the activity of the Spirit with this concept of the church as the unity of believers with one another and with their Lord, "The Body of Christ.")
(II) (12:27 specifically points out that "you," the Corinthian church members, "are The Body of Christ." The body of believers make up an organic unity, a *gestalt*, a larger than the sum-total of the individual members, for the organic Body [church] is indwelt by the Spiritual-Christ.)

TABLE 5

TILLICH'S ADEQUACY TO EXPRESS THE PAULINE DOCTRINE OF THE SPIRIT

Paul:

Paul Tillich:

1.   Divine Power had been exercised in Christ who was crucified and resurrected. The same power was effected in Paul and he wished it to be so in his converts —he even found it so realized in a congre- gation. Paul had seen miraculous signs of the Spirit's power in the church. (II Cor. 13:4; I Thessa. 1:5; Rom. 15:18f; I Cor. 2:4, 4:20f.; II Cor. 6:6f.; Rom. 15:13; I Cor. 12:10 and 28 f.; I Cor.1:24.)

1.   Jesus as the Christ is a creation of the Divine Spirit. The New Being is present in him. New Being is essential being under the conditions of existence conquering the gap between essence and existence. This New Being expresses the same idea which Paul does in the term New Creation. It is equivalent to the experience of being grasped by the Spiritual Presence. It is fragmentarily, though unambiguously, experienced by the Christian. Wherever men are grasped by an ultimate concern, especially in the church, the New Being or the Divine Spirit is manifest and men participate in it. (*Systematic Theology*, I, 118ff.)

2.   The gift of the Spirit came from God as an act of His love, it was bestowed on the faithful as a sign of their adoption as the sons of God. (I Thessa. 4:8; Gal. 3:5, 4:6; I Cor. 2:10, 12; II Cor. 1:22, 5:5; II Thessa. 2:13; Rom. 8:9. 14; 16f.)

2.   The Spiritual Presence is the unity of power and meaning, symbolically it is God Present, the transcendent unity of unambiguous life. It is not created by man but comes into man as an experience of the unity and creativity of the Ground of Being. It comes to man from that ultimate and uncon- ditional basis of things, that transcends both concepts, inside and outside. It comes freely and grasps the being of those who are filled with an ultimate concern.

Paul

3. The Spirit came to the adopted sons as a pledge of the resurrection life. It signified a new creation in them and participation in the eternal life of Christ. (II Cor. 1:22, 5:1-10, Rom. 8:23; II Thessa. 2:13, Rom. 6:11, 8:2, 10f., 23; I Cor. 15:20-23, 43f.; Philip. 1:21f.; 3:9-11.) Christ himself as the last Adam had become a lifegiving Spirit. (I Cor. 15:45.)

4. Paul teaches that Christians must lead holy lives for they are called to sanctification. They are to be spiritual for they are united with Christ in the Body of Christ and have become one spirit with him. Christians are the temple of the Holy Spirit. The virtues of the Christian are the harvest of the Spirit cooperating with him as he obeys his Lord. (I Thessa. 4:3, 7f.; Gal. 6:1; I Cor. 2:15, 3:1,-14:37; Rom.1:11, 7:14; 15:27; I Cor. 2:13, 9:11, 6:15-17, 19, 2:16; 7:40; Rom. 8:27; 12:2, Philip. 2:12f., Gal. 5:22, 6:1; I Cor. 4:21, 12:31-13:1.)

Paul Tillich

3. The experience of being grasped by the Spirit drives the human spirit out of itself towards a successful self-transcendence. It creates, fragmentarily, *now*, the exeperience of the transcendent unity of unambiguous life which overcomes the gap between essence and existence. It is salvatory and healing and points beyond itself to ultimate and unconditional transcendent union with being itself beyond history.

4. The spiritual Presence manifests itself as faith and love. As love it is the state of being driven towards the reunion of the separated. It drives towards holiness in that it is a manifestation of the holy itself —the Divine Ground of Being. The Christian is holy because of the holiness of the New Being which is in him. Holiness is a matter of faith in the working of the New Being within the Christian. One grasped by the Spirit will be driven towards a life of morality based on religious motivation.

Paul

5. The love created by the possession of the Spirit leads Paul to an ethic of love. Christians form a brotherhood, they are the Body of Christ, the family of God. They participate in the Spirit, for the Holy Spirit creates the community. (Phil. 2:1; II Cor. 13:14; Rom. 12:10; I Thessa. 4:9.)

Paul Tillich:

5. The Spiritual Presence is manifest as love. All ethics are ethics of theonomous or creative love. Love is the state of being taken by the Spiritual Presence into the transcendent unity of unambiguous life. It expresses itself by uniting oneself into a center creating the new and driving one toward union with his ground and aim. In order for one to be truly centered, one must treat every other person as a person with an inviolate center. Love includes justice and is an expression of the power of being which drives towards reuniting the separated. It creates true brotherhood among men. Such love is impossible for man unless he is grasped by the Spirit.

6. The marks of the Spirit's activity in the church include the mighty acts done through the apostle, the ecstasies of believers and prophecy. Paul calls these the gifts of the Spirit. However, Paul stresses that the good of the church is of first importance and encourages those spiritual gifts which build up the church while not actually denying the work of Glossolalia. (Rom. 5:18f; II Cors. 12:12; 12:1-7; I Cor. 12:10, 28-31, 13-1f., 8, 14; 12:10, 13:2, 8; 14:6, 22; I Thessa. 5:19f.)

6. Tillich agrees with all of Paul's descriptions and in fact develops his doctrine on the basis of 1 Cor. 1-3 and 12-13. Ecstasy is a favorite word of Tillich's, for to him faith includes an emotive element. Whatever is done in the church or in mankind that heals, saves, reunites, is the work of the Spiritual Presence and the state of its being made manifest.

7. Membership in the church is dependent on the influence of the Spirit. Faith is a gift of the Spirit. The Spirit brings fellowship with God. The Church is a unity because the Spirit works in it as blood does in the human body. Praise and prayer are inspired by the Spirit—prayer would not be possible unless the Spirit interceded for us. The marks of the Spirit in the Christian life are love, meekness, patience, etc. The character of the Spirit is the character of Christ. (1 Cor 12:3.9; 13:2; 12:13, 14:15, Rom. 6:3f., 8:26, 34; 1 Thess 5:17-19.)

8. Paul speaks indifferently of the Spirit as the Spirit of Jesus Christ, of Christ, of God's Son, of God, or of the living God. The Spirit, like God himself, is revealed in Jesus Christ; as Paul says, "The Lord is the Spirit." Thus Paul had no clearly worked out doctrine of the Trinity and certainly identified the Spirit in some sense with the presence of the living Christ.[1]

7. Membership in the Spiritual Community, the hidden essence of the Church, is gained only by being grasped by the Spirit. Faith is the gift of God, for in relation to God, everything is by God. It is the presence of the New Being, or the Spirit that makes the church one, holy and universal. Every true prayer is the result of one's being driven by the Spirit.

8. Tillich accepts the Pauline manner of speaking of the Spirit, saying, "In the divine economy, the Spirit follows the Son, but in essence the Son is the Spirit." Jesus as the Christ is the bearer of the Spirit in the most complete sense. The New Being and the Spiritual Presence are one quality—the presence of the Divine in the world.

---

[1]The above detailed account of Paul's doctrine of the Spirit has been freely adapted from Alan Richardson, *A Theological Wordbook of the Bible* (New York: MacMillan Co., 1953), pp. 241-243.

BIBLIOGRAPHY

Books

Adams, J. L. *Paul Tillich's Philosophy of Culture, Science, and Religion.* New York: Harper Row, Publisher, 1965.

Adler, Mortimer J. *The Conditions of Philosophy.* New York: Atheneum, 1965.

Alter, Robert. *Genesis: Translation and Commentary.* New York: W. W. Norton & Co., 1996.

Althaus, Paul. *The Theology of Martin Luther.* Trans. Robert C. Schultz. Philadelphia: Fortress Press, 1966.

Altizer, Thomas J. J. *The Gospel of Christian Atheism.* Philadelphia: Westminster Press, 1966.

_____. *Mircea Eliade and the Dialectic of the Sacred.* Philadelphia: Westminster Press, 1963.

_____. *Oriental Mysticism and Biblical Eschatology.* Philadelphia: Westminster Press, 1961.

Amiot, Francois. *The Key Concepts of St. Paul.* New York: Herder and Herder, 1962.

Arnal, Jean. *La Notion de l'Espirt. La Doctrine Paulininenne.* Paris: Fischbacher, 1907.

Arndt, William F. and F. Wilbur Gingrich (trans.). *A Greek-English Lexicon of the New Testament,* by Walter Bauer. 4th German ed. Chicago: University of Chicago Press, 1959.

Augustine. *Later Works.* Edited by John Burnaby. Library of Christian Classics. Philadelphia: The Westminster Press, 1955.

Barclay, William. *The Mind of St. Paul.* New York: Harper & Bros., 1958.

Barr, James. *The Semantics of Biblical Language.* Oxford: Oxford University Press, 1962.

Barrett, C. K. *From First Adam to Last.* London: Adam & Charles Black, 1962.

Barth, Karl. *Church Dogmatics.* Vol. 1. Edited by G. W. Bromiley and T. F. Torrance. Edinburgh: T. & T. Clark, 1963.

Barth, K. *The Holy Ghost and the Christian Life.* Translated by R. Birch Hoyle. London: F. Muller, Ltd., 1938.

Bartsch, Hans Werner (ed.). *Kerygma and Myth*. Translated by R. H. Fuller. New York: Harper Torch Books, 1961.

Berkhof, H. *The Doctrine of the Holy Spirit*. Richmond, Virginia: John Knox Press, 1964.

Blass, F. and Debrunner, A. *A Greek Grammar of the New Testament and other Early Christian Literature*. Translated by Robert W. Funk. Chicago: University of Chicago Press, 1961.

St. Bonaventura. "The Triple Way, or Love Enkindled," *The Works of Bonaventura*, Vol. 1: *Mystical Opuscula*. Translated by Jose de Vinck. Patterson, New Jersey: St. Anthony Guild Press, 1960.

Bonhoeffer, Dietrich. *Act and Being*. London: Collins, 1962.

Braaten, Carl E. *Principles of Lutheran Theology*. Minneapolis: Fortress Press, 1983.

Braaten, Carl E. and Robert W. Jenson. *A Map of Twentieth-Century Theology*. Minneapolis: Fortress Press, 1995.

Brown, D. Mackenzie. *Ultimate Concern*. New York: Harper & Row, 1965.

Bulman, Raymond F. and Parrella, Frederick J., editors. *Paul Tillich: A New Catholic Assessment*. Collegeville, MN: The Liturgical Press, 1994.

Bultmann, Rudolf. *Existence and Faith: Shorter Writings of Rudolf Bultmann*. Translated by S. M. Ogden. New York: Meridian Books, 1960.

_____. *Jesus Christ and Mythology*. New York: Charles Scribners' Sons, 1958.

_____. *Theology of the New Testament*. Vol. 1. Translated by Kendrick Grobel. New York: Charles Scribners' Sons. 1951.

Carey John J. ed., *Theonomy and Autonomy. Studies in Paul Tillich's Engagement with Modern Culture*. North American Paul Tillich Society. Macon: Mercer University Press, 1984.

_____. ed., *Kairos and Logos. Studies in the Roots and Implications of Tillich's Theology*. North American Paul Tillich Society. Macon: Mercer University Press, 1984.

_____. *Being and Doing. Paul Tillich as Ethicist*. North American Paul Tillich Society. Macon: Mercer University Press, 1987.

Cockin, F. A. *God in Action*. Baltimore: Penguin Books, 1961.

Come, Arnold B. *Human Spirit and Holy Spirit*. Philadelphia: Westminster Press, 1959.

Cooper, John Charles. "Paul Tillich and NeoPlatonism," in *Studies in NeoPlatonism*, Vol. X. Albany: SUNY Press, forthcoming.

_____. *The Roots of Radical Theology*. Philadelphia: Westminster Press, 1967.

_____. *Radical Christianity and its Sources*. Philadelphia: Westminster Press, 1968.

_____. *The New Mentality*. Philadelphia: Westminster Press, 1969.

_____. *Religion in the Age of Aquarius*. Philadelphia: Westminster Press, 1971.

_____. *Paul for Today*. Philadelphia: Lutheran Church Press, 1971.

_____. *A New Kind of Man*. Philadelphia: Westminster Press, 1972.

_____. *Fantasy and the Human Spirit*. New York: Seabury Press, 1975.

_____. *Why We Hurt and Who can Heal*. Waco: Word Books, 1978.

Cross, F. L. and E. A. Livingston, ed. *The Oxford Dictionary of the Christian Church*. New York: Oxford University Press, 1997.

Crossman, Richard C., *Paul Tillich: A Comprehensive Bibliography, etc.* Metuchen, New Jersey: The Scarecrow Press, 1983.

Davies, W. D. *Paul and Rabbinic Judaism*. London: S. P. C. K., 1962.

De Chardin, Pierre Teilhard. *The Divine Milieu*. New York: Harper Torch Books, 1965.

_____. *The Future of Man*. New York: Harper & Row, 1964.

_____. *The Phenomenon of Man*. Translated by B. Wall. New York: Harper, 1959.

Deissman, Adolf. *Die neutestamentliche formel "in Christo Jesu."* Marburg: N. G. Elevert, 1962.

_____. *Paul – A Study in Social and Religious History*. Translated by W. E. Wilson. New York: Harper and Brothers, 1957.

Dewart, Lindsay. *The Holy Spirit and Modern Thought*. New York: Harper and Brothers, 1959.

Dilley, F. B. *Metaphysics and Religious Language*. New York: Columbia University Press, 1964.

Dillistone, F. W. *The Holy Spirit in the Life of Today*. Philadelphia: Westminster, 1949.

Dodd, C. H. *The Epistle of Paul to the Romans*. (Moffatt New Testament Commentary.) London: Hodder & Stoughton, 1932; New York: R. Long and R. R. Smith, Inc., 1932.

Douglas, John Hall. *Thinking the Faith*. Minneapolis: Fortress Press, 1989.

_____. *Confessing the Faith*. Minneapolis: Fortress Press, 1996.

Dreisbach, Donald F. *Symbols & Salvation*. Lanham, MD: University Press of America, 1993.

Duncan, G. S. *The Epistle of Paul to the Galatians*. (Moffatt New Testament Commentary.) London: Hodder & Stoughton, 1934.

Ebeling, Gerhard. *Word and Faith*. Philadelphia: Fortress Press, 1964.

Eliade, Mircea. *The Sacred and the Profane*. Harper Torch Books. New York: Harper & Bros., 1961.

Enslin, Morton Scott. *The Ethics of Paul*. New York: Abingdon Press, 1957.

Ephermerides Theological Lovanienses. Anius XL. Belgium: The Catholic University of Louvain. June, 1964. Facililus 2.

Farrar, F. W. *The Life and Work of St. Paul*. New York: E. P. Dutton & Co., 1880.

Findlay, J. N. *Hegel, A Re-examination*. New York: Collier Books, 1962.

Flew, Antony and MacIntyre, Alasdair (eds.). *New Essays in Philosophical Theology*. New York: MacMillan, 1964.

Freeman, David Hugh. *Tillich: Recent Studies in Philosophy and Theology*. Philadelphia: Presbyterian and Reformed Publishing Company, 1962.

Fuchs, Ernst. *Hermeneutik*. Bad Cannstatt: R. Millerscttön, 1954.

_____. *Zur Frage nach dem Historischen Jesus*. Tubingen: Mohr, 1960.

Gale, Herbert M. *The Use of Analogy in the Letters of Paul*. Philadelphia: Westminster Press, 1964.

Gertz, W. H. General Editor. *The Dictionary of Bible and Religion*. Nashville: Abingdon Press, 1986.

Gibel, Johannes. *Der Heilige Geist in der heilsverkindigung des Paulus*. Halle: M. Niemeyer, 1888.

Grant, Robert M. *The Bible in the Church, A Short History of the Interpretation of the Bible*. Rev. ed. New York: MacMillan Co., 1963.

Greig, Richard. *Symbol and Empowerment: Paul Tillich's Post-Theistic System*. Macon: Mercer University Press, 1985.

Hamilton, Kenneth. *The System and the Gospel. A Critique of Paul Tillich*. New York: MacMillan, 1963.

Hamilton, William. *The New Essence of Christianity*. New York: Association Press, 1961.

Hamilton, William, and Altizer, T. J. J. *Radical Theology and the Death of God*. New York: Bobbs-Merrill Co., 1965.

Hammond, Guyton B. *Man in Estrangement*. Nashville: Vanderbilt University Press, 1965.

Hammond, Guyton B. *The Power of Self-Transcendence*. St. Louis, MO: The Bethany Press, 1966.

Hartshorne, Charles and Reese, William L. (eds.) *Philosophers Speak of God*. Chicago: University of Chicago Press, 1953.

Hegel, G. F. *On Christianity*. Harper Torch Books. New York: Harper & Bros., 1961.

Hegel, G. F. *Phenomenology of Mind*. Translated by J. B. Baillie. New York: MacMillan Co., 1910.

Heidegger, Martin. *Being and Time*. Translated by J. MacQuarrie and Edward Robinson. New York: Harper, 1962.

Henderson, Ian. *Myth in the New Testament*. Chicago: A. R. Allenson, Inc., 1952.

Hendry, George S. *The Holy Spirit in Christian Theology*. Philadelphia: Westminster. 1956.

Herrmann, Ingo. *Kyrios und Pneuma. Studien zur Christologies der Paulinschen Hauptbriefe*. (Studien Zum Alten and Neuen Testament, Band 2.) Munchen: Kosel-Verlag, 1961.

Hook, Sidney (ed.). *Religious Experience and Truth*. New York: New York University Press, 1961.

Hoyle, R. Birch. *The Holy Spirit in St. Paul*. Garden City, New York: Doubleday, Doran Co., 1929.

Hunter, Archibald M. *Paul and His Predecessors*. New rev. ed. Philadelphia: Westminster Press, 1961.

Jaspers, Karl and Bultmann, R. *Myth and Christianity*. New York: Noonday Press, 1962.

Jaspers, Karl. *Value and Man*. Edited by L. Z. Hammer. New York: McGraw-Hill, 1966.

Johnson, Wayne G. *Theological Method in Luther and Tillich*. Washington, D.C.: University Press of America, 1981.

Johnston, George. *The Doctrine of the Church in the New Testament*. Cambridge: Cambridge Press, 1943.

Kähler, Martin. *The So-Called Historical Jesus and the Historic Biblical Christ*. Translated by Carl E. Braaten. Philadelphia: Fortress Press, 1964.

Kegley, Charles W. and Bretall, Robert (eds.). *The Theology of Paul Tillich*. MacMillan Paperbacks. New York: The MacMillan Co., 1964.

Kelsey, David H. *The Fabric of Paul Tillich's Theology*. New Haven: Yale University Press, 1967.

Killen, R. Allen. *The Ontological Theology of Paul Tillich*. Kampen: J. H. Kok, 1956.

King, Rachel H. *The Omission of the Holy Spirit from Reinhold Niebuhr's Theology*. New York: Philosophical Library, 1964.

Kittel, G. V. *Theologisches Worterbuch zum Neuen Testament*. Stuttgart: W. Kohlhammer, 1935.

Klausner, Joseph. *From Jesus to Paul*. Translated from the Hebrew by William F. Stinespring. Boston: Beacon Press, 1961.

Knox, John. *The Church and the Reality of Christ*. New York: Harper & Row, 1962.

Leibrecht, Walter (ed.). *Religion and Culture*. Essays in honor of Paul Tillich. New York: Harpers, 1959.

Lonnings, Per. *The Dilemma of Contemporary Theology*. New York: Humanities Press, 1962.

Lull, Timothy F. ed. *Martin Luther's Basic Theological Writings*. Minneapolis: Fortress Press, 1989.

Macquarrie, John. *Twentieth Century Religious Thought*. New York: Harper & Row, 1963.

Mahan, Wayne W. *Tillich's System*. San Antonio, TX: Trinity University Press, 1974.

Martin, Bernard. *The Existentialist Theology of Paul Tillich*. New York: Bookman Associates, 1963.

Marty, Martin E. (ed.). *The Place of Bonhoffer*. New York: Association Press, 1962.

Mascall, E. L. *The Secularization of Christianity*. New York: Holt, Rinehart & Winston, 1966.

May, Rollo. *Paulus*. New York: Harper & Row Publishers, 1973.

McKelway, Alexander T. *The Systematic Theology of Paul Tillich*. Richmond: John Knox Press, 1964.

McLean, George F. *Man's Knowledge of God According to Paul Tillich — A Thomistic Critique*. Washington, D.C.: The Catholic University of America Press, 1958.

McNeile, Alan H. *An Introduction to the Study of the New Testament*. Revised by C. S. C. Williams. Oxford: Clarendon Press, 1953.

Metzger, Bruce M. (ed.). *New Testament Tools and Studies*, Vol. 1: *Index to Periodical Literature on the Apostle Paul*. Grand Rapids: Eerdmans Press, 1951.

Michael, J. H. *The Epistle of Paul to the Philippians*. (Moffatt New Testament Commentary.) Garden City, New York: Doubleday, Doran & Co., Inc., 1929; London: Hodder & Stoughton, 1928.

Mondin, Battista. *The Principle of Analogy in Protestant & Catholic Theology*. The Hague: Martinus Nizhoff, 1963.

Morrison, Clinton. *The Powers That Be*. Naperville, Illinois: A. Allenson, 1960.

Moulton, J. H. and Milligan, George. *The Vocabulary of the Greek Testament*. 2nd ed. London: Houghton & Stoughton, 1915.

Moulton, W. F. and Geden, A. S. *A Concordance to the Greek Testament*. New York: Charles Scribner's Sons, 1897.

Muhlen, Heribert. *Der heilige Geist als Person*. Munster: Aschendorff, 1963.

Munck, Johannes. *Paul and the Salvation of Mankind*. Translated by Frank Clarke. Richmond: John Knox Press, 1959.

Nestle, E. *Novum Testamentum Graece*. Stuttgart: Württembergische Bibelanstalt, 1956.

Neugebauer, Fritz. *In Christus: En Christoi*. Göttingen: Vandenhoeck and Ruprecht, 1961.

Newport, John P. *Paul Tillich* (Makers of the Modern Theological Mind, Editor, Bob E. Patterson). Waco, TX: Word Books, 1984.

Nietzsche, F. *The Collected Works of Nietzsche*. New York: Modern Library, 1937.

Nygren, Anders. *Agape and Eros*. Translated by Philip Watson. Philadelphia: Westminster Press, 1953.

———. *Commentary on Romans*. Translated by Carl C. Rasmussen. Philadelphia: Muhlenberg Press, 1949.

O'Conner, D. J. (ed.). *A Critical History of Western Philosophy*. New York: The Free Press, 1964.

O'Meara, T. A. and Weisser, C. D. (eds.). *Paul Tillich in Catholic Thought*. Dubuque, Iowa: The Priory Press, 1964.

Orymski, Wanda (ed.). *Hegel: Highlights*. New York: Philosophical Library, 1960.

Outler, Albert C. (ed.). *Augustine: Confessions and Enchiridion, Library of Christian Classics*. Philadelphia: Westminster Press, 1955.

Pauck, Wilhelm and Marion. *Paul Tillich: His Life and Thought, Vol. 1, Life*. New York: Harper & Row, 1976.

Pelikan, Jaroslav. *The Shape of Death*. New York: Abingdon Press, 1961.

Pederson, Phillip E. ed. *What does this Mean: Luther's Catechisms Today*. Philadelphia: Fortress Press, 1979.

Peterson, Michael, et al, ed. *Philosophy of Religion: Selected Readings*. New York: Oxford University Press, 1996.

Phillips, J. B. *Letters to Young Churches*. New York: MacMillan, 1948.

Plantinga, Alvin (ed.). *The Ontological Argument*. Garden City, New York: Doubleday Anchor Books, 1965.

Plato. *Great Dialogues of Plato*. Translated by W. H. D. Rouse. New York: Mentor Books, 1956.

Pongo, K. T. *Expectation as Fulfillment: A Study in Paul Tillich's Theology of Justice*. Lanham, MD: University of America, 1996.

Porter, Frank C. *The Mind of Christ in Paul*. New York: Charles Scribner's Sons, 1930.

Prenter, Regin. *Spiritus Creator*. Philadelphia: Muhlenberg Press, 1956.

Price, James L. *Interpreting the New Testament*. New York: Holt, Rinehart and Winston, 1961.

Ramm, Bernard. *The Witness of the Spirit*. Grand Rapids: Eerdmans, 1959.

Ramsey, Ian T. *Religious Language*. New York: MacMillan, 1963.

Richardson, Alan. *A Theological Wordbook of the Bible*. New York: MacMillan, 1953.

Richardson, William J. and Heidegger, S. J. *Through Phenomenology to Thought*. The Hague: Martinus Nizhoff, 1963.

Robinson, J. A. T. *The Body – A Study in Pauline Theology.* London: SCM Press, 1957.

Robinson, James M. and Cobb, John B., Jr. *The New Hermeneutic* ("New Frontiers in Theology," Vol. 11). New York: Harper & Row, 1964.

Rome, Sydney and Rome, Beatrice (eds.). *Philosophical Interrogations.* New York: Holt, Rinehart and Winston, 1964.

Ross, Robert R. N. *The Non-Existence of God.* New York: The Mellen Press, 1978.

Rowe, William L. *Religious Symbols and God.* Chicago: The University of Chicago Press, 1968.

Runes, Dagobert D. (ed.). *Dictionary of Philosophy.* Paterson, New Jersey: Littlefield, Adams & Co., 1962.

Schelling, F. *The Ages of the World.* Translated by F. Bolman, Jr. New York: Columbia University Press, 1942.

_____. *On Human Freedom.* Translated by James Gutmann. Chicago: Open Court Publishing Company, 1936.

Scharlemann, Robert P. *Reflection and Doubt in the Thought of Paul Tillich.* New Haven: Yale University Press, 1969.

Schleiermacher, F. *The Christian Faith.* Harper Torch Books. New York: Harper & Bros., 1963. (First published in 1928 in Edinburgh: T. and T. Clark.)

Schweitzer, Albert. *The Mysticism of Paul the Apostle.* New York: Henry Holt & Co., 1931.

_____. *Paul and His Interpreters.* Translated by W. Montgomery. London: Adam & Charles Black, 1948.

Schweitzer, Eduard. "Spirit of God," *Bible Key Words.* London: Adam and Charles Black , 1960.

Scheops, H. J. *Paulus.* Tubingen: Mohr, 1959.

_____. *Paul.* London: Lutterworth Press, 1961.

Scott, E. F. *Colossians, Philemon and Ephesians.* (Moffatt New Testament Commentary.) New York: R. R. Smith, Inc., 1930.

Selby, P. J. *Towards the Understanding of St. Paul.* Englewood Cliffs, New Jersey: Prentice Hall, 1962.

Shields, Philip R. *Logic and Sin in the Writings of Ludwig Wittgenstein.* Chicago: The University of Chicago Press, 1993.

Sittler, Joseph. *The Ecology of Faith.* Philadelphia: Muhlenberg Press, 1961.

Smart, James D. *The Interpretation of Scripture.* Baton Rouge: Louisiana State University Press, 1958.

_____. *The Structure of Christian Ethics.* Baton Rouge: Louisiana State University Press, 1961.

Stace, W. T. *Mysticism and Philosophy.* Philadelphia: Lippincott, 1960.

Stalder, Kurt. *Das Werk des Geistes in der Heilegung bei Paulus.* Zurich: EVZ-Verlag, 1962.

Stauffer, Ethelbert. *New Testament Theology.* Translated by John Marsh. New York: MacMillan, 1955.

Stegmann, Basil. "Christ, the Man from Heaven -- A Study of I Cor. 15:45-47 in the Light of the Anthropology of Philo Judaeus." Unpublished S. T. D. thesis, Catholic University. Washington, D.C., 1927.

Stewart, James S. *A Man in Christ.* New York: Harper, 1963.

Strawson, P. F. *Individuals.* London: Methuen, 1959.

Taylor, Mark. ed. *Paul Tillich: Theologian of the Boundaries.* Minneapolis: Fortress Press, 1991.

Tavard, George H. *Paul Tillich and the Christian Message.* New York: Charles Scribner's Sons, 1962.

Thatcher, Adrian. *The Ontology of Paul Tillich.* Oxford University Press, 1978.

Thomas, G. F. *Spirit and Its Freedom.* Chapel Hill: University of North Carolina Press, 1939.

Thomas, Heywood. *Paul Tillich.* Richmond: John Knox Press, 1966.

_____. *Paul Tillich: An Appraisal.* Philadelphia: Westminster Press, 1963.

Tillich, Hannah. *From Time to Time.* New York: Stein and Day, Publishers, 1973.

Tillich, Hannah. *From Place to Place.* New York: Stein and Day, Publishers, 1976.

Tillich, Paul. *Auf der Grenze: Aus dem Lebenswerk Paul Tillich.* Stuttgart: Evangelisches Verlagswerk, 1962.

_____. *Biblical Religion and the Search for Ultimate Reality.* Chicago: University of Chicago Press, 1964.

_____. *Christianity and the Encounter with the World Religions.* New York: Columbia University Press, 1963.

_____. *The Courage To Be.* New Haven: Yale University Press, 1952.

_____. *Das System der Wissenschaften nach Gegenstanden und Methoden.* Göttingen: Vandenhoeck and Ruprecht, 1923.

_____. *Die Verlorene Dimension: Not und Hoffnung unserer Ziet.* Hamburg: Furche-Verlag, 1962.

_____. *Dynamics of Faith.* New York: Harper Torchbooks, 1957.

_____. *The Eternal Now.* New York: Charles Scribner's Sons, 1963.

_____. *The Interpretation of History.* Translated by N. A. Rasetzki (Part 1) and Elsa L. Talmey (Parts II-IV). New York: Charles Scribner's Sons, 1936.

_____. *The Irrelevance and Relevance of the Christian Message.* ed. Cleveland: The Pilgrim Press, 1996.

_____. *Love, Power and Justice.* New York: Oxford University Press, 1960.

_____. *Morality and Beyond.* New York: Harper & Row, 1963.

_____. *On the Boundary.* New York: Charles Scribner's Sons, 1966.

_____. *Political Expectation.* Edited by James Luther Adams. Lanham, MD: University Press of America, 1971.

_____. *Political Expectation.* Ed. James Luther Adams. Macon: Mercer University Press, 1981 (orig. 1971).

_____. *The Protestant Era.* Abridged ed. Chicago: University of Chicago, 1962.

_____. *The Religious Situation.* Translated by H. Richard Neibuhr. New York: Meridian Books, 1960.

_____. *The Spiritual Situation in Our Technical Society.* Introduced and ed. J. Mark Thomas. Macon: Mercer University Press, 1988.

_____. *The Socialist Decision.* Translated by Franklin Sherman. Washington, D. C.: University Press of America, 1977.

_____. *The Shaking of the Foundations.* New York: Charles Scribner's Sons, 1948.

_____. *The World Situation.* (Facet Books, Social Ethics Series, PBK). Philadelphia: Fortress Press, 1965.

_____. *Symbol and Wirklichkeit.* Göttingen: Vandenhoeck and Ruprecht, 1962.

_____. *Systematic Theology.* Vols. I-III. Chicago: University of Chicago Press, 1951, 1957, 1963.

_____. *The Theology of Culture.* Edited by Robert C. Kimball. New York: Oxford University Press, 1964.

Torrance, R. M. *The Spiritual Quest: Transcendence in Myth, Religion, and Science.* University of California Press, 1994.

Tresmontant, Claude. *St. Paul and the Mystery of Christ.* Translated by Donald Attwater. New York: Harper Torchbooks, 1957.

Trueblood, David E. *Philosophy of Religion.* New York: Harper & Row, 1957.

Unhyein, Anne. *Dynamics of Doubt.* Fortress Press, 1966.

Vahanian, Gabriel. *The Death of God.* New York: George Braziller, 1961.

van Buren, Paul. *The Secular Meaning of the Gospel.* New York: MacMillan Co., 1963.

van Dusen, H. P. (ed.). *The Christian Answer.* New York: Charles Scribner's Sons, 1945.

_____. *Spirit, Son and Father.* New York: Charles Scribner's Sons, 1958.

Watson, Philip. *Let God be God.* London: The Epworth Press, 1954.

Wheat, Leonard F. *Paul Tillich's Dialectical Humanism.* The Johns Hopkins Press, 1970.

Whitehead, Alfred North. *Process and Reality.* Harper Torchbooks. New York: Harper & Bros., 1960

Whiteley, D. E. H. *The Theology of St. Paul*. Philadelphia: Fortress Press, 1964.

Wikenhauser, Alfred. *Pauline Mysticism*. New York: Herder and Herder, 1960.

Windelband, Wilhelm. *A History of Philosophy*. Vol. 1. Harper Torchbooks. New York: Harper Bros., 1958.

Wittgenstein, Ludwig. *Philosophical Grammar*. Berkley: University of California Press, 1978.

_____. *Tractatus Logico–Philosophicus*. Trans. D. F. Pears, and B. F. McGuinness. London: Routledge & Kegan-Paul, 1971.

Wright, George Ernest. *God Who Acts: Biblical Theology as Recital*. ("Studies in Biblical Theology," No. 8.) Chicago: Alec R. Allenson, Inc., 1952.

Yates, J. E. *The Spirit and the Kingdom*. London: SPCK, 1963.

Articles

Allen, J. A. "The 'In Christ' Formula in the Pastoral Epistles," *New Testament Studies*, 1963.

Allen, J. A. "The 'In Christ' Formula in Ephesians," *New Testament Studies*. 1958.

Badcock, F. "'The Spirit' and Spirit in the New Testament," *Expository Times*. Vol. XLV, No. 5 (February, 1934).

Bartling, W. "The New Creation in Christ: A Study of the Pauline Formula," *Concordia Theological Monthly*, Vol. XXI (1950).

Boll, Gerard. "Studies in Texts: II Cor. 3:17-18," *Theology*, Vol. VI (1923).

Buckham, J. W. "Are Christ and the Spirit Identical in Paul's Teaching?" *Expositor*, 8th Series, Vol. XXII (1921).

Cooper, John C. "Mythology and Religion," *Discourse*, Vol. VII, No. 2 (Spring, 1964).

_____. "The 'New Hermeneutic' and Metaphysics," *Bucknell Review*, vol. XIX, no. 1 Spring, 1971.

_____. "St. Paul's Evaluation of Women and Marriage," *The Lutheran Quarterly*, Vol. XVI, No. 4 (November, 1964).

_____. "Paul Tillich's Philosophy of Science," *The Southern Humanity Review*, vol. 2, no.1, Winter 1968.

_____. "The Epistemological Order of Value and Fact," *Ohio Journal of Religion*, vol. 5, no. 1, April 1977.

_____. "The Eternal and the Present (The Writings of Paul Tillich)," *Resource*, vol. 7, no. 6, March 1966.

_____. "Why did Augustine Write Books XI-XIII of the *Confessions?*" *Augustinian Studies*, vol. 2, 1971.

_____. "The Basic Philosophical and Theological Notions of St. Augustine," *Augustinian Studies*, vol. 15, 1984.

_____. "Beyond Existentialism," *South Carolina Academy of Science Bulletin*, 1963.

Grech, Prosper. "II Cor. 3:17 and the Pauline Doctrine of Conversion to the Holy Spirit," *Catholic Biblical Quarterly*, Vol. XVII (1955).

Griffiths, D. R. "'The Lord is the Spirit' (II Cor. 3:17-18)," *Pastoral Theology*, Vol. LV (1943-1944).

Hamilton, William. "The New Optimism from Prufrock to Ringo," *Union Seminary Quarterly Review*, Vol. XXI, No. 2, Part 2 (January, 1966).

_____. "The Death of God Theology," *The Christian Scholar*, XLVIII, No. 1 (Spring, 1965).

Hammond, Guyton B. "An Examination of Tillich's Method of Correlation," *The Journal of Bible and Religion*, Vol. XXXII, No. 3. (July, 1964).

Hoyle, R. B. "Spirit in St. Paul's Experience and Writings," *Biblical Research*, Vol. XI (1926).

_____. "Paul's Doctrine of the Spirit," *Biblical Research*, Vol. XIII (1928).

Hughes, H. M. "II Cor. 3:17," *Expository Times*, Vol. XLV (1933-1934).

Loomer, Bernard M. "Tillich's Theology of Correlation," *Journal of Religion*, Vol. XXXVI, No. 3 (July, 1956).

Losee, John P. "Biblical Religion and Ontology: Has Tillich Established a Point of Identity?" *The Journal of Bible and Religion*, XXXIII, No. 3 (July, 1965), 223-228.

Martin, D. W. "'Spirit' in the 2nd Chapter of I Cor.," *Catholic Biblical Quarterly*, Vol. V (1943).

May, Rollo, et. al. *Pastoral Psychology*, Vol. XIX, No. 181 (February, 1968).

Nuovo, Victor. "Tillich and Emerson," *Journal of the American Academy of Religion*, Vol. III, No. 4.

Ott, Heinrich. "Language and Understanding," *Union Seminary Quarterly Review*, Vol. XXI, No. 3 (March, 1966).

Ralston, D. H. "The Union of Christ with the Believer and the Inference Therefrom," *Union Seminary Quarterly Review*, Vol. XXI (1909-1910).

Richardson, Cryil C. "Discussion: The Tri-Unity of God," *Union Seminary Quarterly Review*, Vol. XXI, No. 2, Part 2 (January, 1966).

Robinson, J. A. T. "The Most Primitive Christology of All?" *Journal of Theological Studies*, New Series, Vol. VII (1956).

Shrayer, M. J. "The Lord is the Spirit," *Religion in Life*, Vol. XX (1951).

Tillich, Paul. "My Belief in Faith," *Realities*, No. 177 (August, 1965), pp. 68-71.

_____. "The Religious Symbol," *The Journal of Liberal Religion*, Vol. II, No. 1 (Summer, 1940).

_____. "Myth and Mythology," in *Die Religion in Geschichte und Gegenwart: Handworterbuch für Theologie und Religionswissenschaft.* Vol. IV (1930). Translated from the German by this writer. Tubingen: Mohr, 1927-1932, 2nd edition.

Tamaru, N. "Motive and Struktur der Theologie Paul Tillich," *N. Z. Systematik Theologie*, III (1961), 1-38.

Wolff, Otto. "Paul Tillich Christologie des 'Neuen Seins,'" *N. Z. Systematik Theologie*, III (1961), 129-140.

Unpublished Material

Cooper, John C. "The Necessity of Ontology in the Hermeneutic Task." Paper delivered before the 1966 meeting of the Southern section of the American Academy of Religion at Decatur, GA.

_____. "Søren Kierkegaard's Use of Scripture." Paper read to the Kentucky Philosophical Association at Spalding University, Louisville, KY, November 9, 1991.

Pitcher, William Alvin. "Theological Ethics in Paul Tillich and Emil Brunner." Unpublished Ph.D. Dissertation, Divinity School, University of Chicago, 1955.

Tillich, Paul. "The Bible and Systematic Theology." Lecture delivered at Washington, D. C.

_____. "Personal Introduction to the Systematic Theology." Collection of Tillich's unpublished papers by James Luther Adams, Meadville Theological School, Chicago, Illinois.

_____. "Systematic Theology." Lectures at Union Theological Seminary, New York City, compiled by Peter H. Johns. (Mimeographed).

Name Index

Scripture Index

The "Spiritual Presence" in the Theology of Paul Tillich
by John Charles Cooper

Published by Mercer University Press
October 1997
Book design by Marc A. Jolley.
Camera-ready pages composed on a Macintosh
    Performa 6300CD, via Microsoft Word 6.0.1.
Text font: Book Antiqua 10/12 and 9/11.
Printed and bound in the United States.
Cased and covered with cloth, smyth-sewn, and printed
    on acid-free paper.